本书得到国家语委重大科研项目
“语言文字科学保护的理论与实践研究”资金资助
课题编号 ZDA125-14

World Language Education and Talents Cultivation

APEC 区域语言教育与高端人才培养

主　编：李宇明
副主编：方　军　杨　军　Adriana de Kanter　赵　旻

北京语言大学出版社
BEIJING LANGUAGE AND CULTURE UNIVERSITY PRESS

图书在版编目（CIP）数据

区域语言教育与高端人才培养 / 李宇明主编．— 北京：北京语言大学出版社，2014.12

ISBN 978-7-5619-3982-6

Ⅰ．①区…　Ⅱ．①李…　Ⅲ．①语言教学—教学研究②人才培养—研究　Ⅳ．① H09 ② C961

中国版本图书馆 CIP 数据核字（2014）第 259261 号

书　　名：区域语言教育与高端人才培养
QUYU YUYAN JIAOYU YU GAODUAN RENCAI PEIYANG

责任印制：姜正周

出版发行：北京语言大学出版社

社　　址：北京市海淀区学院路 15 号　　邮政编码：100083

网　　址：www.blcup.com

电　　话：编 辑 部：8610-8230 3647/3592/3395
国内发行：8610-8230 3650/3591/3648
海外发行：8610-8230 0309/3365/3080
读者服务部：8610-8230 3653/3908
网上订购：8610-8230 3653（国内）/ 3668（海外）
service @blcup.com

印　　刷：保定市中画美凯印刷有限公司

经　　销：全国新华书店

版　　次：2014 年 12 月第 1 版　　2014 年 12 月第 1 次印刷

开　　本：710 毫米 ×1000 毫米　1/16　印张：15.75

字　　数：338 千字

书　　号：ISBN 978-7-5619-3982-6 / H · 14257

定　　价：52.00 元

国际合作，语言先行
——《区域语言教育与高端人才培养》序

[中国]李宇明

展现在读者面前的这部文集，是2012年在北京语言大学举办的首届亚太经合组织（APEC）教育论坛的成果汇编。

亚太经合组织成立于1989年，经20余年发展，已成为亚太地区最重要的经济合作论坛，也是本地区最高级别的政府间经济合作组织。其成立之初衷，是建立成员间经济上相互依存、合作开放的多边贸易体制，减少贸易及投资壁垒，推动本地区经济成长，维护本地区共同的经济利益。事实证明，它在促进亚太地区经济合作和贸易发展上，确实做出了一定的贡献。

亚太经合组织不同于其他经由条约而确立的政府间组织，其运作是通过非约束性承诺和成员自愿来完成的。它强调开放性对话，平等对待各成员意见。从传统的区域联盟视角看，它显得有些松散、低效，但从另一角度看，这也保证了它的协商性与平等性，在这里更易听到不同国家和地区的不同诉求。

亚太经合组织是一个经济论坛，其主题当然是经贸合作。但当亚太地区领导人坐在一起，共同探讨经济合作问题时，他们立刻意识到，优秀人才培养是经贸交流的基础，进而认识到，文化交流相对于经济交流有着更为深远的意义。于是，论题自然地向人文领域延伸，衍生出APEC教育论坛。

APEC 教育论坛，致力扩大成员间的人文交流，分享教育发展改革成果，进而达成教育理念上的共识。作为一个不可阻挡的世界潮流，全球化与区域合作对教育领域的影响极为深刻，教育应具有国际化心态，置身于全球化大环境下及时进行自我调节。早在 2008 年 11 月，在秘鲁举行的亚太经合组织教育部长会议上，各成员体就一致认为：21 世纪的学生必须掌握一些核心能力和技能，包括批判性思维、创新能力、分析和解决问题的能力、终身学习、团队合作、自我管理和自学能力等。获取这些能力，必须进行教育体制改革，转变学习观念，整合知识，提高教育技术水平。亦是在这次教育部长会议上，确立了教育的四个重点领域：数学与科学教育、语言尤其是外语学习、职业和技术教育、信息通信技术与教育体制改革，并就各领域的重点和举措进行了实证研究和政策比较研究。

正如后来所看到的那样，APEC 教育论坛最终把教育交流和人才培养的重点放在了语言上。在新的时代背景下，语言已不仅仅是交际工具，更是一种资源。语言能力和跨文化交流能力，成为各经济体实力的重要组成部分。每个经济体，都需要分享其他经济体的知识和经验，这就要求每一经济体的"经济人"，必须拥有较强的语言沟通能力，才能跨越地域的局限，突破"语言的囚笼"，完成亚太地区真正的交流与合作。在经济全球化、教育国际化和文化多元化浪潮的推动下，亚太经合组织成员之间多层面、多目标、多方式的经贸和文化交往空前广泛，对既熟悉专业又熟练掌握外语的高级复合型人才需求越来越大，这正是高端人才培养的方向所在。

由智利和中国台北牵头进行的研究表明，亚太经合组织成员都面临一个共同问题，即如何有效培养能够使用两种以上语言、顺畅进行跨文化交流的公民。相对而言，东方经济体越来越重视英语教育，低年级就引入英语教学，强调应用能力。而母语为英语的经济体，则较难激发学生学习外语的动机，也缺乏合格的外语师资。为此，亚太经合组织工作组提出了"相互学习语言"的建议。该建议呼吁，编制各经济体共同的英语和其他语言的教学标准，提高外语教师的专业能力，并配置以相应的语言教育政策。自 2004 年开始，亚太经合组织就把成员间相互学习语言定为各经济体教育的首要任务。2008 年举行的第四届 APEC 教育部长会议，把语言教育确定为 2008—2012 年教育合作的优先领域。

正是在此背景下，2012年9月10日—11日，首届“区域语言教育与高端人才培养——亚太经合组织教育论坛”在北京语言大学成功举办。论坛得到了美国、中国、韩国、泰国等国的教育官员、教育专家和语言学家的大力支持，参会的境外人员有87位，其中发展中地区经济体代表14位，发达地区经济体代表8位，自主报名并通过经济体认可的境外参会人员6位，大学校长和相关领域知名专家等59位。

论坛围绕“面向21世纪的区域语言教育与高端人才培养”这一主题，通过大会发言、分论坛交流等多种形式，对外语教育政策与规划、外语教育标准、外语师资培养、外语教学模式以及外语高端人才培养等多个话题进行了探讨。中国、澳大利亚、文莱、加拿大、日本、韩国、马来西亚、墨西哥、秘鲁、菲律宾、中国台北、泰国、美国、越南等14个APEC经济体的教育官员及外语教育领域的知名专家做了大会发言，发表了诸多高见。在“语言教育政策和标准”分论坛上，各成员的教育官员提供了各经济体独特的经验、策略、方法和智慧。在“文化视角下的语言教育与合作”分论坛上，从区域语言教育的课程标准与课程设置，到区域语言高端人才的培养模式，各位专家都贡献了他们的研究心得。

本论坛有助于各成员体了解其他国家和地区的教育理念和教育技术的发展，分享教育实践经验，进一步推动区域语言教育的交流与合作。以此论坛为基础和契机，可以搭建一个国际化的教育研究与合作平台，使亚太地区语言教育与人才培养的交流常态化，提升APEC在外语教育及高端人才培养方面的国际影响力，推动亚太地区经济、社会与文化、教育等方面的合作与发展。

这部文集从语言教育政策与人才培养、跨境/跨文化视角下的语言教育与合作、语言教师的职业发展、信息技术与语言教育项目等方面，探讨了区域语言教育的重要性、可行性以及未来的发展，从一个侧面展示了论坛的多元文化交流与合作的盛况。作为论坛的承办方，我们对论文的作者、出席会议的各位嘉宾和支持、服务会议的各界人士，表示由衷的感谢，并期待本文集能给关心亚太地区经贸、文化、教育交流的读者以有益的启示。

Language Paving the Way for International Cooperation

[People's Republic of China] Li Yuming

The proceedings are based on the first APEC (Asia-Pacific Economic Cooperation) Education Forum held at Beijing Language and Culture University (BLCU) in 2012.

Since its establishment in 1989, after more than two decades of development, APEC has gradually emerged as both the most important economic cooperation forum in the Asia-Pacific Region and a top-level intergovernmental economic cooperation organization in the region. APEC was initiated to set up a multilateral trade mechanism for interdependent economic cooperation and liberalization, removing trade and investment barriers, promoting regional economic growth, and safeguarding the common economic interests of the peoples in this region. It has been proven by facts that APEC has made significant contributions to economic cooperation and trade growth in the Asia-Pacific Region.

Different from other intergovernmental organizations ratified by treaties, APEC functions through non-binding promises and members' free will. APEC emphasizes open dialogs and respect for members' stance on an equal footing. Judged by a conventional regional league, APEC seems a bit loose and inefficient, but observed from a different perspective, it guarantees negotiation and equality so that different demands can be more easily voiced by different countries and regions.

Starting as an economic forum, APEC has concentrated its topics on economic and trade cooperation. During their meetings on economic cooperation, the leaders of the economy came to the natural realization that the training of excellent personnel actually constitutes the basis for economic exchanges, which led to the revelation that cultural exchanges can produce much farther-reaching significance than mere economic exchanges. The APEC topics, consequently, are extended to humanities, giving birth to the APEC Education Forum.

The APEC Education Forum is committed to expanding the people-to-people exchanges between members, sharing the achievements of educational development and reform, and reaching consensus in educational philosophy. As an unstoppable trend, globalization and regional cooperation exert a profound impact on education, requiring every member to be equipped with an international vision to exercise self-adjustment against economic and cultural globalization. As early as November 2008, during the APEC conference of education ministers in Peru, each economy came to the following unanimous understanding: that students in the 21st century must master certain core abilities and skills, including critical thinking, creativity, and the ability to analyze and solve problems, and pursue life-long learning, team spirit, self management and self learning, etc. The attainment of these abilities should entail educational system reform, learning concept transformation, knowledge integration, and technology enhancement. Also during the conference, APEC identified four priorities for education: mathematics and science, language (world language in particular), vocational and technical education, ICT and educational system reform. Empirical studies and contrastive policy research about key issues and action programs in the aforementioned areas have been conducted.

As demonstrated, the APEC Education Forum has always viewed language as the focal point in educational exchanges and personnel training. In this new era of economic globalization, language is more than a communication instrument;

rather, it is a kind of resource. Language ability and cross-cultural communication ability have become important elements of every economy. Every economy finds it necessary to share with other economies knowledge and experience. This requires every "economic man" in every economy to possess strong language communication abilities to reach beyond borders between nations and regions, thus breaking free from the "cage of language", and fulfilling real exchanges and cooperation in the Asia-Pacific Region. With the trend of economic globalization, educational internationalization and cultural diversification, unprecedented extensive economic, trade and cultural cooperation among APEC economies has been going on in a multi-level, multi-purpose and multi-approach manner, creating an increasing demand for top interdisciplinary talents with both specialized skills and proficient world language ability. This is the goal of top talents training.

As shown by the language research led by Chile and Chinese Taipei, all APEC members face a common problem: how to effectively train people who can conduct cross-cultural exchanges by using more than two languages. Relatively speaking, the Eastern economies are attaching increasing importance to English teaching, stressing the inclusion of world language education at early stages, especially the practical application of English. The economies where English is the mother tongue, however, find it hard to motivate their students to learn a world language, resulting in an inadequate supply of teachers of world languages. To address the problem, APEC working groups proposed "mutual language learning" which advocated that a standard of the teaching of English and other languages shared by all the economies be worked out so that teachers' professional competence can be improved in world language teaching and language education policy can be improved. From 2004 on, APEC has given first priority to encouraging its members to learn each other's languages. The fourth APEC education ministers' conference in 2008 identified language education as a priority in educational cooperation for the period of 2008 to 2012.

Against this backdrop, the first World Language Education and Talents Cultivation—APEC Education Forum was held at BLCU from September 10 to 11, 2012. The forum attracted educational officials, experts and linguists from countries and regions such as the United States, China, South Korea and Thailand, with the total number of foreign representatives reaching 87, including 14 from developing economies, eight from developed economies, six volunteer participants who have been approved by other economies, and 59 Presidents of foreign universities and renowned experts in relevant fields.

Centering on the theme "world language education and talents cultivation geared towards the 21st century", the forum, by way of plenary speeches and sub-forum discussions, facilitated explorations into world language education in the following subjects: language policy and planning, educational standards, teacher training, teaching models, and talents cultivation. During the plenary speeches, 14 educational officials and renowned experts in world language education from China, Australia, Brunei Darussalam, Canada, Japan, South Korea, Malaysia, Mexico, Peru, the Philippines, Chinese Taipei, Thailand, the United States, and Vietnam respectively offered their insights and ideas. In the sub-forum on language education policy and standards, educational officials from different economies introduced their unique experience, strategies, methods and wisdom. In the sub-forum on language education and cooperation with a cultural perspective, experts shared their research findings in terms of curriculum standards and setting, and the training model of talents cultivation in world language education.

It is evident that the forum contributed to the understanding of other economies' educational theories and technologies, sharing each other's practical experience and advanced concepts, and further promoting the exchange and cooperation of world language education. This forum served as an opportunity for us to establish an international platform for educational research and cooperation, so that regular research and cooperation in language education and personnel training can be launched in the Asia-Pacific Region to further boost APEC's influence on world language education and talents cultivation, ultimately promoting the economic, social, cultural and educational cooperation and development in this region.

This book covers the importance, feasibility and future of world language education in four specific areas: language education policy and talents cultivation;

Language education and cooperation from a cross-cultural perspective; professional development for language teachers; and information technology and language education project. These fully demonstrate the spectacular exchanges and cooperation of diverse cultures in this forum. We, as the host of this forum, would like to extend our sincere gratitude to the authors, guests and all those who have given support and service to the forum. It is our sincere hope that the proceedings can shed some light to all those who are interested in China and the economic, cultural and educational exchanges in the Asia-Pacific Region.

目 录
Contents

区域语言教育与高端人才培养
——APEC 教育国际研讨会开幕式致辞

[中国]杨　军

尊敬的崔希亮校长、各位 APEC 经济体的代表、各位嘉宾：

大家上午好！

在这秋高气爽的季节，区域语言教育与高端人才培养——亚太经合组织（APEC）教育国际研讨会在北京语言大学隆重开幕。首先，请允许我代表中国教育部国际合作与交流司，对各位远道而来的嘉宾表示诚挚的欢迎！

APEC 是亚太地区机制最完善、层级最高的经济合作官方论坛。自 1991 年加入以来，中国一直积极参与 APEC 教育领域的各项工作，为促进各经济体的教育交流合作，分享各成员优秀教育实践和先进理念，以及巩固和加强 APEC 各成员之间的友好团结发挥了积极的作用。

多年来，语言教育的研究一直是 APEC 教育合作领域支持关注的重点之一。此次会议是 APEC 首次在中国高校召开的以语言教育为主题的会议，其重要性不言而喻。会议以“面向 21 世纪的区域语言教育与高端人才培养”为主题，分设“语言教育政策和标准”和“跨文化视角下的语言教育与合作”两大议题。在一天半的时间里，来自 APEC 12 个经济体的教育官员及语言教育领域的专家将从多个角度交流各经济体在语言教育与高端人才培养方面的现状和存在的问题，分享成功的实践经验，并探讨共同培养 APEC 区域语言人才的合作方式。我相信，本次会议不仅可以帮助各经济体完善 APEC 高端语言人才培养的政策与标准，还能进一步推动 APEC 区域语言教育的交流与合作,从而搭建起一个全方位、多元化的 APEC 区域语言教育研究的新平台。

语言是沟通的工具，是文化的载体，也是合作的桥梁。语言教育应置身于经济和文化全球化的大环境，具有国际化的特征。本着开放的态度，中国政府十分重视学习他国语言。英语已进入中国国民教育体系，成为各级各类学校的必修课程。在中学阶段，我们开办了一些诸如外语中学的特色学校，开设了除英语之外的其他外国语言课程。一些有条件的中小学还鼓励学生学习除英语之外的第二外语。在大学阶段，我们开办了像北京语言大学一样的以语言学习为主要课程的特色大学。我们还支持中国学生到国外学习。1978 年以来，中国赴海外留学的人数已经超过 200 万人。截至 2011 年年底，中国在外留学人员总数已达 142 万。仅 2011 年，中国学生赴海外学习的人数就达近 34 万人，使得近三年年均出国留学人数增长达 23%。中国成为世界上最大的留学生生源国。我们也注重引进海外优质教育资源。目前，中外合作办学机构和项目总数已近 1600 个，数万名中国学生不出国门享受着国外优质教育资源，用他国语言学习专业知识。

同时，随着中国经济的发展和中国影响力的增大，世界各国了解中国的愿望日益增强。为顺应这种趋势，汉语也正在加快走向世界的步伐。越来越多的孔子学院在世界各地建立。截至 2011 年年底，中国的高校与它们的外国合作者已经在 105 个国家建成了 358 所孔子学院和 500 个孔子课堂，带动全球 5000 万人学习汉语，42 个国家和地区将汉语教学纳入了国民教育体系。来华学习的各国留学生也逐年递增，2011 年达到 29 万多人。我们期待着在这次会议上与各位参会代表分享中国的政策、经验和做法，共同探讨语言教学的合作。

此次会议的召开适逢北京语言大学 50 周年校庆，因此意义非同寻常。北京语言大学是一所以语言教学与研究为特色和优势的多学科大学，是中国唯一一所把来华留学生的汉语和中华文化教育作为主要任务的国际型大学，每年都有超过一万名来自世界各地的留学生来校学习，因而有“小联合国”的美誉。目前北京语言大学已成为中国中外语言、文化研究的重要学术基地和培养涉外高级人才的摇篮。这也是我们选择在这里举行此次会议的主要原因之一。

最后，再次感谢各位来宾的出席，预祝会议取得圆满成功，同时也希望各位代表此次北京之行顺利愉快。

World Language Education and Talents Cultivation — Speech at the Opening Ceremony of the APEC Education International Forum

[People's Republic of China] Yang Jun

Dear President Cui Xiliang, APEC representatives and distinguished guests,

Good morning!

In this beautiful autumn with clear skies and fresh air, the APEC Education International Forum on World Language Education and Talents Cultivation is now opened at Beijing Language and Culture University. First of all, on behalf of the Department of International Cooperation and Exchange of the Ministry of Education of China, I would like to extend a warm welcome to all guests from afar.

APEC is an official forum for economic cooperation, which has the most complete system and the highest level of collaboration in the Asia-Pacific Region. Since becoming a member of APEC in 1991, China has always been actively participating in all activities in the APEC educational field and has played an active role in promoting educational exchanges and cooperation, sharing excellent educational practice and advanced ideas, as well as cementing friendship and fostering solidarity between all APEC members.

For many years, research into language education has been one of the major focuses of APEC's work in the field of educational cooperation. This forum is the first time that APEC has held a conference with the theme of language education at a Chinese university, which demonstrates the significance of this topic. The theme of the forum is "Regional Language Education and High-End Talents Cultivation in the 21st Century," and the two related topics are "The Policies and Standards of Language Education" and "Language Education and Cooperation from a Cross-Cultural Perspective." During the next one and a half days, officers and experts in the field of language education from 12 APEC members will exchange ideas about the status quo and existing problems in world language education and talents cultivation from various perspectives, share valuable experiences of success, and discuss the means of cooperation in co-training APEC regional language talents. It is my firm belief that this forum cannot only help APEC members to perfect the policies and standards of high-end language talents training, but can also promote the exchange and cooperation of APEC regional language education, which will set up a comprehensive and diversified new platform for APEC regional language education.

Language is a tool of communication, a carrier of culture and a bridge for cooperation. Language education should be put in the environment of economic and cultural globalization, featured by internationalization. With an attitude of opening up to the outside world, the Chinese government attaches great importance to the study of other languages. English has entered into the Chinese national educational system and become a compulsory course for schools at all levels. In the period of high school, we have set up some schools with special features, such as foreign language schools, in which courses concentrating on other foreign languages other than English are available. Those primary schools and high schools with better resources encourage their students to learn a second foreign language in addition to English. In the phase of higher education, we have set up some universities with special features, such as Beijing Language and Culture University, whose major courses are about language study. We also support Chinese students to study abroad. Since 1978, the total number of students studying abroad has exceeded two million. The number of students studying abroad currently (up to the end of 2011) is 1.42 million. In 2011 alone, the number reached approximately 340,000 students, with an average increase of 23% within the last three years. China has become the biggest source country of overseas students. We also pay attention to bringing in educational resources with a high level of expertise. At present, the number of joint school-running organizations and programs between China and foreign countries has reached 1,600, which makes it possible for tens of thousands of students to get easy access to foreign educational resources with high quality training and study their majors via a foreign language without going abroad.

At the same time, with the development of China's economy and the increase of China's influence, more and more countries would like to get to know China. In order to conform to this tendency, the Chinese language is quickening its steps towards the world. More and more Confucius Institutes are being set up all over the world. By the end of 2011, with the assistance of foreign cooperation, Chinese universities have set up 358 Confucius Institutes and 500 Confucius Classrooms in 105 countries, thus involving over 50 million people in the learning of Chinese. Moreover, 42 countries and regions have incorporated Chinese teaching into their national educational system. The number of foreign students studying in China is also increasing year by year, and reached over 290,000 in 2011. We intend to share the policy, experience and methods of Chinese education and discuss the cooperation in language teaching with all representatives in this forum.

Coincidentally, the forum falls on the 50th anniversary of the founding of Beijing Language and Culture University; therefore, it is doubly significant. Beijing Language and Culture University is a multidisciplinary university with language teaching and research as its feature and advantage. It is the only international university in China that takes teaching foreign students Chinese language and culture in China as its main task. Each year, there are more than

10,000 foreign students from all over the world coming to study in this university, which enables it to earn the fine reputation as a "Mini-UN." Nowadays, Beijing Language and Culture University has become an important academic base for the research into language and culture across China and other countries, as well as the cradle of high-end talents concerning foreign affairs. This is also one of the reasons why we chose to hold the forum here at this university.

Finally, I would like to show my heartfelt thanks again to all distinguished guests. I wish the forum a great success and all representatives a happy time in Beijing!

语言教育政策与人才培养

Language Education Policy and Talents Cultivation

The Leading Role of APEC in Language and Culture Education

[The United States] Adriana de Kanter and Bridget Belknap

Abstract: This paper focuses on "The Leading Role of APEC in Language and Culture Education". The need for language and culture education is critical for a globalizing world, in which every citizen needs strong communication skills for economic growth and mutual understanding. This paper focuses on APEC, a trade and economic organization which operates with English as its official language, but which has made learning each other's languages an education priority since 2004. This is because key research shows the advantages of introducing international languages to children, the positive relationship between language and cultural learning, and the benefits and necessity of technology innovation to language learning. New research needs to be undertaken on the economic benefits of learning more than one language and the need to consistently teach languages from K-12 in an articulated system—all of which are included in the New Directions/Recommendations section of the paper.

Keywords: APEC Language and Culture Education; technology innovation

Background

In a world that relies increasingly on the development of knowledge to drive economic growth, 21st century skills such as critical thinking, pattern recognition and communication have high value in the workplace. Every economy has best practices and can share its knowledge and experiences with other economies to the benefit of all. To do so effectively, citizens of these economies must understand one another's languages and cultures.

Today's learners, youth and adult, need strong interpersonal and communication skills that enable them to function in teams that may have members spread across more than one location, even across two or more economies. Just as technology continues to revise the way products and resources are developed and brought to market, it continues to facilitate new methods of collaboration across multiple sites. Workers and learners now connect in virtual meeting and learning spaces, using cloud computing to build solutions to theoretical and real-life problems. For these collaborations to succeed, the collaborators must, metaphorically and actually, speak the same language. In addition, workers and learners must have an understanding of the cultural norms of the people they are working with across the globe.

APEC Agenda Motivation

The 2012 Pre-Ministerial Symposium Thematic Overview Paper identified four goals for the Ministers including an emphasis on 21st century skills (e.g., mathematics, science, language and culture education) within three broad themes: globalization, innovation and cooperation.

— Globalization: language and intercultural education will provide citizens with the necessary competencies to know how to successfully adapt and adjust to cultural contexts. Intercultural education primarily aims to train individuals in the skills and attitudes necessary to become a truly intercultural person.

— Innovation: language and intercultural education makes innovation possible from the very heart of the various cultures and their creative experience. In this respect, multiculturalism is key to innovation and problem-solving because it draws from diverse ways of thinking.

— Cooperation: language and intercultural education is the cornerstone of enabling dialog and exchange between cultures.

Success in a knowledge-based economy is a primary goal of education. To achieve success, students must master future skills, such as fluency in a foreign language to navigate commerce in multiple economies. Foreign language education is a critical component for students to achieve college and career outcomes in a globalizing society.

Currently, businesses conduct commerce in more than one economy and in the future must continually adapt to changing economic conditions. Workers must be able to communicate and negotiate in more than one language. A 2005 survey of international executive recruiters found that nearly 88 percent of recruiters in Asia and 95 percent of recruiters in Latin America agreed that speaking two or more languages fluently is necessary for success in a competitive job market (Korn and Ferry, 2005). Recruiters also felt that knowing a foreign language would become increasingly important in the next decade and would give business executives "a significant competitive advantage" (Korn and Ferry, 2005). Education can respond to emerging reality by providing authentic language instruction supported by teacher training and innovative instructional technology. Knowing a foreign language also promotes cross-cultural collaboration and communication, providing an ideal setting for cooperation across multiple economies.

The official language in APEC is English, yet we speak more than 100 languages. Because of its diversity, APEC has made learning each other's languages an education priority since 2004. Our work in this priority is best illustrated by three major activities:

- In 2010, APEC held the APEC-SEAMEO Language Conference, entitled: "Language Education: An Essential for a Global Economy," to discuss the relevance of a multilingual education in a global economy. The overall consensus from the conference was that multilingual education is becoming increasingly important not only for the purpose in and of itself, but also for economic success in a global workforce.

- APEC also implemented the Best Practices Language Applications Lesson Study project, which analyzed the best practices for professional development in language education using lesson study. A DVD Workshop on Lesson Study, called Study of Best Practices in Teaching and Learning Languages in APEC Economies, was prepared for key language educators and primary and secondary school language teachers in APEC Member Economies. Distribution of the DVD provides widespread access to examples of lessons used to teach languages so that teachers have access to professional development materials from the cultural perspectives of member economies.

- Additionally, APEC set out the Strategic Plan for English and Other Languages project, which addressed language education in each of the major dimensions of learning, such as content standards, assessment (including performance standards), curriculum and instruction, policy, and exchange programs. Activities in this project included collecting language learning standards from the member economies, creating a consumer checklist for what to expect in an English language and Mandarin Chinese language program, promoting and extending the APEC E-Language programs, and inventorying students' foreign language assessments.

These projects have sought to emphasize the importance of language and culture education and their specific connections to economic placement and opportunities.

English has become a standard international language. English is important for trade and commerce: as the numbers of English speakers in a non-English speaking country increase, the amount of trade between the US and the non-English speaking country increases (Melitz, 2005). Additionally, English has become increasingly important for diplomacy: key international bodies such as the United Nations (Secretariat), the Asia-Pacific Economic Cooperation (APEC), the Association of Southeast Asian Nations (ASEAN), the International Criminal Court, and the North Atlantic Treaty Organization for Economic Cooperation and Development have adopted English for their working language. Thus, knowing English can be beneficial in both industry and diplomacy and can provide a multitude of additional opportunities for a job seeker.

Many non-English speaking APEC economies have already instituted programs that place special focus on learning English, as this is the primary language of the global economy. As a part of a mid-1980s economic strategy, Singapore required all students to learn English and use English as the official language of instruction (Suarez, 2005). China uses a program of teaching students content instruction using a foreign or second language with the intent of mastering the language, as well as the subject knowledge (Xiong and Shao, 2009). There are actually more people learning English in China than in any other economy, including the US. English has become a standard international language, making it critical to trade, commerce, and diplomacy. Knowing English can be beneficial in a variety of sectors and can provide a multitude of additional opportunities for a job seeker. Researchers in the US have found that having English as a second language is one of the biggest economic success indicators of immigrants or minority groups in the US, Canada, and Australia.

Learning about a foreign culture in conjunction with that culture's language provides an important context that in turn helps engage students and create more authentic learning experiences. This cultural understanding promotes increased global awareness of and respect for cultural differences. Research has shown (Guo, 2007) that there may be some hesitation to trade or engage with people from outside of one's own religious or cultural group. Therefore, raising awareness about others' cultures and religions and trying to break down these barriers can help to increase trade. Language and cultural competencies contribute toward the accomplishment of APEC goals to develop a labor force that can meet the job opportunities that economic integration offers. If we give students the tools necessary to be able to do this, they will have unique opportunities to cross religious and cultural lines.

Key Research

As the nature of work changes, so must education priorities. Studies in the US and Canada find that introducing children to foreign languages benefits ultimate proficiency in those languages, cognitive development, and performance in other content areas and on standardized assessments (Lazaruk, 2007; Soderman, 2005; Stewart, 2005; National Education Association, 2007; Jackson and Malone, 2009).

The cultural aspect of learning a language results in myriad benefits too (National Education Association, 2007). Learning about a foreign culture in conjunction with that culture's language provides an important context that in turn helps engage students and create more authentic learning experiences. This cultural understanding promotes increased global awareness of and respect for cultural differences (Jackson and Malone, 2009). Effective communication in a foreign language requires full fluency and proficiency when students graduate from high school.

Elementary/primary and secondary foreign language programs must be well articulated and use a sequenced curriculum that builds on learner knowledge from year to year and maximizes instructional impact (American Council on the Teaching of Foreign Languages, 2011; Pufahl and Rhodes, 2011; Lenker and Rhodes, 2007). O'Connell and Norwood (2007) argue for enhanced articulation of elementary/primary and secondary language programs, (a) to provide learners with opportunities for more advanced level and more in-depth area and language studies, and (b) to help students who reach fluency in foreign languages and cultures experience enhanced career opportunities and competitive advantages in the workforce. Singapore has a strong example of a language program that is comprehensive and well-articulated. Children are provided with content and language instruction in English and a "mother tongue" through all levels of schooling (Rubdy and Tupas, 2009). Such examples of a systematic approach to language learning support APEC economic interests, as workers who can communicate well in multiple languages are more competitive.

According to the Partnership for 21st Century Skills, global awareness and multilingual proficiency will be essential in preparing students to both find opportunities for themselves in the global marketplace and to be engaged as effective citizens of the world. A central part of this education is utilizing technology in an educational framework—to both facilitate teaching and give children experience with 21st century technology that they will need to be able to work with in their future careers and endeavors.

Technological competence is a current reality that will only continue to grow. Technology is changing; in addition to equipping students with the skills to use current technology, educators must provide them with the skills to prepare for future technology. In secondary schools in the US, using classroom-based technology to teach foreign language has increased significantly (Pufahl and Rhodes, 2011). In China, a recent study found that teaching a language through a computer-based gaming approach increased language proficiency and student motivation to learn the target language (Green, Sha and Liu, 2011).

Technology as an integral aspect of instructional strategy reflects shifting trends and paradigms in education and addresses practical concerns such as teacher shortages and budget restrictions (Nielson, Gonzalaz-Lloret, and Pinkney, 2009; Winke, Goertler, and Amuzie, 2010). Distance courses and blended online (hybrid) courses create a flexible teaching model in which one instructor can reach multiple classrooms in multiple schools. This allows more students to participate, including those in rural or low-income areas, and more languages to be offered, without increasing the demand for personnel.

To promote cooperation and collaboration, educators and policy makers should examine successful foreign language programs and policies from other economies. The average age for the introduction of second languages merits consideration. In the APEC region, second language instruction typically begins in Grade 3, while in China's Hong Kong SAR, the Chinese mainland, Malaysia, Singapore, and Thailand, second language instruction starts in Grade 1 (Chen, Sinclair, Huang and Eyerman, 2011). Most European Union (EU) countries introduce foreign language instruction in primary grades, and recent efforts have encouraged school systems to require instruction in two foreign languages (Commission of the European Communities, 2008). In 2007, 60 percent of EU secondary students were studying at least two foreign languages (Eurostat, 2009). In the US, only an estimated 41 percent of secondary students are enrolled in a foreign language (Pufahl and Rhodes, 2011).

Students must reach advanced proficiency in languages and cultures to be competitive job candidates in a global economy. Instructional programs must be well articulated and designed based on successful, evidence-based programs that are already producing bilingual and trilingual students. There is a lack of research into effective instructional models and strategies for teaching foreign languages (Jackson and Malone, 2009). Starting in early elementary grades, researchers should further investigate the extent to which different program interventions impact language learning and other content learning over time. As more and more technology is implemented in the classroom, additional studies should be conducted to determine how technology is implemented and how technology-based interventions influence learning.

New Directions/Recommendations

Learning a foreign language has cognitive and academic benefits and can help to advance cultural study and careers in a global market, with the extra benefit of improving general learning. Additional studies are needed to determine the most effective policies, programs, and strategies for teaching foreign languages. Findings from these studies can inform the design of coherent, consistent, and well-integrated models for teaching foreign languages at the elementary, secondary, and post-secondary levels. The models should also reflect the demands of an increasingly digital society by incorporating effective and innovative instructional technology.

Action 1: Research the economic benefits and advantages of foreign language acquisition for individuals and communities with detailed analyzes of:

- Different market sectors and what foreign language skill gaps exist within those sectors;
- What levels of proficiency are required to achieve different levels of economic gains/wage earning potential.

Action 2: Examine systematic approaches to language learning including examining articulation of language programs from K-16, including:

• Comparisons of how different economies align key system components (i.e. textbooks, teacher development, assessments, etc.) to systematically implement language programs over the academic career of students;

• Comparisons of how different economies differentiate foreign language instruction for students on various academic and vocational pathways.

Action 3: Support programs implementing models infused with instructional technology innovation, including:

• The exploration and replication of successful instructional methods from other economies and support experimental and other rigorous research studies to determine the effectiveness of specific program interventions to maximize their impact on foreign language teaching;

• Identifying promising practices in teacher preparation and teacher development for blended learning environments for language instruction;

• Identifying promising practices on using virtual environments to facilitate cooperative learning models of foreign languages, including cooperation on the classroom level and cooperation on the individual student level.

Action 4: Enhance the portal on the APEC wiki devoted to language acquisition and multi-cultural education that provides the most up-to-date research, issue briefs, articles, and commentaries from the APEC member economies.

References:

[1] American Council on the Teaching of Foreign Languages. (2011). *Characteristics of Effective Elementary School Foreign Language Programs*. Accessed December 1. http://www.actfl.org/i4a/pages/index.cfm?pageid=3655.

[2] Andrade, C., R., JR. Kretschmer, and L. Kretschmer. (1989). Two Languages for All Children: Expanding to Low Achievers and the Handicapped. In Muller, K. E. (Ed.) *Languages in Elementary Schools*, 177-203. New York: The American Forum for Global Education.

[3] Armstrong, P. W. and J. D. Rogers. (1997). Basic Skills Revisited: The Effects of Foreign Language Instruction on Reading, Math and Language Arts. *Learning Languages* (Spring): 20-31.

[4] Chen, H., P. Sinclair, S. Huang, and L. Eyerman. (2011). *APEC EDNET Project Seminar on Language Standards and Their Assessment: Background Research Paper*. Asia-Pacific Economic Cooperation. Accessed December 1. http://www.apecknowledgebank.org/file.aspx?id=959.

[5] Commission of the European Communities. (2008). *Multilingualism: An Asset for Europe and a Shared Commitment.* Communication from the Commission to the European Parliament, the Council, the European Economic and Social Committee and the Committee of the Regions. Brussels. http://ec.europa.eu/languages/pdf/comm2008_en.pdf.

[6] Curtain, H. and C. A. Dahlberg. (2004). *Languages and Children: Making the Match: New Languages for Young Learners, Grades K-8*. Third Edition. New York: Longman.

[7] Dumas, L. S. (1999). Learning a Second Language: Exposing Your Child to a New World of Words Boosts Her Brainpower, Vocabulary and Self-Esteem. *Child* (February): 72, 74, 76-77.

[8] Eurostat. (2009). *European Day of Languages* [News release], September 24. http://epp.eurostat.ec.europa.eu/cache/ITY_PUBLIC/3-24092009-AP/EN/3-24092009-AP-EN.PDF.

[9] Garfinkel, A., and K. E. Tabor. (1991). Elementary School Foreign Languages and English Reading Achievement: A New View of the Relationship. *Foreign Language Annals* 24 (5): 375-382.

[10] Green, P., Sha, M. and Liu, L. (2011). *The US-China E-Language Project: A Study of a Gaming Approach to English Language Learning for Middle School Students.* RTI International. Retrieved from: http://www.ed.gov/about/offices/list/opepd/ppss/reports.html

[11] Guo, Rongxing. (2007). Linguistic and Religious Influences on Foreign Trade: Evidence from East Asia, *Asian Economic Journal*, 21 (1): 101-21.

[12] Holobow, N., F. Genesee, W. Lambert, and L. Chartrand. (1988). *The Effectiveness of a Partial Immersion French Program for Students from Different Ethnic and Social Class Backgrounds.* Montreal: McGill University, Department of Psychology.

[13] Jackson, F. H., and M. E. Malone. (2009). *Building the Foreign Language Capacity We Need: Toward a Comprehensive Strategy for a National Framework.* Washington, DC: Center for Applied Linguistics.

[14] Lazaruk, W. (2007). Linguistic, Academic, and Cognitive Benefits of French Immersion. *The Canadian Modern Language review/La revue canadienne des langues vivantes* 63 (5): 605-628.

[15] LeLoup, J. W. and R. Ponterio. (2003). Second Language Acquisition and Technology: A Review of the Research, *ERIC Digest* (Washington, DC: Center for Applied Linguistics, ERIC Clearinghouse on Languages and Linguistics).

[16] Lenker, A. and N. C. Rhodes. (2007). Foreign Language Immersion Programs: Features and Trends over 35 Years. *The ACIE Newsletter* 10 (2):1-8.

[17] Masciantonio, R. (1977). Tangible Benefits of the Study of Latin: A Review of Research. *Foreign Language Annals* 10: 375-382.

[18] Melitz, J. (2005). *Language and Foreign Trade*. University of Strathclyde Working Paper (revised version of CEPR Working Paper No. 3590).

[19] National Education Association. (2007). The Benefits of Second Language Study. Regarding World Language Education. NEA Research. December.

[20] Nielson, K., M. Gonzalaz-Lloret, and K. Pinkney. (2009). *Learning Foreign Languages at a Distance: Characteristics of Effective Online Courses*. College Park: University of Maryland Center for Advanced Study of Language.

[21] O'Connell, M. E., and J. L. Norwood (eds.) (2007). *International Education and Foreign Languages: Keys to Securing America's Future*. Committee to Review the Title VI and Fulbright-Hayes International Education Programs. Washington, DC: National Academies Press. Retrieved from Catalog: American University database. Partnership for 21st Century Skills "Skills Framework." http://www.p21.org/overview/skills-framework.

[22] Pufahl, I. and N. C. Rhodes. (2011). Foreign Language Instruction in US Schools: Results of a National Survey of Elementary and Secondary Schools. The American Council on the Teaching of Foreign Languages. *Foreign Language Annals*, 44 (2): 258-288.

[23] Rafferty, E. A. (1986). *Second Language Study and Basic Skills in Louisiana*. Baton Rouge: Louisiana Department of Education. (ED283360). 80-85.

[24] Rubdy, R. and Tupas, T. R. F. (2009). Research in Applied Linguistics and Language Teaching and Learning in Singapore (2000-2007).

[25] Salaberry, M. R. (2001). The Use of Technology for Second Language Learning and Teaching: A Retrospective. *The Modern Language Journal*, 85 (i).

[26] Saunders, C. M. (1998). *The Effect of the Study of a Foreign Language in the Elementary School on Scores on the Iowa Test of Basic Skills and an Analysis of Student-Participants' Attitudes and Abilities*. Unpublished dissertation. University of Georgia.

[27] Soderman, A. K. (2005). Language Immersion Programs for Young Children? Yes, but Proceed with Caution. *Kappan*, 91: 54-61.

[28] Stewart, J. H. (2005). Foreign Language Study in Elementary Schools: Benefits and Implications for Achievement in Reading and Math. *Early Childhood Education Journal*, 33 (1): 11-16.

[29] Winke, P., S. Goertler, and G. L. Amuzie. (2010). Commonly Taught and Less Commonly Taught Learners: Are They Equally Prepared for CALL and Online Language Learning? *Computer Assisted Language Learning*, 23 (3): 199-219.

亚太经合组织在语言文化教育领域的引领作用

[美国] Adriana de Kanter and Bridget Belknap

摘要： 本文主要阐述了亚太经合组织是如何引领语言和文化教育的。为了促进经济发展和相互理解，生活在全球化社会中的公民需要掌握沟通技能，因此面向公民开展语言与文化教育至关重要。本文主要介绍亚太经合组织在语言与文化教育方面开展的工作。该组织的活动以经济和贸易为中心，英语虽然是其官方语言，但是自 2004 年以来却坚持把互相学习组织内他国语言作为教育的首要任务。这是因为，以往的重要研究表明：吸引儿童学习外语有利于其认知发展，学习语言和该语言中的文化存在着正向的关系，借助创新技术可促进语言的学习，而且也很有必要这样做。本文最后提出了下一步的研究方向和建议，包括学习一种以上语言产生的经济效益，12 年制教育体系中有必要精心制定、自始至终开设语言学习课程，向学生传授多种语言。

关键词： 亚太经合组织中的语言与文化教育；技术创新

Language Education Policy for the Cultivation of Language Talents

[Malaysia] Hisham Hj. Rahmat

Abstract: This paper aims to describe the language education policy known as the MBMMBI —*Memartabatkan Bahasa Malaysia Memperkukuh Bahasa Inggeris* policy: To Uphold Bahasa Malaysia and to Strengthen English Language policy, which is currently implemented in Malaysia to meet the objective of ensuring that each child can master both the Malay and English languages well and fluently. The overall objective of this policy is to produce Malaysians who are proficient in both languages to enable them to function effectively in all aspects of communication. This is indeed crucial as Malaysia aspires to become a high-income developed nation by the year 2020. Through the MBMMBI's soft landing approach, the reversion of the medium of instruction from English language to Bahasa Malaysia (Malay language) in all the national schools, from English language to Chinese language in the Chinese national type schools, and from English language to Tamil language in the Tamil national type schools for the teaching of mathematics and science is done on a gradual basis to make allowance for pupils' readiness and their cognitive ability. This paper outlines the strategies to strengthen the proficiency of English language, the second language, amongst Malaysian pupils. In discussing the implementation of the strategies, several factors and challenges such as teacher capacity building, provision of supplementary teaching and learning materials as well as the provision of language laboratories are discussed. In line with the introduction of this policy, the importance of cultivating the talents of Malaysian pupils for the local and global competitive demands for the workforce in the future is also highlighted.

Keywords: MBMMBI; English education; teacher capacity building; provision of supplementary teaching and learning materials

Introduction

Malaysia aims to become a developed high-income nation by the year 2020. In achieving this vision, various initiatives are drawn up and implemented to ensure that Malaysian human capital meets the challenges of the 21st century. It is believed that without the skilled and knowledgeable workers who are creatively, innovatively and intellectually responsive to the new demands of global economic changes, a country would not be able to advance greatly in today's competitive world. These global economic changes have indeed propelled many countries around the world to undertake education reforms to address social and economic issues, which include the need to advance in the science and technology field as well as in the information and communication technology related fields. Thus, it is imperative for all countries and regions, as well as the APEC members, to prepare their human capital with the 21st century skills in the millennium age, which includes developing the language talents to ensure the social and environmental stability as well as the economic prosperity of every nation.

The MBMMBI Policy — the Overall Objectives

In addressing the need to prepare the language talents of the 21st century, Malaysia introduced the MBMMBI—*Memartabatkan Bahasa Malaysia Memperkukuh Bahasa Inggeris*: To Uphold Bahasa Malaysia and to Strengthen English Language policy. The overall objective of this policy is to produce Malaysians who are proficient in both the Malay (Bahasa Malaysia) and English languages to enable them to function effectively in all aspects of communication. Thus, this policy has to ensure that each child can master both languages well and fluently. This is in reality a challenging task especially in upholding Bahasa Malaysia as the language of unity amongst the many races in Malaysia as well as developing proficiency in the English language, a second language amongst the Malaysian pupils. Inevitably, proficiency in the English language is important as

English is the international language of communication. Mastering the language and similarly cultivating language talents are vital communicative prerequisites as it has become a commercial commodity for one nation to compete locally and globally. Developing language talents for a variety of purposes ensures that a competitive workforce meets the demands for new technologies in the 21st century.

The Definition of MBMMBI

"To uphold Bahasa Malaysia" means to place the language in its rightful position especially as it is the national language of Malaysia as enshrined in Article 152. Bahasa Malaysia is also the main medium of instruction based on the Education Act of 1996.

"To strengthen the English language" means to enhance the command of the language as a compulsory language to be learned, the language of communication and the language of knowledge acquisition.

The Soft Landing Approach of the MBMMBI Policy

The MBMMBI policy is implemented in stages from the year 2010. During the transitional period, the teaching of mathematics and science is conducted in English and/or Bahasa Malaysia in the national primary and secondary schools. As for the Chinese national type schools, these subjects are taught in English and/or Chinese language. The subjects are taught in English and/or Tamil language in the Tamil national type schools. This choice of language for the teaching of mathematics and science takes into consideration teachers' and pupils' readiness to adjust to the change in the policy.

The soft landing approach of the MBMMBI policy enables primary and secondary school pupils who have learnt mathematics and science in English in or before 2010 to continue to do so until they complete Form 5 (16+ years of age).

With the soft landing approach, the teaching and learning of mathematics and science will be carried out fully in Bahasa Malaysia in 2016 in primary schools and in 2021 in secondary schools. This is indeed a key strategy in upholding Bahasa Malaysia as the main medium of instruction in MOE's national primary and secondary schools.

MBMMBI Strategies — How Is the MBMMBI Policy Implemented in Schools?

The MBMMBI policy is carried out in schools through reinstating Bahasa Malaysia as the medium of learning and teaching of science and mathematics, increasing the proficiency of Bahasa Malaysia and English language through extra teaching and learning periods as well as increasing the teaching capacity and human resource. Sufficient teaching and learning materials as well as the appropriate equipment are provided to create and sustain a conducive learning environment for school-going pupils in Malaysia. In addition to these strategies, information technology and communication is integrated in the teaching and learning of the two important languages in the Malaysian classrooms.

It is the main aim of this paper to focus on the strategies to strengthen the command of the English language, the second language in Malaysia:

1) Primary School English Curriculum Transformation

In 2011, a new primary school curriculum known as *Kurikulum Standard Sekolah Rendah* — KSSR was introduced for Year 1 pupils (6+ years of age). This standard-based curriculum emphasizes mastering basic literacy and strengthening English through the modular approach.

Furthermore, the curriculum emphasizes Back to Basics, which involves strengthening the mastering of basic English by focusing on phonics as well as incorporating enjoyable learning elements in the Language Arts module. The learning of grammar within context is given specific emphasis in the Grammar module.

The Language Arts Module stresses language appreciation and the learning of English through an entertaining way. Attractive and effective language teaching and learning is done through activities such as singing, jazz chants, choral speaking, drama, music and other teaching aids. Aesthetic reading materials, such as Children's Contemporary Literature, Structured Preliminary Reading materials and Extensive Reading are provided to expose pupils to various genres of English.

2) Quality English Language Teachers

It is important that the Ministry of Education (MOE) ensures that quality instruction is delivered in the Malaysian classrooms. In realizing this goal, teachers who teach the English language must be English-optioned to ensure that pupils receive quality instruction in the Malaysian schools. The MOE has planned and carried out various training programs to support the MBMMBI policy.

English-optioned teachers are required to attend in-service professional development courses to enhance and keep abreast with state-of-the-art pedagogy skills, and acquire the latest knowledge and technological skills.

Courses, such as Certificate in the Practice of English Language Teaching (C-PELT) for Non-Option English Language Teachers, are held to help teachers enhance their pedagogical skills as well as develop their English language proficiency. For those non-option teachers of English who do not follow the C-PELT course, another course entitled Reinforcing English Language Teaching for Non-Option English Language Teachers (RELTNOTe) is tailored for this group.

3) Native Speaker Program—Recruitment of Native Speakers as Mentors and Training Fellows

In building the teachers' capacity and developing competent English language teachers, 360 native speakers from English-speaking countries are recruited to work as mentors to teachers from 1,800 primary schools. These mentors have been specially selected to work collaboratively with the teachers from six zones throughout the country.

In enhancing the pedagogical skills of English language lecturers in Malaysia, five Institutes of Teacher Education have been identified as the Centers of Excellence for the English language, and native speakers known as Training Fellows are recruited to work closely with the lecturers.

The Native Speaker Program was implemented from 2011 to 2013 and the performance of the program was evaluated based on the Key Performance Indicators set by the MOE.

4) The Fulbright ETA—English Teaching Assistants (ETAs)

In 2011, 50 Fulbright English Teaching Assistants (ETAs) worked with English language teachers from 50 schools. Through this program, the ETAs from the United States of America assist teachers from English Language low-performing schools in the three states of Terengganu, Pahang and Johor. In 2012, a batch of 75 ETAs was recruited under this program. It was observed that through this program, pupils were motivated to communicate with the native speakers and gain confidence in speaking English.

5) Recruitment of Retired English Teachers on a Contract Basis

The MOE also recruited 600 retired teachers of English on a contract basis from 2011 to 2013 to work in primary schools that were short of English language teachers, especially those in rural areas. Every consecutive year beginning in 2011, a cohort of 200 teachers were inducted to the latest development in curriculum change, especially the new KSSR—Standard Curriculum for Primary School, which was introduced in 2011 for the Year 1 pupils. These contracted teachers, formally teachers of English, were trained on the new elements of the KSSR such as language arts, phonics, back to basics and other pedagogical elements.

6) Provision of Sufficient Teaching and Learning Materials: Digital Materials and Supplementary Reading Materials

Digital materials in the form of stand-alone compact discs (CDs) which can be used with all computers are provided to all schools. These materials can be used by teachers as teaching materials as well as learning materials for pupils to acquire English. Fun elements have been infused in the lessons provided on the CDs. Apart from these materials, supplementary extensive reading materials are provided for pupils to read.

7) Provision of Language Laboratories

With the introduction of the MBMMBI policy in 2011, another initiative was implemented and this involved the upgrading of the current multimedia laboratories to function as language laboratories in schools. These laboratories were equipped with audiovisual tools, and digital materials which emphasized the acquisition of language skills were provided.

8) Determining the English Model

The standard British English Model is used as a guide so that each teacher can refer to the same standard when it comes to pronunciation, writing and grammar.

9) School Leadership—Principals and Headmasters as Effective Curriculum Managers

Headmasters and principals are given more exposure relating to their roles as curriculum managers. The objectives and demands of the English curriculum are clearly shared and their engagement is ensured in planning suitable programs to achieve the set objectives.

10) English Language Support Activities

Various English language support activities are held at school, district, state and national levels to ensure pupil participation in the co-curricular activities. Choral speaking, storytelling, debate, drama, public speaking, and essay writing competitions are some of the activities held to develop the language talents of Malaysian children. Pupils also participate in international competitions to develop language skills in the cultivation of language talents.

This list of strategies is not exhaustive as there are other initiatives that are being piloted before they are implemented nationwide.

MBMMBI Implementation Committees

In monitoring the progress of all the strategies planned and implemented, six implementation committees are formed:

1. Curriculum Development Committee: It develops the standard curriculum document and implements curriculum transformation (Curriculum Development Division).

2. Textbook and Materials Committee: It provides textbooks and supplementary reading and digital materials (Textbook Division and Educational Technology Division).

3. Teacher Training and Development Committee: It conducts pre-service and in-service training (Teacher Education Division/Institute of Teacher Education, Malaysia).

4. Personnel Committee: It recruits retired teachers on a contract basis (Human Resource Management Division).

5. Publicity Committee: It plans publicity and mass media strategies to disseminate information on the MBMMBI policy to the general public (Corporate Communication Unit).

6. Logistics Committee: It plans and coordinates the provision of infrastructure, language laboratories and financial allocation (Finance Division).

Challenges and Opportunities

The implementation of any education policy has its own challenges and this inevitably leads to interim and improvement measures being taken to overcome prevailing issues. During the transition period of the soft landing approach of the MBMMBI policy, pupils' readiness to the change of the language of science and mathematics has been given its due attention to ensure a smooth and gradual implementation of the policy. Pupils who prefer to learn science and mathematics in Bahasa Malaysia are allowed to study these subjects fully in Bahasa Malaysia in the national primary and secondary schools. The need for these pupils to develop their English language proficiency to ensure their communicative and competitive abilities to seize the opportunities for future undertakings is done through various MBI—*Memperkukuh Bahasa Inggeris*, Strengthening the Command of the English Language Initiatives, some of which have been mentioned earlier. Thus, the development of the language talents of all the pupils in the Malaysian classrooms is given its adequate emphasis in the implementation of this policy.

Providing English-optioned teachers in the rural and remote schools is still a challenge. Pupils in these areas still grapple with their lack of ability to communicate in English. Teaching English and developing the language proficiency amongst the rural and remote school pupils is indeed where the main challenge is despite the current initiatives being implemented. The lack of opportunity to immerse in English, the second language, has been the challenge for many years and as such, serious attention to addressing this challenge has been given and it is a main focus of the MBMMBI policy.

Whenever a new curriculum change is implemented, inducting teachers to the new elements of the new curriculum has always been a challenge. More conceited and collaborative efforts to empower the District Education Office to play a bigger role are currently being planned to solve the recurring issue of cascade model and school-based training of teachers.

The Importance of Cultivating Language Talents and Recommendation

It is undeniable that school-going children of APEC members have to develop essential language talents to communicate functionally for various social and economic purposes in the 21st century. Member economies that invest poorly in this aspect will be at a losing end. Multi-talented and multi-skilled individuals who are able to carry out various challenging tasks will reap better social and economic opportunities in the future.

APEC members need to synergize efforts for regional cooperation and further international growth. Sharing expertise and skills for the cultivation of language talents amongst member economies is essential for the achievement of common goals in the arena. Sharing implementation issues and lessons learnt of every APEC member through regional forums and workshops will promise lucrative social and economic returns in the future. Activities that promote regional growth need to be systematically planned to ensure the social and economic well being of APEC members.

Conclusion

The implementation of the MBMMBI policy in Malaysia takes into consideration the important views of the stakeholders, namely the relevant NGOs (Non-Governmental Organizations), education-related agencies and associations, statesmen, academicians, parents, teachers and pupils alike. Thus, opinions and views through roundtable discussions and other mediums as well as research-based data were sought before this policy was introduced. The Ministry of Education of Malaysia is confident that with all the appropriate measures taken and with the support and commitment of all the stakeholders involved, especially the teachers as the key change agent, the objective of producing pupils who are fluent and confident in using both Bahasa Malaysia, the national language, and the English language, the international language, can be achieved. Continuous monitoring and ongoing evaluation of all the MBMMBI programs implemented provide the check and balance to analyze the strengths and weaknesses of the programs implemented for further improvement. The cultivation of language talents through various activities organized under this MBMMBI policy will ensure the provision of talented individuals for further challenging tasks in the ever competitive global world. All APEC members need to synergize efforts and work collaboratively towards achieving this common goal through the sharing of expertise and experiences that are unique in every APEC member.

References:

[1] Corporate Communication Unit, Ministry of Education, Malaysia. (2012). Ministry of Education policies, Frequently Asked Questions. http:www.moe.gov.my (August, 2012).

[2] Ministry of Education, Malaysia. (2010). To Uphold Bahasa Malaysia and to Strengthen the English Language. http://www.moe.gov.my (August, 2012).

语言人才培养的语言教育政策

[马来西亚] Hisham Hj. Rahmat

摘要：本文旨在描述马来西亚正在实施的“保护马来语和强化英语”的语言教育政策。首先阐述的是该语言政策的意义和重要内容。鉴于马来西亚有志于在 2020 年成为高收入的发达国家，因此这个政策意义重大。该政策的总目标是要培养能够流利使用两种语言、有效应对各种交流场合的马来西亚人。考虑到学生在适应语言政策变化的意愿和认知能力上存在差异，因此借助该政策中的“软着陆”方法，在国立学校、华语学校和泰米尔语学校，数学和自然科学课程的教学语言将采取逐步过渡的方式，从英语回归到马来语、华语和泰米尔语。本文还概述了在马来西亚学生中强化英语作为第二语言的具体策略，也探讨了诸如教师能力建设、补充性教学材料的提供和语言实验室建设等几个因素以及面临的挑战。本文最后强调：为了满足本国和全球市场对未来劳动力竞争性的需求，培养马来西亚学生的语言能力十分重要。

关键词：MBMMBI；英语教育；教师能力建设；补充性教学资料的提供

中国语言生活的时代特征

[中国] 李宇明

摘要：中国语言生活具有如下一些重要的时代特征："双言双语"的语言生活初步形成；虚拟语言生活在快速发展；中国"语言地图"在快速改写；快速的城市化进程急需语言规划；国内、国外两个语言大局需统筹兼顾。准确把握、深入认识这些语言国情，处理好语言关系，管理好语言生活，有效提升公民语言能力和国家语言能力，最大限度地获取各种"语言红利"，履行好国际语言义务等等，是国家语言规划的重要任务，也有许多崭新的学术课题。

关键词：语言生活；时代特征；语言规划

中国现代化的进程起步于清代晚期。在艰难曲折地走向现代化的风雨历程中，中国语文现代化思潮迭浪而兴，语文现代化运动接踵而起，并形成了不同时期的语言规划，促进语言生活逐渐现代化。

政府的职责之一就是管理语言生活。管理好语言生活，必须全面深入地了解语言生活的状况，准确把握语言生活的时代特征，在此基础上方能制定包括语言政策在内的科学的语言规划。进入 21 世纪，中国语言生活的基本状况如何，发展到了什么样的阶段，有哪些基本的时代特征，这是做好当今中国的语言规划必须考察的。

不过，语言生活这一话题学界讨论还不充分，语言国情的诸多方面还不怎么清楚，要全面准确地认识当下语言生活的时代特征还存在较大的学术困难。就当前的认识水平看，笔者认为中国语言生活最为重要的特征有如下四个方面：

一、“双言双语”（多言多语）① 的语言生活初步形成

（一）中国古代的“单言单语”生活

总体上看，中国古代的语言生活是“单言单语”型的。汉民族共同语的书面形式形成很早。“雅言”“通语”在秦汉时代已经存在，其后又有代行民族共同语职能的官话。但是，汉民族的口语在古代基本上是方言，即便是全国有大体相似的读书音和官场音，能够操读书音、官场音的人并不多，对全民的口语交际影响也不大。古代的中国是农业国，民众“乐土重迁”，交通、通信不发达，除了饥荒、战乱和有计划的移民之外，整体上看，人口活动的半径、流量和频率也都相当有限，因此能够操两种及多种方言的人数也不会很多，汉民族基本上是“单言生活”。

对于古代少数民族语言生活的研究，成果更是有限。哪些民族语言有方言差异，有多大程度上的方言差异，这些民族的成员操单言、操双言的情况如何，都不大清楚。但是根据当时人口流动的情况推测，有方言差异的少数民族，其语言生活也基本上应当是单言的。

中国是一个多民族国家，在边境地区，在民族杂居地区，在国家的政治中心，在专门处理民族事务和涉外事务的机构中，在许多民族的执政班子里，自古就有懂得两种或多种民族语言的人，也有懂得某种国外语言的人。但是双语人（包括多语人）在全民中必然是少数，双语使用的地域和社会领域必然不多，中国古代基本上是单语生活。

因此可以说，中国古代虽然存在一些双言双语人，有些地区、有些领域存在双言双语生活，但总体上看，语言生活是“单言单语”的。

（二）百年来语言统一的成就

现代意义上的语言统一运动，以 1911 年清朝《学部中央教育会议议决

---

① 在本文中，作为学术概念使用的“语”和“言”是不同的。“语”是语言，“言”是语言的变体，包括地方方言和共同语；方言是语言的地方变体，共同语是语言的高级变体。根据掌握语和言的数量，可以把人分为单言人、双言人、多言人和单语人、双语人、多语人等。为讨论问题的方便，一般情况下不严格区分双言人和多言人、双语人和多语人，说“双言人”时往往包含了“多言人”，说“双语人”时往往包含了“多语人”。根据社会交际使用“语”和“言”的数量，也可以把语言生活分为单言生活、双言生活、多言生活和单语生活、双语生活、多语生活等类型，同样为讨论问题的方便，语言生活一般情况下不严格区分双言生活和多言生活、双语生活和多语生活，说“双言生活”时往往包含了“多言生活”，说“双语生活”时往往包含了“多语生活”。

统一国语办法案》[②] 为标志。《统一国语办法案》承继了清末切音字运动的成果，开启了具有深远影响的国语运动。1949 年以后新中国持续地大力推广普通话，台湾光复之后台湾地区的华语普及，香港、澳门回归之后的普通话教育，以及新加坡 1979 年开始并持续 30 余年的讲华语运动，都是当时国语运动的纵向的历史延伸和横向的地域延展。

语言统一的百年历程，成就辉煌。这辉煌的成就表现在如下几个方面：

第一，确立了“以北京语音为标准音、以北方话为基础方言、以典范的现代白话文著作为语法规范”的汉民族共同语。而且，普通话在实践中和法律上都发展为国家通用语言，发挥着国语的职能。

第二，制定并推行了注音字母和汉语拼音方案。在广播、电视、电影等有声媒体不发达的时代，这些拼音工具对推行汉民族共同语的标准读音是不可缺少的；在当今有声媒体广泛普及的时代，这些拼音工具仍在发挥着多方面的重要作用。

第三，培养了大量的双言双语人，形成了双言社会和部分地区的双语社会。据统计，上世纪末祖国大陆能够使用普通话的比例为 53.06%[③]，随着时间的推移，现在能够使用普通话的人数应当达到了 70%[④]。台湾地区能够讲华语的人数比例更高。香港、澳门特区能够讲普通话的人数也在不断增加。当然，在普通话推广过程中，也出现了一批只会讲普通话不会讲方言的新的单言人，这种现象值得关注、值得研究。

就全国范围来看，普通话与汉语方言“共存共用”的局面已经形成。普通话是国家通用语言，主要用于教育、公务、新闻出版、大众服务等高层次、跨地区、跨民族、大范围的交际，汉语方言主要用于家庭、社区交际和乡土文化活动等方面。

有些民族由于各种各样的历史原因，已经放弃了自己的语言而转用汉语，如回族、满族等。但他们的语言转用，常常是因居住地不同而转用不同的汉语方言；随着普通话的推广，这些民族也形成了用汉语的双言社会。有些民族在保持本民族语言的同时也使用汉语，他们所使用的汉语也多是汉

② 见文字改革出版社编（1958）。

③ 见中国语言文字使用情况调查领导小组办公室编（2006）图 1。

④ 根据谢俊英等（2011：6）的报告，语言文字应用研究所 2010 年运用与“中国语言文字使用情况调查”（1999 年 8 月—2001 年 9 月实施）相近的方法，对河北、江苏、广西三省（区）进行了普通话普及情况的调查，发现这三省（区）能够用普通话交谈的比例达到了 70%—80%。

语方言；随着普通话的推广，这些民族成为双语双言民族，能够讲汉语方言，也能够讲普通话。有些单语民族随着普通话的推广，其成员也逐渐掌握了普通话，开始发展为双语民族。概言之，随着普通话的推广，汉族和转用汉语的少数民族由单言社会发展为双言社会；原来只讲本族语的民族发展为双语民族，原来的双语民族发展为双语双言民族。

不能忽略的是，中国许多少数民族语言也有方言的分歧。几十年来，这些有方言分歧的少数民族语言，也有了不少发展变化，比如蒙古语、壮语等都确立了本民族共同语的语音标准，并且还先后开展了标准音的测试。通过学校教育、标准音测试等，这些民族也出现了越来越多的掌握本民族共同语和本民族方言的人，在一些地区或领域也形成了民族的“双言”生活，并呈现不断发展的趋势。

（三）一百多年来外语教育的影响

中国现代意义上的外语教育，起码可以上溯到清末京师同文馆（1862年）和上海广方言馆（1863年）的建立以及洋务学堂中外语课程的设立。[⑤]此后，中国建立了现代学校制度，有了专门的外语院校，一般学校开设外语课程，一些教会学校使用外语作为教学媒介语，还有各种外语培训班、预科班以及社会上各种形式的外语学习。现在，据说外语学习者超过3亿人。

百多年来的外语教育，培养了大批的外语专门人才，同时也使许多受过一般教育的人有了外语知识或一定的外语能力，使单语人成为双语人或三语人。当然，由于特定的历史环境决定了中国有大规模的外语教育，有一定数量的双语人，但是基本上没有外语生活。从长远的发展来看，公民的外语水平还会不断提高，对外语的学习、利用还会加强，但是仍然不大可能形成外语生活。这很不同于曾经做过西方殖民地的中国香港、新加坡、印度、巴基斯坦以及一些阿拉伯国家、非洲国家；这些地区和国家，原来宗主国的语言或是官方工作语言，或在教育、商务等领域中继续应用。

（四）“双言双语”社会的语言问题

研究“双言双语”人和“双言双语”社会的特点，做出科学的语言规划，是时代提出的新课题。就语言生活的这一时代特征而言，有如下几个方面的问题值得注意：

⑤ 参见高晓芳（2006）。

1. 应当对“双言双语”社会给予积极评价。由“单言单语”人发展为“双言双语（多言多语）”人，由“单言单语”生活发展为“双言双语（多言多语）”生活，是社会的进步、教育的进步、语言生活的进步，应当正确评价它，积极促进它，不断完善它。我们习惯了“单言单语”社会，形成了思维惯性，对“双言双语”社会缺乏必要的认识，因此，在认识上和实践中都会遇到许多新问题，都会有许多不适应，需要逐渐建立一系列的新理念，需要逐渐形成适合中国国情的“双言双语”社会的语言规划，需要采取一系列的新政策、新举措。

2. 要处理好“语言关系”。“单言单语”社会的主要矛盾是克服语言交际障碍，“双言双语”社会的主要矛盾是处理好语言关系，具体到中国当前的国情而言，就是处理好中华民族各语言、各方言的关系，处理好母语与外语的关系。要保证国家通用语言在高层交际中发挥作用，同时也要发挥其他的语言和汉语方言的作用，构建和谐的语言生活。

3. 探讨建立公民语言能力标准。中国的教育实践和用人实践，已经基本形成了“双言双语”社会对公民语言能力的要求，即：

（1）汉族和一些转用汉语的民族，其成员应当具有“双言双语”的能力，即掌握普通话和某种汉语方言，并具有一定的外语能力；

（2）没有转用汉语的少数民族，其成员应当具有“三语”能力，即掌握母语和国家通用语言，并具有一定的外语能力；

（3）受过研究生教育的精英人才，应当掌握两门外语。

应当把这种实践“物化”为教育标准，并进而形成公民的语言能力标准。“双语”能力或“三语”能力，已经是许许多多国家的教育标准，是国际发展的大趋势。

二、现实与虚拟两个空间的语言生活相互促进

（一）虚拟语言生活的产生与发展

在人类漫长的历史中，语言生活只有现实语言生活，只存在人与人的交际，即“人－人交际”。在牧民、农民、猎人、驯兽师和骑兵那里，人类也可能用有声语言或是特殊的符号、身姿同动物进行交际，但这种交际不是真

正的语言交际，起作用的不是语义而是符号，与人类的交际不在一个性质层面上。⑥

人类在20世纪上半叶发明了计算机，之后不久就尝试让其进行语言翻译，从此开始了艰难而又充满魅力的语言处理之路，发展人类与机器的交际，即“人－机交际”。计算机语言处理技术不断发展和普及，各种语言技术产品逐渐发明并进入日常语言生活，人与计算机的语言交际逐渐形成。“人－机交际”由使用符号交际到趋近于语音、文字交际，由技术人员与计算机交际发展为一般人与计算机交际。特别是随着互联网的发明并逐渐商业化，机器之间的信息传输（“机－机交际”）开始出现且迅速发展起来，人类在现实世界的基础上又构建起一个虚拟世界，同时在现实语言生活的基础上产生了虚拟语言生活。

（二）虚拟语言生活产生的巨大效应

虚拟语言生活对社会的影响是广泛、巨大而深远的。

首先，人类的语言交际形式发生了巨大的变化。虚拟语言生活是由现代语言技术做支撑的，现代语言技术以计算机语言处理为基础，它的逐步发展和快速普及，使语言交际在“人－人交际”的基础上又发展出“人－机交际”和“机－机交际”。到了现在，“人－人交际”也越来越多地依赖机器的帮助，形成了“人－机－人”（包括“人－机－机－人”）的混成式交际。在过去，书写是受过教育的公民必须具备的素养；而混成式交际的发展，使得现代语言技术成为公民应当具备的语言素养。

其次，语言进入国家的“硬实力”范畴。现代语言技术的发展在相当大的程度上依赖于语言文字知识，一些语言文字知识还转化为信息工业的标准。现代语言技术的发展虽然只有几十年的历史，但已经孕育了一批语言新职业，如语言速录师、语言工程师、字库设计师等；产生了一批语言新产业，如语言文字的输入与识别、计算机字库的建设、语言文字的传输与输出、自动翻译、语言文字信息的检索与加工、电子阅读等高新技术所形成的产业，由此而形成了宏富的语言经济。同时像打字员、字模铸造、纸质信件通信、电报等一些传统的语言职业和语言产业，也在蜕变或消逝，从而带来社会经

⑥ 参见李宇明（1989）。

济结构的变化。语言是国家的“软实力”已有共识，但仅有此等认识是不够的，应当看到语言已经发展为国家的“硬实力”。[⑦]

第三，虚拟语言生活对现实语言生活的影响越来越大。虚拟语言生活是在现实语言生活的基础上产生的，但反过来又在影响现实语言生活，而且这种影响越来越大。其主要表现如：

1. 以新词语为代表的许多语言新现象，首先在虚拟语言生活中聚集萌生，然后进入现实语言生活。虚拟空间成为新词语等新语言现象的主要滋生地和繁衍区。

2. 产生了电子邮件、BBS、QQ、博客、微博、微信等许多新的信息传播方式，网络逐渐成为信息的集散地和“反应堆”，以新媒体的身份深刻地影响着现实语言生活。

3. 人类在现实生活中的许多活动，都尝试着迁移到网络上去运行，如电子政务、电子商务、电子学务、电子出版、电子娱乐等等，构成了当今的虚拟生活。这些虚拟生活往往都伴随着现代语言技术进行，成为虚拟语言生活的组成部分。

4. 网络已经成为人类最大、更新最快的信息贮存库，纸媒出版物（包括辞书）、图书馆、档案馆、博物馆的许多职能，将越来越多地让位于网络。但是，网络的信息有许多是需要过滤、挖掘和整理的，应充分认识网络信息贮存库的作用，努力发展网络信息挖掘技术，及时有效地利用网络信息。

特别是随着云计算、物联网由概念逐渐变为现实，互联网正在发生质的跃变，其功能将更加强大，其对现实生活的介入将更为全面而深入。与之相应，虚拟语言生活将更为发达，其对现实语言生活的影响也将更为全面、深入和强烈。

（三）虚实语言生活背景下的语言规划

过去的语言规划，主要处理语言与人的关系，现在必须要处理语言、人、机器三者之间的关系。过去只考虑现实语言生活的问题，现在需要考虑两个空间的语言生活问题。由于虚拟语言生活产生时间不长，对它的研究还较为浮浅，因此虚拟语言生活还较少进入语言规划者的视野，这显然是落后于时局的。在虚实两个空间的语言生活的背景下，语言规划应当注意如下一些问题：

---

⑦ 参见李宇明（2011）。

1. 促进虚拟语言生活的健康发展。应当以积极的态度来看待虚拟语言生活，不能无视它的存在与发展，更不能把它仅仅作为现实语言生活的附庸，用现实语言生活的观念去看待它，用管理现实语言生活的办法去管理它，甚至用削足适履的方法去限制它。语言规划应当促进虚拟语言生活快速而健康地发展。

中国虚拟语言生活的网络空间，应当尽可能地适合国人的生活习惯，最大限度地适合中华语言文字的使用习惯。这关系到硬件、软件和各种语言信息技术：一方面，需要拥有更多的信息技术方面的知识产权；另一方面，在软件设计、语言文字应用乃至各种细微末节上，都要充分重视国人的文化习惯，与人“友好”。

要不断提升国人虚拟语言生活的质量。从发展眼光看，虚拟语言生活不是少数人或某一部分人的语言生活，而应当是大多数人的语言生活，具有普惠性。到 2011 年 9 月底，中国互联网用户已突破 5 亿，互联网普及率接近 40%。我们应当帮助更多的人步入虚拟语言生活，减少“信息边缘化”的人群。应当放开思路，设想在虚拟空间中可以过哪些语言生活，并有计划地孕育它、发展它。应当着意建立虚拟语言生活的各种运行规则，建立合理的秩序，着力提高虚拟语言生活质量，并把这些规则、这种秩序尽力向外延展，为国际虚拟语言生活做出中国人的贡献。

2. 虚实语言生活相互促进。研究虚拟语言生活对现实语言生活的影响，例如：电脑的使用是否会带来书写水平的减退？怎样看待书写能力的减退？影响汉字发展演变的主要动因是书写，“书写”方式的演变对汉字的发展演变会带来什么影响？人们的阅读习惯、信息获取习惯、语言表达习惯等都会发生一些什么样变化？通过这些研究，采取一定措施，减少其负面影响，扩大其积极作用。同时要努力做好虚实两界语言生活的沟通，相互促进，保证语言生活的和谐。

3. 更加重视“语言资源”的理念。不仅把语言看作“问题”，而且把语言看作文化资源和经济资源的理念，称为“语言资源”理念。在现代语言技术快速发展的背景下，语言资源理念得到了突显和新阐释。今天的语言规划，必须在语言经济学的支撑下充分重视、尽力保护、全面开发语言资源，促进现代语言技术的发展，促进语言职业和语言产业的发展，充分发挥语言对社会的经济贡献，收取“语言红利”。

三、城市与乡村的语言生活正在发生巨变

（一）快速的城市化进程

当前，中国社会最为突出的变化是快速发展的城市化（或称“城镇化”）进程。新中国早期的城市化率很低，且长期徘徊不前。1950年城市化率为11.2%，1978年为17.92%，年增长率约为0.23%。改革开放之后，城市化进程不断加速。1980年城市化率为19.4%，1998年为30.42%，2008年为45.68%，年增长率超过13%。[8] 2009年中国城市化率已达47%，2011年大约为50%。世界城市化率2000年为48%，估计现在也为50%左右，这就是说，中国的城市化已经与国际平均水平大体相当。

2009年底召开的中央经济工作会议，要求继续促进大中小城市和小城镇的协调发展，并放宽中小城市和城镇户籍限制。国务院批转的发改委《关于2010年深化经济体制改革重点工作的意见》，提出要“深化户籍制度改革，加快落实放宽中小城市、小城镇特别是县城和中心镇落户条件的政策。进一步完善暂住人口登记制度，逐步在全国范围内实行居住证制度”，这将更加方便农业人口逐步向城镇转移。2011年3月5日公布的中国“十二五”规划纲要草案指出，“十二五”期间还将积极稳妥地推进城镇化，到2015年城市化率提高到51.5%。可以预计，中国城市化进程还将飞速发展，2050年之前可能达到70%以上，向先进国家的城市化水平靠近。

城市化使农民变成市民或是“农民工”，使许多农村变成城镇，使小城市变为大城市，使大城市变得更大，激发了它们成为国际化大都市的雄心，并逐渐形成若干城市群。这些变化将使中国的“语言地图”快速改写，语言生活发生前所未有的重大变化。

（二）城市语言规划

城市需要建设规划，也需要语言规划，其实可以认为城市语言规划就是城市建设规划的有机组成部分。城市语言规划主要有如下几个方面的内容：

第一，城市语言生活中主导性的语言文字。主导性的语言文字，是指在政府公务、教育、新闻出版、大众服务等领域主要使用哪种或哪些语言文字。依照《国家通用语言文字法》，中国城市的主导性语言文字应当是国家通用

---

⑧ 参见范恒山等（2009）。

语言文字。在民族自治地方，主导性语言文字还包括自治地方的民族语言文字。

第二，对新老市民、进城务工人员进行语言培训与指导。城市语言生活与农村语言生活有很大不同，对于新市民和进城务工人员，在使用的语言或方言、同周围交换信息的内容与方式等方面，都需要进行指导或培训，以便使其尽快适应城市语言生活。由于时代的发展变化、郊区人口向城市中心区的移动，以及新市民和大量进城务工人员的涌入，老市民也面临新的语言生活，也会出现焦虑等各种不适应，严重时还会发生新老群体的语言冲突乃至社会冲突。因此，对于一些发展较快的城市，需要有计划地指导老市民适应新的语言生活。

第三，社会语言服务。社会语言服务已经具备为城市发展规划而服务的信息服务功能。社会语言服务的内容十分广泛，包括道路街巷、公共单位的各种牌匾标示，以及商贸、旅游、交通、邮政、金融、医疗、文化娱乐等领域的语言文字应用。特别是一些特殊的社会语言服务，更是城市语言规划所应特别考虑的，比如对盲、聋等残障人士的语言服务，对语言不通的外来人士的语言服务，包括对外国来华人员的外语服务等。

第四，通过语言特色展现城市文化风貌。城市建设应当有各自的文化特色，而不同的文化特色不仅表现在外部建筑上，也体现在文化内涵上。语言及其负载的文化艺术是展现城市文化风貌的重要资源，例如报纸、广播、电视适当地体现地方语言文化，带有地方特色的语言文化博物馆，曲艺、歌谣、传说等地方语言文化的收集整理与展示、传承等等，都能展现城市文化风貌。

（三）保存当今的“语言地图”

伴随着城乡地图的快速变化，在不长的时间里，中国“语言地图”必将大幅度改写。这种改写也许无法避免，但应当用多媒体技术把现代语言实态记录下来，留下语言的有声数据，留下今日语言地图的轮廓，以此作为“科学保护各民族语言文字”的重要举措。2011 年 9 月 6 日，在纪念中央文史研究馆成立 60 周年座谈会上，冯骥才先生指出，五千年历史留给我们的千姿万态的古村落的存亡，已经到了紧急关头。每座古村落都是一部厚重的书，可是没等我们去认真翻阅它、阅读它，便在城镇化大潮中很快消失不见了。语言和方言也是一部部厚重的书，许多中华语言（包括方言）所面临的状况，不会比冯骥才先生描述的古村落的状况好，而且更加不为人所关注。中华语言及其各种方言的濒危与消亡，是国家语言资源的严重流失，是中华文化不可复现性的损失。

提倡双言双语制度。这既是对中国已经初步形成的“双言双语”生活的认定，也是解决语言沟通和语言保存的治本之策。掌握国家通用语言可以顺畅进行地区间、民族间的交际，同时传承民族母语、传承方言，可以保存语言文化的多样性景观。在城市化率较低、城市化进程较为缓慢的时期，在国家通用语言文字普及程度较低的时期，推广普通话是国家语言文字工作的主要任务。而当今在大力推广和规范使用国家通用语言文字的同时，也必须认真考虑语言保护的各种问题，“两条腿走路”。

当然，保存当今的“语言地图”，也还有其他办法，比如在可能的条件下建立“语言保护区”，以便对濒危语言或濒危方言进行“活态语言”保护。通过非物质文化遗产的保护项目，对与非物质文化遗产关系密切的一些语言或方言进行保护。鼓励有条件的地方建立语言文化博物馆，或在博物馆、展览馆中专辟语言文化展室。互联网的发展为语言保护提供了新手段，可以建立虚拟的语言文化博物馆，用现代信息技术进行语言文化的收集、保存与展览、开发等。

总之，在快速的城市化进程中，会产生一些新的语言矛盾，出现一些新的语言问题。在此境况下，必须认真思考它会对国家的语言面貌产生何种影响，会有哪些新的语言问题需要解决，会有哪些特殊人群需要特殊的语言服务，怎样通过科学的语言规划和有效的语言行动，来保证城市化进程的顺畅前行，保障城乡二元语言生活的和谐。

四、国内和国外两个大局统筹兼顾

改革开放开启了中国新时期的国际化进程，30余年的改革开放，使中国人有了更多的国际语言生活和外语需求，汉语也伴随着国家走向世界的步伐快速向世界传播，语言文字事业逐渐形成了国内和国外两个大局。当代中国的语言规划必须兼顾国内和国外两个大局。

（一）推进中华语言的国际传播

随着国家的改革开放和国家国际地位的提升，中华语言也加快了向海外传播的步伐，不少外籍人士已经把汉语看作仅次于英语的第二大商务用语。

为加快中华语言的国际传播，需要注意几个方面的问题：

第一，科学推进汉语在国际上的传播。衡量其是否科学，大概有以下几个可以考虑的指标：

1. 能否满足世界各国学习汉语的需求；

2. 能否为汉语学习者带来学习之后的应有的实际效益；

3. 在教学标准、教材教辅、教学方法、考试、师资供给、教学声望等方面，能否赶上当前向外传播较好的语言；

4. 国家是否收到了应得的“语言传播红利”，包括经济利益和文化利益等；

5. 汉语传播事业能否可持续发展。

这些指标，标志着汉语国际传播的理想状态。要达到如此的理想状态，就需要分析古今中外语言传播现象，研究语言传播规律，据此制定汉语国际传播规划，并在实践中不断调适完善。

第二，协调好与海外华语的关系。海外华语是汉语走向世界的先遣队，普通话的规范标准、汉语作为第二语言的教学标准，都应考虑到海外华语的存在现状，最大限度地实现本土与海外的语言沟通，使“以普通话为基础的全世界华人的共同语”这一“大华语”的概念⑨，在本土与海外的语言沟通中发挥作用。华语之间的协调，进而可以发展为各地华语教育机构的协调，其理想状态是形成同盟关系，联合制定教学标准，编写教材和教辅材料，研讨教学方法，协调考试办法，共认考试结果，促进华语教学事业的良性发展。

第三，与国内语言文字事业结合起来，形成合力。国内语言文字事业是汉语研究、汉语教育和普通话推广的大本营，拥有丰厚的人力资源和智力资源，将这些资源转换为汉语国际教学资源，会源源不竭，可持续发展。这方面的结合，也是语言文字事业的国内大局和国外大局协调发展的最为重要的体现。

同时，汉语的国际传播也要同中国少数民族语言的国际传播结合起来。我国许多少数民族语言，如蒙古语、藏语、维吾尔语、彝语、傣语、满语等，国际上都有数量不等的学习者和研究者。汉语国际传播同少数民族语言的国际传播，应有所统筹，共同发展，形成中华语言国际传播的磅礴阵势。向外传播少数民族语言，满足国际需求，既是中国的国际义务，同时也关乎国家安全。

⑨ 见李宇明主编（2010）《全球华语词典》前言。

（二）提升国家外语能力

国家在处理海内外各种事务时，都需要得到合适的语言支援。能否得到合适的语言支援，取决于国家的语言能力，包括国家的外语能力。过去中国的外语学习，除了外交的需求之外，主要是向西方学习先进的科学文化，因此外语语种单寡，教学的重点是外语的标准语和书面语，外语界的学术研究也侧重在外语教学上。在国门封闭的时代，这种情况尚能基本适应国家的需求，但就当今中国改革开放的形势及国家的未来发展看，已经远远不能满足国家需求。

随着中国改革开放和国际地位的提升，外国朋友来华工作、学习、开会、旅游甚至定居者与日俱增，一些大型的运动会、博览会、商贸洽谈会、学术会议等也常在中国召开。中国需要为他们提供必要的外语服务。外语服务涉及诸多方面的问题，比如公共服务领域的外文标示、说明文字及口语服务等，许多外国人聚集社区的外语服务等，重大国际会议、会展的外语服务等，非通用外语语种人才的培养和社会工作者的外语培训等。

中国的海外事务越来越多，比如，到各种国际组织中任职服务，国际维和、反恐、救灾等人道主义合作，劳务输出，国际经贸、科技、文化活动，塑造国家的良好国际形象，争取国际话语权等等，海外事务对国家的发展越来越重要。当今的国家利益已超出本土，如何用世界各国人民习用的语言介绍真实的中国，减少误解与冲突，如何通过语言保护国家的海外利益和出国人员的安全，已是必须考虑的国务大事。正因如此，我们需要全方位地了解世界，仔细地研究世界，学会进行“国际游戏”。这些都需要精通更多语种的外语人才，需要更多的兼通多门外语或兼通某种专业的复合型外语人才。

提升国家的外语能力，已成为国家发展之大计。要尽快了解各行业的外语需求，盘点国家的外语人才状况，成立具有多方协调能力的外语管理机构，制定合适的外语发展战略，制定国际化人才的语言培育规划，拿出具体有效的措施，尽快解决外语语种单寡、外语人才单纯的问题。

（三）解决好跨境语言问题

跨境语言问题，既是国内语言问题，也是国外语言问题。解决好跨境语言问题，是睦邻戍边的需要，也是提升国家语言能力的重要环节。中国的跨境语言（包括跨境方言）估计超过 30 种，情况错综复杂。跨境语言处理得当，境睦边安，中华文化与科学技术能够自然延展，四邻受惠；处理不好，会损失语言资源，削弱语言能力，诱发各种语言矛盾，出现文化“倒灌”现象，带来国家安全方面的种种隐患。

当前，我们对跨境语言的重要性认识不足，对跨境语言的现实情况不太了解，特别是这些语言在邻国的使用情况。应当利用多种方式开展跨境语言的调查研究，科学制定跨境语言政策，有计划地培养跨境语言人才。做好跨境语言工作，就等于为国境铺设了一条新的安全线，为四邻架设了一座座友谊桥。

（四）履行国际语言义务

作为一个负责任的大国，必须履行一系列国际义务，其中包括语言方面的国际义务。国际领域的语言事务主要是：对人类面临的主要语言问题进行研究，利用国际力量来正确对待这些问题，合理解决这些问题；建立健全国际语言秩序，化解语言矛盾，为各国的语言规划进行咨询或建议，帮助世界人民过好语言生活。据笔者陋见，当前最需关注的有如下三个方面：

第一，维护语言权益。语言权益是人权的重要组成部分。个人、民族、国家都拥有各种语言权益，这些语言权益需要国际社会通过公约、倡议等各种方式来维护。比如移民的语言权益、弱小民族的语言权益、发展中国家的话语权问题等。

第二，保障语言沟通。国际社会需要相互沟通，因此需要科学规划国际多边组织、跨国的地区组织等的工作语言，需要通过公平的国际标准等保障互联网上的语言传输。通过沟通增进了解，增加互信，减少误会。

第三，保护濒危语言。语言是文化的贮存库，语言的消逝是人类文化不可挽回的损失。据估计，人类现存的6,000种左右的语言，有90%可能会在本世纪消逝。面对这种“文化劫难”，人类需要采取切实的措施，尽量延缓这些语言的消亡，或是进行“活态”保护，或是通过现代信息技术将这些语言的资料保存下来。

五、结　语

双言双语社会的逐渐形成、虚实两个空间语言生活的分野与连通、城乡语言规划问题及“语言地图”的快速改写、国内外两个语言大局的统筹兼顾，构成了当下中国主要的语言国情。认识这种语言国情，准确地把握这种语言国情，是国家语言规划的基础，也有许多崭新的学术课题。

在这种形势下，语言与国家的关系提到了新高度。语言与国家认同、民族认同、地区认同，语言与国家安全，语言与国家的创新能力，语言与国家信息化发展，语言对社会的经济贡献等，成为政界学界常议之话题。语言矛盾呈现易于激化的态势，许多社会的、文化的冲突往往伴之以语言冲突，或者直接表现为语言冲突。这种倾向在世界许多国家也都有明显表现，甚至引发政府危机和“语言战争”。此外，语言生活的多需求，对语言服务的要求越来越多样，越来越迫切，必须尽快建立政府指导、社会参与、多种机制并发的社会语言服务体系。

语言规划就是要解决国家和人类发展中遇到的各种语言问题。当今之世，要求我们必须站在国际化的角度关注中国的语言生活，站在信息化的高度观照现实语言生活，站在世界大国的立场做中国语言规划，努力提升公民的语言应用能力，尽快提升国家的语言能力，切实履行国际领域的语言义务，促进中国乃至世界语言生活的和谐。

参考文献

[1] [以] 博纳德 • 斯波斯基（2011）张治国译，《语言政策——社会语言学中的重要论题》，北京：商务印书馆。

[2] 陈章太（2009）语言资源与语言问题，《云南师范大学学报（哲学社会科学版）》第 4 期。

[3] 戴庆厦主编（1993）《跨境语言研究》，北京：中央民族学院出版社。

[4] 戴庆厦（2010）语言关系与国家安全，《云南师范大学学报（哲学社会科学版）》第 2 期。

[5] 范恒山、陶良虎主编（2009）《中国城市化进程》，北京：人民出版社。

[6] 高晓芳（2006）《晚清洋务学堂的外语教育研究》，北京：商务印书馆。

[7] 郭龙生（2008）《中国当代语言规划的理论与实践》，广州：广东教育出版社。

[8] 何俊芳、周庆生（2010）《语言冲突研究》，北京：中央民族大学出版社。

[9] 李现乐（2010）语言资源和语言问题视角下的语言服务研究，《云南师范大学学报（哲学社会科学版）》第 5 期。

[10] 李宇明（1989）人对动物语言交际的特点，《语言学通讯》（华中师范大学）第 2 期。

[11] 李宇明主编（2010）《全球华语词典》，北京：商务印书馆。
[12] 李宇明（2011）语言也是“硬实力”，《华中师范大学学报（人文社会科学版）》第5期；《新华文摘》第23期。
[13] 屈哨兵（2010）关于《中国语言生活状况报告》中语言服务问题的观察与思考，《云南师范大学学报（哲学社会科学版）》第5期。
[14] 谢俊英、李卫红、姚喜双、魏 晖（2011）普通话普及情况调查分析，《语言文字应用》第3期。
[15] 王建勤（2010）美国“关键语言”战略与我国国家安全语言战略，《云南师范大学学报（哲学社会科学版）》第2期。
[16] 文秋芳、苏 静、监艳红（2011）国家外语能力的理论构建与应用尝试，《中国外语》第3期。
[17] 文字改革出版社编（1958）《清末文字改革文集》，北京：文字改革出版社。
[18] 赵蓉晖（2010）国家安全视域的中国外语规划，《云南师范大学学报（哲学社会科学版）》第2期。
[19] 中国语言文字使用情况调查领导小组办公室编（2006）《中国语言文字使用情况调查资料》，北京：语文出版社。

The Time Characteristics of the Chinese Language

[People's Republic of China] Li Yuming

Abstract: The Chinese language situation has the following important time characteristics: the initial formation of a language featuring bilingualism, the rapid development of the virtual language, the fast rewriting of the Chinese language map, the urgent need for language planning in rapid urbanization, and the coordination of the domestic and foreign language situation in general. It is important for national language planning to accurately grasp and deeply understand the national situation of these languages, handle well language relations, manage language situation, effectively improve the language abilities of the citizens and the nation, maximize various "language bonuses", and fulfill international language obligations. In today's world, we need to pay close attention to China's language situation from an international perspective, observe real language situation in terms of information development, establish China's language planning from the standing of a world power, and strive to improve citizens' application of languages so as to enhance the country's language abilities for the better fulfillment of its international language obligations and the harmony of language situation in China and around the globe.

Keywords: language planning; language policy; monolingual; multilingual

Language Education Strategy, Language Education and Talents Cultivation in the Philippines

[The Philippines] Anna Marie Baligod-San Diego

Abstract: The Philippines is home to 110 known languages. Our country is an archipelago made up of more than 7,000 islands. Our natural landscape helped create unique cultures and languages that mark each region and province. These are some of the reasons which make our nation and our language situation unique.

Language is identified as a means to bind any group of people together. Realizing the potential effects of language, our constitution has mandated to have a national language — Filipino. The constitution also recognizes that since it is a very young language, it has great potential to evolve, "and it shall be further developed and enriched on the basis of existing Philippino and other languages". Our law made explicit mention that subject to provisions of law and as Congress may deem appropriate, the government "shall take steps to initiate and sustain the use of Filipino as a medium of official communication and as language of instruction in the educational system. For the purposes of communication and instruction, the official languages of the Philippines are Filipino and, until otherwise provided by law, English. The regional languages are the auxiliary official languages in the regions and shall serve as auxiliary media of instruction therein."

This provision in our constitution is now open to various interpretations, and has inadvertently created confusion among our people. The present administration is very keen on spelling out and formulating steps that would help eradicate this confusion without sacrificing whatever language gains we have so far. We have special programs that enhance the use of both our national language, Filipino, and our second official language, English.

At this time, we are at the brink of change. Our government has foreseen the possible effects of globalization, which is why it has encouraged the Department of Education

(DepEd) through the Bureau of Secondary Education to expand its Special Program for Foreign Languages. It boasts programs for language learners of German, French, Japanese, Spanish, and Mandarin. And soon, it will also open language programs for language learners of Arabic and Korean.

All learners and their trainers will come together during the National Festival of Talents, a culminating activity that will pit the best of each region with each other.

This paper seeks to explain how these various language programs function and help our students and teachers, including their training and selection. It also presents a clear picture on how the DepEd works through enhancing the teaching and learning of our national and official languages.

In the light of the Mother Tongue-Based Multilingual Education (MTB-MLE) introduced at the primary level, this paper shows the department's plan to strike a good balance on all the language concerns of its stakeholders.

Keywords: Filipino; Special Program for Foreign Languages; language education policy; talents cultivation; MTB-MLE

The Philippines is home to 110 known languages. Our country is an archipelago made up of more than 7,000 islands. Our natural landscape helped create unique cultures and languages that mark each region and province. These are some of the reasons which make our nation and our language situation unique.

Language is identified as a means to bind any group of people together. Realizing the potential effects of language, the Philippine constitution has mandated that Filipino be the national language. The constitution also recognizes that since it is a very young language, it has great potential to evolve, "and it shall be further developed and enriched on the basis of existing Philippine and other languages." Our law made explicit mention that subject to provisions of law and as Congress may deem appropriate, the government "shall take steps to initiate and sustain the use of Filipino as the medium of official communication and as language of instruction in the educational system. For the purposes of communication and instruction, the official languages of the Philippines are

Filipino and, until otherwise provided by law, English. The regional languages are the auxiliary official languages in the regions and shall serve as auxiliary media of instruction therein."

This provision in our constitution is now open to various interpretations, and has inadvertently created confusion among our people. The present administration is very keen on spelling out and formulating steps that would help eradicate this confusion without sacrificing whatever language gains we have so far. We have special programs that enhance the use of both our national language, Filipino, our second official language, English, and the other regional languages.

In 2012, the Department of Education issued an order that mandates all public schools to implement Mother Tongue-Based Multilingual Education (MTB-MLE), specifically in kindergartens, Grades 1, 2 and 3 as part of the K to 12 Basic Education Program. MTB-MLE is the effective use of more than two languages for literacy and instruction.

MTB-MLE aims to develop the following areas:

1. Language development which establishes a strong education for success in school and for lifelong learning;
2. Cognitive development which focuses on Higher Order Thinking Skills (HOTS);
3. Academic development which prepares the learner to acquire mastery of competencies in each of the learning areas; and
4. Socio-cultural awareness which enhances the pride of the learner's heritage, language and culture.

This department edict is based on another department order that came out in 2009 and institutionalized MTB-MLE as a fundamental educational policy and program in DepEd in the whole stretch of formal education, including pre-school, and in the Alternative Learning System (ALS). It further explains that local and international researches are consistent with the Basic Education Sector Reform Agenda's (BESRA) recommendations and it affirms the benefits and relevance of MLE. These researches present the following findings:

1. Learners learn to read more quickly in their first language (L1).

2. Pupils who have learned to read and write in their first language learn to speak, read and write in the second language (L2) and third language (L3) more quickly than those who are taught in a second language or third language first; and
3. In terms of cognitive development and its effect in other academic areas, pupils taught to read and write in their first language acquire such competencies more quickly.

Based on these, DepEd is now more determined to rectify the provisions of the former language programs in order to ensure the improvement of the performance of Filipino students academically.

MTB-MLE is just one of the provisions of the new K to 12 curriculum of the country. This will only be implemented during the students' primary years. Concepts in maths, health and sciences will be taught in their mother tongue but Filipino will gradually be introduced once the students have reached Grade 1 and English will also be used before that grade level ends. This is a direct contradiction to what was practiced before K to 12.

Once students reach Grade 4, the primary languages of instruction will be Filipino and English. These languages will be used until the learners reach Grade 12.

At present, our government has foreseen the possible effects of globalization, which is why it has encouraged the Department of Education (DepEd) through the Bureau of Secondary Education (BSE) to carry out the implementation of the Special Program in Foreign Language (SPFL). The program covers German, French, Japanese, Spanish, and Chinese Mandarin languages with the support of various program partners.

Aside from these curricular innovations, the department continues to support the teaching of the language elective, journalism. Since grade school, students are taught not only the rudiments of writing journalistic articles, but also how to lay out and publish their school papers. All public secondary schools in the country have both English and Filipino school papers while grade schools have an option of choosing to publish their school papers in either English or Filipino, but they need to reserve a special section where the other language is used.

The students are immersed in different trainings and forums to prepare them for a possible career in journalism whether in print or broadcast. These same students undergo the assessment test so as to organize their school papers' editorial board.

Talents Cultivation

One of the oldest and the longest running academic contests in the country is the National Schools Press Conference (NSPC). This is a nationwide event where about three thousand students and teachers from seventeen regions of the country gather together and compete in both English and Filipino. On an interesting note, the NSPC is the only school-based competition that is backed by a law, the Campus Journalism Act of 1991 or the Republic Act 7079, which guarantees the teaching and training of teachers and students from grade school, high school and college levels.

The NSPC is composed of two major group contests and individual contests for both Filipino and English. The Group contest is composed of the Campus Papers category, Radio Script Writing and Broadcasting, and the Collaborative Publishing category.

In the Individual Journalism contests, all the Department of Education's regional offices shall field in their top seven winners from their regional press conference on the following journalistic categories: news, features, editorial, sports, photojournalism, editorial cartooning and copy reading, and headline writing.

The NSPC, as a competition, is the culmination of various school, district, division and regional contests that the campus journalists have gone through the whole school year. From the winnings of each region, the points are added and the region which garnered the highest number of points will be declared national champion.

Since the offering of the foreign language program in 2009, the Bureau of Secondary Education's Staff Development Division has developed an event to promote the teaching and learning of a foreign language by way of exhibits, contests, and cultural presentations also known as Festival of Talents for the Special Program in Foreign Language to encourage more students to join the program.

Booths showcasing different language and cultural activities to promote the foreign language are set up. There is a food festival with games (to exhibit culinary skill, live cooking can be done) and fun activities to promote the language. Quiz Bee and an Oratorical contest are also part of the event.

A Cosplay or Characters on Parade is a competition where students of a foreign language don a national costume, or take on a literary or a pop culture character of the country that he or she represents. Each contestant is required to talk about the costume, characters and the country in the language he or she has studied. The judges come from the partner agencies (Instituto Cervantes and AECID, Japan Foundation, Alliance Française de Manille, Goethe Institute, Confucius Institute, and Angeles University Foundation).

One of the highlights of this event is the cultural presentation, an activity which showcases talents (e.g. dancing, singing, acting, etc.) of the students studying foreign language by using the foreign language and culture that they have learned.

Lastly, one of the special activities in this week-long event is the Festival of Talents in Filipino. In this celebration of skills and talents, students engage in a variety of activities and competitions that are all delivered in the national language, Filipino. Like all the other events, this is projected to showcase the ability of the students to communicate properly and effectively in Filipino. They are to compete against the best from each region in poetry, essay writing and a poetic or literary debate called Balagtasan.

Balagtasan is derived from the name of Francisco Balagtas, a noted Filipino poet and hero who is also considered as the nation's equivalent to William Shakespeare. Using rhyme and meter — with a dash of wit, sarcasm and drama — debaters from the affirmative and negative sides present their arguments before the audience, their facilitator cum arbiter and the board of judges. The facilitator cum arbiter gives the introduction about the debate topic and the competing debaters. There are three rounds of constructive speeches on three different arguments and each of them is followed immediately by a response from the opposing debater. After three rounds, a final rebuttal speech is given by each debater, after which the facilitator cum arbiter presents the strengths and weaknesses of the arguments presented by both sides.

In 2013, the main event of the Filipino Festival of Talents was the contest on the creation of a two-minute movie trailer. The team from each region was asked to write a script and produce a movie trailer about a theme or topic that was given on the day of the contest.

This five-day celebration of talents showed how effective these language programs were. The Department will continue to find ways to provide avenues to make language learning fun and exciting for the students. Science and Health Reporting in the NSPC, storytelling contests in the foreign language and maybe, the creation of short movies in Filipino are some of the other activities that may eventually be included in the Grand Festival of Talents.

The future of language education and talents cultivation in the Philippines will be definitely bright and wonderful. In the near future, we may be able to see the schools in the provinces sponsoring activities to celebrate their own language and culture, where students are introduced to old songs, myths, history, dances, and unique traditions of their province. These can only happen through local government and community support. It is about the time that the younger generation be given a chance to appreciate who they are, so that they are able to set a clear perspective of what they will be in the future.

Going back to the basics, accepting our unique qualities and respecting our cultural diversity may hold the keys in making the Filipinos see and use our language gains to improve our country's performance. The language activities and events created by the Department of Education through the efforts of Bureau of Secondary Education have challenged our students to become better communicators not only in English, our official language, and Filipino, our national language, but also in other languages that are offered to our students.

And we are hopeful that our children will eventually become multi-lingual so as to help them succeed in the 21st century.

菲律宾的语言教育战略、语言教育及人才培养

[菲律宾] Anna Marie Baligod-San Diego

摘要：本文主要介绍了菲律宾的语言教育政策及外语人才的培养方案。菲律宾是一个多种族、多民族、多语言的国家，政府将菲律宾语定为民族语言及第一官方语言，英语为第二官方语言，其他地方语言为官方语言之外的辅助交际用语。本文重点介绍了菲律宾的语言教育政策。菲律宾曾经实施以菲律宾语和英语作为基础教育阶段的双语教育政策，2012 年颁布了一项新的语言教育政策，即“基于母语的多元语言教学”，这里的母语指的是地方原住民语言。该政策从 2009 年的语言教育政策延伸发展而来，教育部希望通过实施该政策，开发学生的语言和认知能力，树立社会文化观，也希望由此带动学生学习第二语言，甚至第三语言。在全球化的浪潮下，菲律宾政府也注意到除菲律宾语和英语之外的其他语言的重要性，如德语、法语、日语以及汉语，并开展前述语言的项目培训，以培养掌握更多语言的人才。本文也描述了政府为培养外语人才开展的项目和活动，包括促进语言学习的各种项目和系列庆祝活动，以期通过展览、竞赛以及文化演讲等形式来检验外语教学以及学生学习的水平，并展示菲律宾语言教育政策的成果。本文最后强调，语言教育在菲律宾充满了生机和活力，政府致力于不断完善和发展语言教育政策，努力培养适应 21 世纪需要的掌握多种语言的人才。

关键词：菲律宾语；专门外语项目；菲律宾的语言教育政策；外语人才的培养；基于母语的多元语言教学

Language Education Strategy/Planning for the Cultivation of Language Talents

[Malaysia] Tunku Ireneza Marina bt. Tunku Mazlan

Abstract: This paper aims to describe the language education strategy for the cultivation of language talents in Malaysia. Malaysia was among the first to join the Asia-Pacific Economic Cooperation (APEC), which was established in 1989. In 2010, Malaysia launched the New Economic Model (NEM), which aims for the country to reach high-income status by 2020 while ensuring that growth is also sustainable and inclusive. The economic growth the NEM envisions is primarily driven by the private sector which moves the Malaysian economy into higher value-added activities in both industry and services. To achieve these goals, Malaysia needs to develop and retain a first-world talent base in supporting the country's transformation into a developed nation. Therefore, the educational system is critical in strengthening the competitiveness of the country in an increasingly competitive global market. The Ministry of Education has initiated educational transformation particularly in upgrading English competency amongst the younger generation for the future workforce. The policy To Uphold Bahasa Malaysia and to Strengthen English Language or its famous acronym in Bahasa Malaysia MBMMBI aims to develop pupils into proficient and confident users of L1 and L2, namely Bahasa Malaysia and English language. English is taught as a second language in all Malaysian primary and secondary schools. The mastery of English is essential for pupils to gain access to information and knowledge written in English. In line with the government's policy on strengthening English, the new curriculum known as the Standard-Based English Language Curriculum for Malaysian Primary Schools has been designed to provide pupils with a strong foundation in the English language. Language skills are taught in a systematic manner in order for pupils to use language proficiently and confidently in various contexts. English language is primarily used for international trade, business, information technology, medical research and technological enhancement to name a few. Malaysia aspires to produce innovative individuals with a creative and innovative mindset in order to spur our technologies equivalent to technologies from developed nations. As such, the Ministry of Education is embarking on honing through the cultivation of language, primarily English language, in order to compete at the global market.

Keywords: language education strategy; cultivation of language talents; Malaysia; New Economic Model (NEM); educational transformation; MBMMBI; potential talents

Introduction

Asia-Pacific Economic Cooperation (APEC) promotes regional understanding amongst members in the region. APEC has become the avenue as the leading forum to facilitate economic growth, cooperation, trade, investment and education among member economies. Member economies realize that in order to thrive, a vision must be made known to each other and shared amongst members in the region. Malaysia was among the first to join APEC, which was established in 1989.

APEC economies are more interrelated than ever before in facing the unrelenting challenges of globalization. The demands of the global economy require that APEC members place greater emphasis on innovative human resource development strategies. A common understanding has emerged concerning the idea that an educated and skilled workforce plays an essential role in ensuring the sustainable growth in the 21st century. Human capital lies at the core of innovation and a productive high-income economy. No economy can succeed without a highly skilled talent base that is able to rapidly respond creatively to economic changes, and is centerd on developing and utilizing knowledge.

The Malaysian government has adopted the creation of a fully developed economy by the year 2020 as a principal goal, emphasizing that the development should be economic, political, social, spiritual, psychological, and cultural. In realizing this aspiration, Malaysia launched the New Economic Model (NEM) in 2010, which aims for the country to reach high-income status by 2020 while ensuring that growth is also sustainable and inclusive. The economic growth the NEM envisions is primarily driven by the private sector which moves the Malaysian economy into higher value-added activities in both industry and services. To achieve these goals, Malaysia needs to develop and retain a first-world talent base in supporting the country's transformation into a developed nation.

In order to develop the necessary human resource base to reach this goal, the country must strengthen the educational system. Education in Malaysia is, in fact, changing very rapidly, responding to the emerging focus on lifelong learning, the growing emphasis on learning, as opposed to teaching, and the development of new delivery systems. With respect to elementary and secondary education, the country has shifted its focus on the provision of basic education for all to the provision of quality education for all in the 21st century, developing new principles and integrating education at all levels of schooling.

Changes are also being made in the nation's higher education and training systems, such as 1996 legislation that allows the establishment of private universities and branch campuses of foreign universities and efforts to provide financial assistance to students. Finally, in the non-formal educational sector, there is an increased emphasis on updating human resources and meeting individual and business needs for job advancement and higher wages.

Ministry of Education (MOE) Initiatives

The Ministry of Education, Malaysia (MOE) has launched various initiatives to intensify human capital development through training and education programs. The Ministry has initiated educational transformation in developing the language talents by particularly upgrading English competency amongst the younger generation for the future workforce.

The policy To Uphold Bahasa Malaysia and to Strengthen English Language, or known as the MBMMBI policy, aims to develop pupils into proficient and confident users of L1 and L2, namely Bahasa Malaysia and English language. English is taught as a second language in all Malaysian primary and secondary schools in line with its status as a second language. The mastery of English is essential for Malaysian pupils to use in everyday life, for knowledge acquisition and for future workplace needs. With globalization, all Malaysians will need to be proficient in English as a medium for communicating with people from other countries. The use of English in ICT (Information and Communication Technologies) has been included to enable learners to access knowledge on the Internet and network with people both locally and overseas.

In line with the government's policy on strengthening English, the Curriculum Development Division develops the standard document and implements curriculum transformation for primary schools. The English Language Curriculum for Primary Schools aims to equip pupils with basic language skills to enable them to communicate effectively in a variety of contexts that are appropriate to the pupils' level of development. This is in line with the goals of the National Philosophy of Education, which seek to optimize the intellectual, emotional and spiritual potential of pupils.

The new curriculum known as the Standard-Based English Language Curriculum for Malaysian Primary Schools has been designed to provide pupils with a strong foundation in the English language. The curriculum is based on modular structure, which is reflected in the organization of the content and learning standards. It emphasizes the development of basic language skills, namely listening, speaking, reading, and writing.

However, this modular approach does not exclude integration of skills; rather, they are developed strategically to enhance pupils' development of specific language skills. In addition, the introduction of the Language Arts module provides pupils with an opportunity to incorporate, experiment and apply what they have learnt in the four language skills through fun-filled, activity-based, and meaningful experiences.

The approach adopted in the standard-based curriculum is underpinned by the following principles:

1) Back to basics

It is essential for teachers to begin with basic literacy skills in order to build a strong foundation of language skills. Basic listening and speaking are introduced in order to help pupils enrich their understanding of the language. The strategy of phonics is introduced in order to help pupils begin to read and a good foundation in penmanship will help pupils acquire good handwriting.

2) Learning is fun, meaningful and purposeful

Lessons, which emphasize meaningful contexts and the integration of language skills, allow pupils to learn by doing fun-filled activities. Contextualised as well as purposeful activities will promote the fun element in language learning.

3) Teaching is learner-centerd

Teaching approaches, lessons and curriculum materials must suit pupils' different needs and abilities. It is important that appropriate activities and materials are used by pupils with different learning capabilities so that their full potential can be realized. The mastery of learning strategies will ensure that pupils master all learning standards in order to help them acquire the language.

4) Integration of salient new technologies

In line with growing globalization, technology is used extensively in our daily communication. Hence, emergent technologies can be used in language learning in order to enhance communication. Information available on the Internet and other electronic media will be vital for knowledge acquisition. Networking facilities will be useful for pupils to communicate and share knowledge.

5) Assessment for learning

Continuous assessment is an integral part of learning which enables teachers to assess whether pupils have acquired the learning standards taught. Formative assessment is conducted as an ongoing process, while summative assessment is conducted at the end of a particular unit or term. A range of activities can be utilized in order to assess pupils' performance orally or in writing. The formative and summative assessments will be used to gauge pupils' performance.

At present, the English language curriculum for secondary schools in Malaysia is organized in a manner that reflects the way English is used in everyday life. The aims of the Integrated Curriculum for Secondary Schools in Malaysia (or known as KBSM) are to further develop the potential of the individual in a holistic, balanced and integrated manner, encompassing the intellectual, spiritual, emotional and physical aspects in order to create a balanced and harmonious human being with high social standards. Language for interpersonal, informational and aesthetic purposes in the English syllabus has been outlined. These areas incorporate the integration of the four language skills of listening, speaking, reading, and witing. The language content outlines the grammar, the sound system and the word list to be taught, while the section on educational emphases incorporates worldwide developments in education such as thinking skills, ICT skills and the theory of Multiple Intelligences.

Language for interpersonal purposes enables learners to establish and maintain friendships and to collaborate with people in undertaking certain things. Language for informational purposes enables learners to use the English language to obtain, process and give information. Language for aesthetic purposes enables learners to enjoy literary texts at a level suited to their language proficiency and develops in them the ability to express themselves creatively.

The literature in English program in the Integrated Curriculum for Secondary Schools is offered as an elective subject for study at the upper secondary school level. The study of literature also allows students to engage with relationships, ideas, places, times, and events. This will lead them to a better understanding of themselves, of the people around them and of the world at large. Literature in English refers to literary works in English, including translated works. The literary works offered for study in the program are drawn from short stories, novels, poems as well as dramas.

Literature was officially included in the Malaysian ELT (English Language teaching) syllabus in the year 2000. The inclusion of the literature in the English language curriculum denotes the acknowledgement of the Ministry of Education, Malaysia on the role and importance of literature in Malaysian ELT. The addition of literature in Malaysian ELT is to benefit students in three areas, namely language development, cultural enrichment and personal growth. In Malaysian ELT, literature is featured not only in primary and secondary language education, but in tertiary English language education as well.

English for Science and Technology is introduced as an elective at the upper secondary school level. The English for Science and Technology syllabus lays the foundation in the use of English in the fields of science and technology not only for the present, but also for further studies at the tertiary level. This program does not aim to teach the subject matter of science. Rather, it is designed to help students develop an ability to grasp the basic concepts and ideas in science and to understand the methods of scientific thoughts and enquiries in English common to all kinds of scientific and technical discourses. The knowledge gained not only enhances personal learning, but also enables learners to think critically of issues in science and technology.

Challenges and Opportunities

The implementation of any new curriculum such as KSSR has its own challenges. It is known that curriculum implementation cannot be ideally executed as a number of constraints operate during the process. These may include teacher factors (their qualifications, motivations, skills, content, clarity, etc.), pupil factors (motivation to learn, readiness for schooling, interest in school and learning, etc.), school factors (class size, management, facilities, school complex, etc.), and other factors, such as language of instruction, insufficient learning materials, teaching aids, attitudes of teachers and learners, etc. The Curriculum Development Division strongly suggests group work as a teaching-learning strategy, but large-sized classes of approximately 40—50 students hinder teachers from practicing it. Students are usually taught as a class even when they are organized into groups. Group work, which is intended to be a pedagogical change, is not functioning as suggested by planners, but is treated as simply a reorganization of seating arrangement of students. Teachers' attitude is another constraint to effective curriculum implementation. Some teachers prefer traditional approaches despite having been exposed to new curricular concepts and student-centerd teaching approaches.

The emphasis is on examination results. Schools focus on academic excellence in public examination, while parents are concerned about their children's grades and test scores. As a result, learning is directed towards preparing students for examinations. Teachers are overdependent on commercially produced materials rather than teacher-made materials. These commercially produced materials may not be suitable to the students' abilities. Wrong placement of teachers is also a barrier to effective curriculum implementation. Qualified teachers do not teach the subject of their option, but are made to teach other subjects. Some teachers cannot teach effectively as they do not have the requisite knowledge and skills to teach the subjects assigned to them. The weakness in the dissemination strategy is another constraint. The cascade system of using key personnel has resulted in the dilution of messages, which the curriculum planners and developers have conceptualized.

One strength in the practice of curriculum development is the collective and participative nature of decision making on curriculum matters. Although certain agencies are responsible for the school curriculum, the actual planning, development and other related activities are shared out. The participation of various stakeholders ensures that related activities are coordinated.

The national curriculum is an integrated curriculum emphasizing the holistic development of the students. It provides opportunities for the students to develop basic skills, knowledge, values, attitudes, interests, and talents. Specifically, the national curriculum develops skills in the following aspects:

- Social skills;
- Intellectual skills;
- Physical skills;
- Spiritual skills;
- Aesthetic values (creativity and appreciation);
- Moral values;
- Information and Communication Technologies (ICT) skills.

The emphasis given to the curricular programs thus exposes the students to relevant skills needed by the nation. The national curriculum ensures that the youth of the nation today are well prepared to face an increasingly competitive and challenging world of tomorrow.

For the successful implementation of the national curriculum, concerted efforts are made to expand infrastructure support and physical facilities, such as libraries, science laboratories, workshops for subjects like living skills and home science to schools. Various measures aimed at improving teaching and learning processes are also implemented.

The Ministry of Education ensures the availability of suitable teachers to implement the curriculum. Qualified and trained teachers teach the students. The pre-service and in-service training courses are provided to the teachers by the Ministry of Education to enhance the quality of the delivery system. The professionalism of the teachers from diverse subject specializations is given emphasis.

Textbooks and other instructional materials reflecting innovative teaching and learning strategies are made available to all schools. Students from the lower income group and disadvantaged areas are given student-aid through the textbook loan scheme. In addition, specific materials are prepared for students and reference materials are also readily available.

Conclusion

As APEC member economies, our journey is towards a common goal. Sharing implementation issues and lessons learnt of every APEC member through regional forums and workshops will promise productive social and economic returns in the future. Educational cooperation can be capitalized amongst APEC members. Conventions of experts from member economies, particularly on cultivation of language talents, is also an avenue for knowledge sharing in order to strengthen education systems in the region. Cooperation on research, curriculum and teaching can be maximized, noting the importance of internationalizing educational institutions in preparing students to succeed in an interconnected world. The robust educational relationship among APEC member economies supports the growing ties in every field and the importance of cultivation of language talents to ensure a peaceful and prosperous future amongst APEC members.

语言人才培养的语言教育战略和规划

[马来西亚] Tunku Ireneza Marina bt. Tunku Mazlan

摘要：本文旨在描述马来西亚培养语言人才的教育战略。首先介绍“保护马来语和强化英语”语言教育政策的产生背景。2010 年，马来西亚启动新经济模式（NEM），即在确保经济增长具有可持续性和包容性的前提下，国家在 2020 年成为全球高收入国家。要实现该目标，马来西亚需要培养并拥有发达国家必需的人才储备。作为未来的劳动力，这一代年轻人需要提升英语能力，因此教育部启动了“保护马来语和强化英语”的教育改革政策。该语言教育政策旨在将学生培养成能够流畅并自如地使用第一语言（马来语）和第二语言（英语）的人才。本文还描述了马来西亚英语教学的现状。中小学阶段的英语教学是第二语言教学。遵照“强化英语”的政策，有关部门设计完成了“基于标准的马来西亚小学英语教学大纲”（KSSR）。新大纲以帮助学生打下牢固的英语基础为目标，要求以系统的方式将各项语言技能教授给学生，使学生在国际贸易、商务、信息技术、医学研究和技术进步等领域中能够流畅而自如地使用英语。本文最后提到政府有志于培养具有创造性思维和创新倾向的创新型人才，以促进马来西亚和发达国家保持相同的科技发展水平。为此，教育部正在通过培养学生的语言能力，主要是英语能力做好相应的准备，以保证马来西亚在全球市场的竞争中获胜。

关键词：语言教育战略；语言人才的培养；马来西亚；新经济模式；教育改革；“保护马来语和强化英语”；潜在人才

Thailand's Regional Language Education and Talents Cultivation

[Thailand] Usanee Watanapan

Abstract: This presentation firstly describes the needs for regional language education in Thailand; then it discusses in detail the policy and developmental strategies for regional language education in this country. In the globalization process, to ensure students to communicate fluently in international settings, the 2001 national core basic education curriculum was promulgated, providing that English as the first foreign language is compulsory throughout the basic education and that other world languages as second foreign languages are widely opened as selective courses. With the rapid growth of the Asian economy, Asian languages such as Chinese, Japanese, and Korean, have become popular in schools and universities. Meanwhile, the ASEAN integration inspires the Thai government to encourage their people to learn ASEAN languages as well. The Ministry of Education launched a series of strategies and plans to improve students' language proficiency through the Office of the Basic Education Commission (OBEC). This presentation also introduces the curriculum and standards for regional language education. According to the 2001 national standard-based curriculum, the foreign language content standards have been designed in four strands: Communication, Cultures, Connection, and Communities. Besides considering the characteristics and standards of some foreign languages, the contents and standards of the foreign language courses are all based on those of English, which have been developed for 12 years. Finally, the presentation discusses the teacher training and team building, textbook research and development, the teaching methods and assessment for regional language education.

Keywords: curriculum and standards for regional language education; teacher training; teaching methods and assessment

The Needs for Regional Language Education

The foreign language education in Thailand has not been obviously a national priority until the 21st century economic liberalization and globalization as well as the emergence of the coming ASEAN Community in 2015. Actually, English as a foreign language has long been introduced in schools as a selective course from upper primary education (Grades 5—7) up to compulsory in secondary and tertiary levels. Other Western languages like French and German have also long been taught as the selective courses in upper secondary level (Grades 10—12). The 21st century brings about high competition in international economy and flow of digital information, whereas it needs harmonized global cooperation in various aspects to maintain global stability, security and peace. English and other languages of big economies become more essential to the development and future of the country.

Dating back to mid 1980s—mid 1990s, Thailand reached the highest economic growth. Political economy policy was friendly to foreign trade, foreign direct investment and other international business. Thailand's economy became outstanding in Southeast Asia, achieving an average growth rate of nearly 10% per year. On the contrary, Thailand's financial crisis in 1997, which was followed by economic hardship, taught Thai society a good lesson. These two opposite phenomena, remarkable success and failure, including various dimensions of change at the global level, have greatly affected Thailand as opportunities and threats for development. High economic competition, leapfrog advances in technologies, social and cultural changes, free movement of people across borders, changes in environment and natural resources, and the advent of Asian Miracle have driven Thailand to set their National Economic and Social Development Plans, since the 8th (1997—2001) to the present (11th) aiming at people-centerd development so as to improve the country's competitiveness. Foreign language competency is considered as one of the essential tools to the key success that enables Thai people to cultivate communication and relations in the world community, to access the world's knowledge and to cope with the international challenges.

As a result, the 2001 national core basic education curriculum was promulgated, providing that English as the first foreign language is compulsory throughout 12 years of basic education, and that other world languages as second foreign languages are widely opened as the selective courses so as to prepare students to be able to communicate in the international environment. The Asian languages such as Chinese, Japanese and Korean, become more popularized not only in higher education as in the past, but also in today's basic education because of those countries' economy growth that influences international relations. Meanwhile, the ASEAN integration inspires the Thai government to encourage its people to learn ASEAN languages as well. Other foreign languages which are actually taught in higher education, such as Spanish, Russian and Italian, are now offered down to secondary education. Time cannot be wasted until students step to higher education since global challenges are always changing. To tackle such challenges and move forward to the benefit of the country, foreign language competency should be cultivated at an early age from basic education.

The Policy and Developmental Strategies for Regional Language Education

Even though the national basic education curriculum of English and other foreign languages has been periodically revised in accordance with global changes, the language proficiency of Thai people is not adequate to cope with the dynamic international competition and intense globalization. Many factors are still constrained in foreign language education. As a result, periodically some interventions have been issued as flagship projects to tackle such phenomena, for instance, (1) the 2003 Cabinet Decision on English Language Development; in 2006, two initiatives of five-year strategic plans (2006—2010) were approved by the cabinet, namely (2) the English Language Teaching and Learning Reform, and (3) Chinese Language Teaching and Learning Promotion; (4) the 2012 English Speaking Year Program. The Office of the Basic Education Commission (OBEC) is the major body utilizing these concrete tools to drive better language proficiency in public schools. Within each strategy of either English or Chinese, clear measures were set for implementation since its inception up until now. The English Language Institute undertakes English language development for basic education (Grades 1—12); and the Book Translation and Chinese Language Promotion Institute is responsible for Chinese language development, recently including other foreign languages.

English

The 2003 Cabinet Decision provided that the Ministry of Education (MOE) carry out the project to develop English language practical skills and increase efficiency of English language teachers, especially in 30 designated provinces for tourism. The relevant strategies were as below:

Strategy 1: In all schools of these 30 provinces, teachers of English language were required to use English as a medium of instruction throughout their lessons.

Strategy 2: Expanding and encouraging the English Program (EP) and Mini English Program (MEP).

Strategy 3: All schools in the 30 provinces were required to manage English camps as an extra-curricular activity.

Strategy 4: Developing English language proficiency of teachers in primary, secondary, and vocational schools so that they meet the required criteria.

Strategy 5: Expanding English Resource and Instruction Centers (ERIC) from 88 to 175 centers (one in every Education Service Area) and improving the existing 76 Self-Access Learning Centers as well as the English Teachers' Club so that they serve as ERIC networks.

Strategy 6: Providing additional support — supporting and coordinating with institutions in and outside Thailand so that English language teachers could further their study abroad at their own expense; providing e-books and encouraging the use of the Internet for English teaching and e-learning; broadcasting English programs on educational TV (ETV) and distance TV; and encouraging self-made teaching media.

The English Language Strategic Plan (2006—2010)—entitled the English Language Teaching and Learning Reform, was issued for continuously improving English competency. This plan involves four main strategies:

Strategy 1: Changing attitudes towards teaching English for communicative purpose;

Strategy 2: Creating equality in learning English with good quality;

Strategy 3: Developing English teaching and learning for communicative purpose;

Strategy 4: Creating a good English learning atmosphere and learning opportunities outside the classroom.

Under each strategy, various flagship projects and activities have been more widely implemented for students, teachers, supervisors, principals and the people concerned. Resource materials together with inspiring environment and methodologies have been developed to support learning and teaching activities. Students have been encouraged to use and show their proficiency in English, for instance, in speech contests, drama contests, young tourist guides, concerts, exhibitions and other stage shows both at regional and national levels. English camps and academic fairs for language promotion are widely organized to enhance students' excellence. There is a great demand for English native speakers. Nevertheless the programs previously initiated have still been undertaken.

The English Program—Basically, at the basic education level, schools in Thailand are administered by different organizations, e.g. the Office of the Basic Education Commission (OBEC), the Office of the Private Education Commission (OPEC), local municipalities and Bangkok Metropolis. The public schools under administration of OBEC are categorized into 6 graded groups: (1) Premium Schools, (2) Regional Science Schools, (3) World-Class Standard Schools, (4) Quality District Schools, (5) Sub-district Schools, and (6) Community Schools. To cultivate talented students, some schools with high academic potential in categories 1, 2, 3 and 4 offer the English Program (EP) and the Mini English Program (MEP) as special classes. Under EP, all subjects except Thai language, religion and Thainess are taught in English more than 18 hours a week by native speakers or other foreign teachers who have got over 550 TOEFL scores. As for MEP, the number of hours for teaching in English must not be less than 15. In other types of schools, namely English Intensive Schools, science and math are tought in English by Thai teachers.

The English Resource and Information Centers (ERIC) were set up in potential schools over the country as networking centers for teaching enhancement and professional development. ERIC networks in different areas often organize trainings, workshops and conferences for exchanging and sharing their best practices of teaching methods. Generally, annual in-service trainings are organized at least twice a year during vacations at home and abroad. Scholarships, in terms of incentives with cost sharing between teachers and OBEC, for short/medium courses abroad are normally provided for master teachers every year. ICT for education and teacher trainings are organized face-to-face and via e-learning or online, in- and out- of-school activities, free TV programs (e.g. Teacher TV, e-Distance TV).

The English Speaking Year Program 2012—According to the emergence of the ASEAN community and ASEAN Charter, English will be a working language in ASEAN community. This puts more pressure on Thai society, which has a weak point on English literacy to speedily improve English proficiency for Thai people. The Ministry of Education initiated the 2012 English Speaking Year Program as an intervention to accelerate the English spoken language for officials, people and students as well. Recently, the government emphasized the policy and focal points for English teaching, which led to three MOE's urgent plans: (1) Strengthening the development of quality of foreign languages: primary and secondary school children must be able to speak English and Chinese better within three months; (2) Improving language teachers' quality through international cooperation: more teachers of native English and Chinese are going to be hired and Thai teachers be trained to teach English and Chinese better; (3) (Information and Communication Technologies) application: teachers are encouraged to use ICT to upgrade learning results of students.

Other Foreign Languages

Under the education policy, OBEC realizes the importance of equipping Thai citizens with language abilities; hence, they initiate and implement the Second Foreign Language Promotion project, which involves Chinese, Japanese, Korean, French, German, Spanish, Russian, and ASEAN languages (Vietnamese, Cambodian, Burmese, and Malay). The policies on supporting effective teaching and learning foreign languages have been implemented through seeking cooperation from relevant organizations and private and public education institutions offering foreign language courses at home and abroad.

Chinese

At present, the Chinese language is the most popular second foreign language in Thailand. Based on the 2006—2010 Strategic Plan on Chinese Language Teaching and Learning Promotion, a lot of support from the Chinese government flooded into basic education up to higher education through the main organization, called Hanban. To implement this strategic plan into practice, four strategies have been carried out.

Strategy 1: Developing the administration and management system—setting up 38 Chinese Promotion Networking Centers in potential schools over the country so as to strengthen language competency among networking schools. Annual budget is allocated to facilitate organization of learning and teaching activities in the networking centers. The Translation and Chinese Language Promotion Institute of OBEC is the main body working cooperatively with the Hanban Representative Office in Bangkok to find agreed solutions. Hanban and the Thai MOE agreed to set up eleven Confucius classrooms in public and private schools and gave annual financial support to organize activities with networking schools. (Twelve Confucius Institutes were previously established and affiliated to universities.)

Strategy 2: Developing teaching and learning—because of lack of teachers of Chinese, voluntary teachers of any subjects have been trained to teach Chinese whilst hundreds of Chinese volunteers are also annually recruited to teach the Chinese language in Thai schools. Every year, Thai teachers of Chinese are provided with Thai and Chinese scholarships to be trained at home and abroad. To sustain the long-run Chinese instruction by Thai teachers, the Chinese and Thai governments joined hands in recruiting graduates of Chinese major, 100 candidates per year in 2008—2010 to study one-year pedagogical courses in Thailand, and another one-year Chinese language course in China. So far, 300 new Thai teachers of Chinese have become the strong workforce in Chinese teaching. In addition, a number of other teachers out of this project have been recruited to supply school needs.

To equip enough support for Chinese language education, the OBEC as the core organization of basic education has developed the Chinese language curriculum and produced Chinese language textbooks, entitled *Experiencing Chinese* together with supporting materials for Grades 1—12. The teaching materials were published by China's Higher Education Press (HEP) under the authorization of Hanban and China's Ministry of Education. Not only the printed materials, but the digital interactive learning system was also developed to help self-study.

Strategy 3: Supporting academic assistance—promoting Chinese teaching and learning activities in all networking centers; organizing Chinese language and cultural camps and language/speech contests at the networking centers at regional, national, and international levels; provision of scholarships to visit China by the Chinese government for school principals, heads of foreign languages, and teachers in every April and October. The new teachers with a major in Chinese have been provided with short-term scholarships back to China to fulfill additional knowledge in language and materials usage.

Strategy 4: Developing talented learners to cultivate Chinese educational and cultural asset—seeking for annual Chinese scholarships to provide for 15—25 Grade 12 students who have good Chinese proficiency and high academic results to further their undergraduate studies in Chinese language and other fields in China. The winners of various Chinese competitions and contests are ranked to get scholarships to Chinese camps in China (i.e. Yunnan, Xiamen, Guangzhou, Beijing, etc.).

So far, the promotion of the Chinese language is successful due to great support from the Chinese government. The quality of Chinese teaching and learning is continuously upgraded. Chinese can be counted as the third language in Thailand after Thai, the mother tongue, and English, an international language. Thailand is also counted by Hanban as a model of successful Chinese language education in the Asian region. A recent survey shows that at the basic education level, there are more than 700 public schools (administered by the OBEC), 600 private schools, and 430 schools (administered by Bangkok Metropolis) offering Chinese language subject to around 600,000 students.

Japanese

Due to the leading economic power of Japan, especially in the auto industry and electric industry intensely which has invested in Thailand, a Japanese language education policy therefore comes into account basic education and Japanese has become one of the most popular languages among Thai students. According to a recent survey in public schools, it is worth noting that there are now 230 public secondary schools offering Japanese to around 50,000 students. There are 150 Thai teachers of Japanese who are not Japanese majors, but have received a one-year intensive Japan Foundation training at home or abroad, 30 new teachers with a major in Japanese, and 50 native Japanese teachers. The OBEC promotes the development of Japanese language education in many aspects with strategies similar to those of the Chinese language:

Strategy 1: Developing the administration and management system—establishing networking centers for developing Japanese teaching and learning. The OBEC helps allocate necessary funding for the networking centers to promote various activities within and among networking schools. At present, there are 27 centers nationwide, each of which is approximately funded US$ 6,500—7,000 annually. All the networking centers are encouraged to organize annual meetings, which provide a platform for presenting their works and discussing strategies/direction of developing Japanese teaching and learning as well as solving problems. To build network for reaching effective development of Japanese language education at the basic education level, the OBEC coordinates with the

Japan Foundation and the JICA, which are key partners in promoting Japanese in Thailand. Professional associations concerning Japanese affairs and educational institutions in Thailand also support with academic assistance.

Strategy 2: Developing teaching and learning—The OBEC organizes annual professional development training which lasts one week during the summer vacation. Such training is supported by the Technology Promotion Association (Thailand-Japan) and the Japan Foundation. The OBEC also initiates the project of training new Thai teachers who are Japanese majors and recruiting them as teachers for public schools. This project is in a process of submitting for the Cabinet approval. The JICA provides Japanese volunteers to help develop Japanese teaching every year, but the number is still smaller than that of Chinese and Korean. The Japanese standard-based curriculum has been developed in accordance with the Basic Education Core Curriculum 2008. Instructional materials have been produced by the Japan Foundation in cooperation with the Technology Promotion Association (Thailand-Japan) to meet the Thai educational and cultural contexts .

Strategy 3: Supporting academic assistance—academic reinforcement is carried out through the following activities: annual linguistic competitions and speech contests, exhibition of students' works/activities, Japanese language and cultural camps, Japanese language training, to prepare for the national examination and JF tests, workshops on Japanese teaching and IT training for teachers, scholarships to participate in language and cultural camps as well as study visits to Japan.

Other Second Foreign Languages

For other second foreign languages: Korean, French, German, Spanish, Russian, and ASEAN languages, the implementation and methods vary, depending on different contexts and support from Thailand and abroad. For instance, the German language has been developed through cooperation with the Goethe Institute; the French language through the Alliance Française; Spanish, Russian, and ASEAN languages through Thai universities which have international cooperation and exchange programs with overseas institutions.

Because of the Asian economic miracle, the number of students selecting East Asian languages has increased, whilst the number of students studying Western languages has declined. This demonstrates that economy and language are closely related. The languages play an important role in international relations, especially in economic terms. Economic power truly impacts on the popularity of the language so that with the Korean leapfrogging economy, Thai school students are encouraged to study Korean language. Korean language education just started in basic education only two years ago in an active manner. Even though there are now no teachers with a major in Korean, the OBEC has cooperated with Thammasat University, where East Asian Studies are offered, to train teachers of other subjects to teach basic Korean. Meanwhile, procurement of Korean volunteer teachers to teach in OBEC schools has been managed by the Korean MOE. 2011 was the first year that Korea sent 54 volunteer teachers, to Thailand. Parallel recruitment of new Thai teachers of Korean language for OBEC schools is underway. The Korean curriculum in accordance with the 2008 national core curriculum has already been developed.

Since ASEAN integration through critical aspects of political and security purposes, economic co-development, and socio-cultural binding, the learning ASEAN languages becomes more essential for Thailand's future and strength of the relations. However, the education of these languages is just at its initial stage in cooperating with universities. It needs a lot of improvement. At the moment, for lack of teachers of these languages, OBEC schools hire native speakers of these languages to teach the languages and build the ASEAN cultural environment in schools to raise ASEAN awareness and solidarity. The OBEC also set up some language networking centers for these languages along the borders of the country, starting from 2012.

The OBEC has been constantly updating databases on these foreign languages for the purpose of efficient and effective administration and management, as shown on the last page.

The Curriculum and Standards for Regional Language Education

According to the 2001 national standard-based curriculum, which was later revised by breaking down its standard indicators from key stage level into grade level and promulgated in 2008, the foreign language content standards have been designed in four strands (4 Cs), i.e., 1) Communication—four linguistic skills of listening, reading, speaking, and writing; 2) Cultures—understanding of target languages and cultures, comparing and contrasting those to their own; 3) Connection—accessing to and integrating with other subject matters across the curriculum; and 4) Communities—using the languages in actual situations beyond the classroom at local and international communities.

English content standards and standard indicators have been developed for the 12-year curriculum and are used as a core concept for designing other foreign language curriculums; however, they are additionally customized to meet the nature and standards of those target languages. To date, the foreign language curriculums of Chinese, Japanese, Korean, and German have been completed for implementation. The ASEAN languages such as Vietnamese, Burmese (Myanmar), Cambodian (Khmer) and Bahasa Malay/Indonesian are going to be designed. Even though the curriculums of latter mentioned languages have not come out, teachers apply the core concepts of foreign language curriculums to design their learning units.

The Teacher Training and Building Team for Regional Language Education

The teacher is the key success of student achievement. But in general Thai valuation, a teaching career ranks lower than other careers. Lack of quality teachers of foreign languages is a major problem, especially English in spite of the fact that English is compulsory at every grade level. Many teachers of English are not graduates or English majors. They lack confidence in their English. As for other foreign languages, the availability of teachers of target languages is the same. But the other languages are the selective courses; schools can offer those language courses when they are in readiness. The system of teacher recruitment to serve the urgent need for foreign language development takes time and long procedures with strict controls and regulations. Basically, to solve problems with regard to teachers and teaching, two major types of in-service training have been organized: 1) Training teachers who major in those target languages to obtain continuous professional development; and 2) Training teachers of other subjects to teach basic foreign languages for beginners' classes. In special science and math classes taught in English, science and math teachers have to be trained the English language used in science and math classes, too. IT skill is an integral part of teaching and learning skills; hence the teachers are trained to use IT in their learning and teaching and are encouraged to guide their students to use IT in a proper and effective way. Teachers who prefer to use IT can improve their own language competency; and IT can help them create a good learning environment. Many teachers learn how to teach and create their lessons from the Internet, such as YouTube and other web applications. Some use online teaching or blend learning between face-to-face and online education. Some create their webpages to be platforms among their groups of teaching or between themselves and their students.

Actually, teachers attend face-to-face trainings, e-trainings, and on-job trainings in Thailand and in the countries of target languages. The training is often assisted by organizations and institutions of native languages and Thai universities offering foreign language courses. Local and global study visits are also provided to teachers with good performance, so as to increase vision and enhance teaching profession.

For lack of Thai teachers of foreign languages, every year, over 1,200 Chinese volunteers are selected and sent by Hanban to teach in Thailand from Grade 1 up to higher education. To sustain a long-run Chinese language development, the OBEC and Hanban jointly have provided scholarships to train 300 new Thai teachers majoring in Chinese, as previously mentioned. This strategy is valuable for language development; therefore the new teachers with a Japanese or Korean major using be soon recruited using the same procedures. Native Japanese and Korean volunteers supported by their governments also play an important role in their language teaching in Thai schools now. The success partly depends on cooperation between Thai and foreign governments.

Textbook Research and Development

A concrete project on textbook research and development is the production of the Thai edition of Chinese textbooks, namely *Experiencing Chinese* and its supporting instructional materials. This project was realized through cooperation between the Chinese Higher Education Press (HEP, under the authorization of Hanban and China's Ministry of Education), Thailand's Office of the Basic Education Commission (OBEC) and Thailand's Kurusapa Press (KP). Pursuant to the Chinese strategic plan carried out by the Ministry of Education, it is an important tool opened to meet the Chinese international policy. The Chinese government (via Hanban) has provided great support on Chinese language education in Thailand. Textbook production is one of many projects that Thai and Chinese organizations have worked cooperatively on textbooks to suit the Thai cultural and educational contexts. A series of *Experiencing Chinese* for Grades 1 to 12, including students' books, audio CDs, workbooks and teachers' manuals, are a core material implemented in schools in accordance with the Chinese language curriculum. Apart from the printed materials, a digital interactive learning system for student self-access is also customized, based on the contents of the textbooks. The textbook production started its research procedure in 2005 and completed main publications in 2011; some production of more supporting materials is still in process. Another series, namely *Creative Chinese*, produced by Yunnan Normal University in cooperation with the OBEC and KP, forms an alternative for secondary education.

As for Japanese language education, the Thai edition of textbooks has been produced and revised to meet the Thai contextual curriculum and culture by the Japan Foundation and the Technology Promotion Association (Thai-Japan).

The Teaching Methods and Assessment

At the basic education level, teachers of foreign languages are encouraged to improve their teaching methods through the communicative approach instead of focusing on the grammar-translation method and the memorization of new words. However, in practice, a lot of teachers cannot easily manage this paradigm shift in teaching, nor in assessment. The grammar-translation method is still traditionally practiced since the entrance examination to universities still emphasizes grammar rules. However, the Basic Education Core Curriculum 2008 stipulates that assessment and evaluation should develop learners and reflect learners' performance. Formative and authentic assessment should be the correct way to trace and help improve students' performances. In the classroom, where teachers can create an appropriate communicative environment using authentic language and natural expressions of real-life situations, it would lead to the authentic assessment. More task-based assignments are introduced for individuals and groups.

The summative assessment in terms of tests is conducted at at least four levels: classroom, school, education service areas, and national. At the school level, tests are still practiced at mid-terms and the final exams. As English is a compulsory subject, it is stipulated that students must do the English test at critical grades. At education service areas, the English tests are done in Grades 2, 5 and 8. At the national level, the national test is stipulated for Grades 3, 6, and 9. In Grade 12, students have to do the Ordinary National Educational Test (O-NET) and the Advanced National Educational Test (A-NET). For the international assessment of foreign languages, students personally may apply for tests, such as TOEFL, YCT, HSK, JLPT, and TOPIK.

Database

These data include numbers of schools offering foreign language courses, numbers of teachers, and students:

Language	No. of Schools		No. of Teachers				No. of Students		
	Lower secondary	Upper secondary	Major	Non-major	Native speakers	Total	Lower secondary	Upper secondary	Total
Chinese	340	389	350	100	600	1,050	199,140	120,287	319,427
	Total: 712 schools - Bkk: 105 - Other provinces: 607								
Japanese	74	230	30	150	50	230	16,200	33,800	50,000
	Total: 230 schools - Bkk: 47 - Others: 176								
Korean	29	45	15	29	43	87	4,712	5,318	10,030
	Total: 45 schools - Bkk: 8 - Others: 37								
French	57	262	502	-	15	517	5,322	50,190	55,512
	Total: 280 schools - Bkk: 111 - Others: 169								
German	-	30	24	18	11	53	945	5,160	6,105
	Total: 30 schools - Bkk: 14 - Others: 16								
Spanish	-	2	2	-	1	3	-	150	150
	Total: 2 schools - Bkk: 1 - Other: 1								
Russian	-	5	-	-	-	-	-	89	89
	Total: 5 schools - Bkk: 5 - Others: -								
Burmese	3	35	2	13	19	34	3,990	6,426	10,416
	Total: 35 schools - Bkk: 1 - Others: 34								
Vietnamese	20	21	3	5	5	13	2,254	2,473	4,727
	Total: 21 schools - Bkk: - - Others: 21								

Language	No. of Schools		No. of Teachers				No. of Students		
	Lower secondary	Upper secondary	Major	Non-major	Native speakers	Total	Lower secondary	Upper secondary	Total
Cambodian	5	4	2	2	4	8	1,357	519	1,876
	Total: 5 schools - Bkk: - - Others: 5								

**N.B. Some schools offer foreign languages at both lower and upper secondary levels.

泰国的区域语言教育和人才培养

[泰国] Usanee Watanapan

摘要：本文首先描述了泰国产生区域语言学习需求的过程，继而详述了泰国区域语言教育的政策和发展战略。在全球化的进程中，为了保证学生在国际环境中具备流利的沟通能力，2001 年颁布的国家教学大纲规定，泰国基础教育阶段英语作为外语属于必修课，其他世界语言作为第二外语允许学生广泛选修。伴随着亚洲经济的迅速增长，汉语、日语和韩国语等亚洲语言在大中小学受到学生的欢迎。与此同时，受到东盟经济共同体成立的启发，泰国政府鼓励学生学习东盟国家的语言。同时，教育部出台了系列战略和规划来提高学生的语言熟练程度，基础教育委员会（OBEC）是实施这些战略和规划的主要机构。本文还介绍了区域语言教育的大纲和标准。根据 2001 年颁布的国家标准大纲，外语学习内容包含交流、文化、联系和社区四个方面。除了顾及某些外语的自身特点和标准之外，外语课程的内容和标准均参照拥有十二年发展历程的英语教学大纲。本文最后讨论了区域语言教育的师资培训及队伍的建立、教材的研发、教学方法与评价等方面的政策。

关键词：区域语言教育的大纲和标准；教师培训；教学方法与评价

The Developmental Strategies for Regional Language Education

[Australia] Cathryn Hlavka

Abstract: This lecture focuses on the developmental strategies for regional language education. The Australian government recognizes the vital importance of increasing the languages capabilities of Australian students, in particular, in Asian languages. However, Australian language research consistently identifies two challenges to increasing language studies, including a low student demand for languages and a limited supply of Asian language teachers, and the Australian government is undertaking to develop language education in Australia through: 1) Developing a high quality language curriculum; 2) Increasing the demand for learning Asian languages; 3) Supporting quality teaching in Asian languages; 4) Developing innovative resources and the necessary infrastructure to support language teaching.

Keywords: regional language education; developmental strategies; a limited supply of Asian language teachers; low student demand for languages; language education in Australia

The Australian government recognizes the vital importance of equipping young Australians with the knowledge and skills to engage with people in our region in their own language and understands that these skills must be a core element of the Australian school curriculum. As a result, the Australian government is committed to increasing Australian students' languages capabilities, in particular, in Asian languages, through multiple strategies in partnerships with all governmental and non-governmental education providers in Australia.

Australian language research consistently identifies two challenges to increasing language studies, including a low student demand for languages and a limited supply of Asian language teachers. In cooperation with state and territory and non-government education authorities, the Australian government is undertaking to develop language education in Australia, through:

1) Developing a high quality language curriculum;

2) Increasing the demand for learning Asian languages;

3) Supporting quality teaching of Asian languages;

4) Developing innovative resources and infrastructure to support language teaching.

Developing a High Quality Language Curriculum

The new Australian school curriculum has been developed by the Australian Curriculum, Assessment and Reporting Authority (ACARA).

The *Shape of the Australian Curriculum: Languages* by ACARA has been designed to guide the development of a languages curriculum from Foundation to Year 10.

The new Australian school curriculum will not only provide curricula for a number of Asian languages, but also build capability in intercultural understanding and give Australian students the opportunity to study Asia and Australia's engagement with Asia as one of the cross-curriculum priorities across different key learning areas.

Increasing the Demand for Learning Asian Languages

Since 2007, building a demand for Asian languages and cultures has been funded by the Australian government through programs such as the National Asian Languages and Studies in Schools Program. This program provided funding of over $62 million over four years from 2008—2009 to 2011—2012 to build momentum towards increasing the number of Australian students proficient at learning the languages and understanding the cultures of China, Indonesia, Japan and Korea.

The Australia-China BRIDGE (Building Relationships through Intercultural Dialog and Growing Engagement) project is another successful program which partners Australian schools with schools in Indonesia, China and South Korea. Using electronic communication to effectively maintain contact between students from the partner schools, BRIDGE schools report substantially increased interest in language learning as a result of the project and at least two have begun offering the partner school's language on the basis of participation in the program.

Building Asia-relevant capabilities to future career opportunities is also an important challenge. The *My Future* website, which offers 20 video vignettes of articulate, interesting Australians who have worked in Asia or who do business with Asian clients, is aiming to address this. The videos have been highly successful in engaging students when used directly in presentations and conference-style activities.

Parents Understanding Asia Literacy is another project funded through the National Asian Languages and Studies in Schools Program, which aims to increase parental support for the teaching of Asian languages.

Supporting Quality Teaching of Asian Languages

A significant consideration for implementing the Australian curriculum is the supply and availability of qualified teachers of Asian languages.

The Endeavour Language Teacher Fellowships Program provides opportunities for practicing and training language teachers in Australian schools and universities to improve their linguistic and cultural skills through intensive short-term in-country study programs. Since 2004, over 1,500 practicing and pre-service language teachers have participated in 11 language programs, including visits to countries and regions in Asia such as Indonesia, China, Korea, Japan and Vietnam.

Developing Innovative Resources and Infrastructure to Support Language Teaching

21st Century ICT (Information and Communication Technologies) are changing educational resources and in turn teaching and learning practices. The Australian government has recognized the benefits of harnessing technology and has provided substantial funding to support substantial changes to our classrooms:

- \$4 million towards the Supporting the Australian Curriculum Online project, which aims to develop and procure high quality digital resources to support the implementation of the Australian Curriculum;
- The National Broadband Network will address issues of teacher supply, build the student demand for languages and cultural capabilities, as well as engage students in online opportunities between countries.

区域语言教育的发展战略

[澳大利亚] Cathryn Hlavka

摘要：本文首先概述区域语言教育的重要性和现存的问题。澳大利亚政府已经认识到学生提高语言能力，尤其是亚洲国家语言能力的重要性，但是，相关的语言研究一直有一个共性，即亚洲语言教学面临教师资源有限和语言学习需求低迷的挑战。澳大利亚政府正在通过多项措施来促进澳大利亚区域语言教育的发展，包括开发高质量的语言教学大纲、增加亚洲语言的学习需求、支持高质量的亚洲语言教学、开发创新型教学资源和必备的基础设施等。

关键词：区域语言教育；发展战略；有限的亚洲语言教师资源；低迷的语言学习需求；澳大利亚的语言教育

跨境/跨文化视角下的语言教育与合作

Language Education and Cooperation from a Cross-Cultural Perspective

Needs for Regional Language Education

[The United States] Timothy Greene and Donald McCloud

Abstract: Globalization continues to create a demand for managers and workers who can communicate in multiple languages. Many of our current students recognize this growing need. American students—and at Western Michigan University (WMU), especially the global and international studies majors—seek to enhance their language abilities in French or Spanish by adding a "non-Western" language such as Chinese, Japanese or Arabic. At the same time, we are seeing at WMU an enormous growth in the number of students coming from abroad—almost anywhere in the world—to learn or improve their English. WMU's non-degree English language programs and short-term specialty professional language programs are among our fastest growing programs, reflecting the understanding of students around the world that no matter what their native languages are, they must have at least basic competence in English if they are to be successful in today's globalized markets.

This concept of global demand for multiple language fluency is widely recognized in most of the major metropolitan areas in the United States and around the world. It is, however, much less commonly recognized in smaller towns and rural areas throughout the world. Some of the difficulty is a matter of lack of access, but some are lack of understanding related to deep-seeded and long-standing parochialisms.

It is already clear that a "one size fits all" approach for Chinese language and culture courses will not work, and as Confucius Institute programs continue to expand and reach out to smaller and more rural school districts, there will be a greater need to offer a variety of program options from which school districts may select the most feasible. Feasibility may be connected to financial constraints or may be more social and political, but in all cases, the Confucius Institute programs will have to adapt to local needs and sensibilities to be successful.

This presentation will examine some of the financial and social constraints facing many local school districts and suggest some ways in which Confucius Institute programs may need to devise program alternatives that aid and support local school programs.

Keywords: regional language education; US education structure; implement of language programs

It is a great pleasure for me to be here today to talk with you about the progress, prospects and challenges ahead for our Confucius Institute, and to share some of our experiences in developing our program. The Confucius Institute at Western Michigan University was established in July, 2009. Our main focus has been providing Chinese language instruction to first and second grade students at schools within the Portage Public School system. We also provide adult language courses in Kalamazoo, and Chinese cultural experiences on the WMU campus to over 25,000 students. These instructional experiences could potentially impact over 200,000 citizens in the surrounding areas.

Consideration and discussion of developing regional language policies in the US is essential in a country with a large and diverse population. A single unified approach towards educational policies would create major difficulties.

Traditionally, educational structures in the US are highly decentralized. To add some perspective, the State of Michigan has over 500 local and fairly autonomous school systems within the state. The state population of approximately 9.9 million people includes approximately 1.5 million students at the elementary, middle and high school levels. In the US education system, there is greater local oversight and control of schools than at the state or national levels. Historically, education in the US has been governed by local school districts. This also includes the authority to levy taxes that affects the value that can be added to the students in the school system.

So let me set the stage with a historical perspective.

It was not until 1979 that the US Department of Education was created by President Jimmy Carter to establish policy and enforce federal education laws. Until then the US systems of K-12 and higher education were very autonomous.

Early universities in the US were typically private or religious-based institutions, which helped to preserve the tenants of the Separation of Church and State. There was no expectation that the federal government would play a role in the development of national educational policy. In contrast, many other countries in the world have educational policies defined and administered through a national ministry of education.

The influences of Federal government involvement in US education policy have been more macro in nature and impact. Four examples specific to higher education will help to illustrate this point:

First, in 1862 Congress passed the Morrill Act that became commonly known in the US as the "Land-Grant Act." The Morrill Act set aside federally held public land in each state to be used to create an agricultural-mechanical college, which would be accessible to everyone. The cost of educating students at these institutions was subsidized by each state. This legislation created an educational model linking teaching and research with public service for the first time. This linking of purpose and outcome was a key factor contributing to the productivity and growth of the US in the late-19th and early-20th centuries. Institutions created under the Morrill Act are today considered to be among the most prestigious universities in the US, and in some cases, in the world. These include the University of Illinois and Urbana-Champaign, Texas A&M University, Purdue University, and the University of California-Davis. Similarly, the US has also established Sea-Grant Institutions and Historical Black Colleges and Universities (HBCU) since 1862.

Another example of the Federal government involvement in higher education can be witnessed in the Servicemen's Readjustment Act, passed by Congress in 1944. Congress created the "G.I. Bill of Rights" to provide scholarships to soldiers returning from active duty in World War II. In retrospect, many have attributed the "G.I. Bill" with the democratization of higher education in the US, as many men and women were provided with access to a college education. The US has in turn benefitted incalculable socio-economic benefits from the education and increased productivity of multiple generations of service veterans. The "G.I. Bill" is currently providing additional professional training and financial supports for thousands of veterans of the Iraq and Afghan Wars.

Third, the Federal government helps provide research funding to higher education institutions. Funds are made available through the National Institutes of Health (NIH), National Science Foundation (NSF), Department of Defense (DoD), National Endowment for the Arts (NEA), National Endowment for the Humanities (NEH), Department of Education (DoE), and other government agencies to American universities to support research and service. As much as half of the total research support for some of our institutions in the US is derived from federal grants and contracts. Industry also provides important research funding in key fields, but does not compare to federal support in volume or breadth. Similarly, many states also provide research and service funding, as do major corporations and foundation boards, including the Ford, Keck and Kellogg Foundations.

The fourth major effort that the Federal government contributes is through Pell Grant funding. The grants are made available to need-based students for as much as $5,600 per year, and have greatly benefitted college accessibility for low-income students.

In the K-12 school systems, the Federal government has also imposed both influence and control primarily through funding. Mandates like "No Child Left Behind" and programs supporting federally subsidized free breakfast and lunch for students both set policy and enforce it through federal funding.

Taking advantage of this significant and growing dependence on federal research funding and direct student funding, the government in Washington has devised an indirect approach to influencing and shaping education policy. Establishing what have become known as "federal mandates", the government codified a series of regulations specifying standardized procedures and policies, with the receipt of federal funding contingent upon compliance with these regulations. The vast majority of American universities and K-12 school systems have accepted the federal directives as a necessary requisite for receiving federal research and other funding.

When considering regional language policies in the US, it must first be recognized that there are three functional levels of bureaucracy to consider: the

Federal Department of Education, the Department of Education in each state, and the local governing school board. In some states, there are also municipal or county administrative units that intervene in the decision and policy making processes.

There are significant variations in the degree to which states assert control over local school districts. The State of Michigan is less aggressive than some other states, with policies that set minimum curricular standards for high school graduation, as well as other area requirements for teacher certification and teacher continuing education. More than 500 independent school boards remain largely in control of curriculum, personnel and other issues for each respective school district.

In recent years, the Federal government has begun to assert influence in the provision of grants, contract awards and other financial supports. These grants, in many cases, go to the state, and with those grants come specific expectations. Common practice stipulates that a school district must comply with certain regulations in order to continue receiving financial support from the Federal government.

It should be noted that federal engagement in local school curriculum and other areas is a hotly contended political issue across the country, where conservative political leaders tend to argue in favor of local control while more liberal political leaders tend to argue for more uniformity of curriculum and academic standards for all schools. Such educational reform packages as "No Child Left Behind", first introduced under President George W. Bush, have significantly expanded federal influence in public schools throughout the US.

The primary issue of concern is the fragmentation of decision making and the autonomy of local school districts. The question of regional policy quickly becomes a question of which level and which region. Often in our system "regional" is the equivalent of "state level" and the bureaucratic structures for policy at the state level are already in place.

Local policies and boards control the effects of K-12 curriculum to a greater extent with lesser influence from state and federal agencies. This impacts the ability of the Confucius Institute to implement Chinese language instruction within a school system. Each school system has a School Board that sets overall policy and budget within the constraints of the state's Department of Education. The

State's Department of Education influences some funding, minimum curriculum standards (primarily at the high school level), length of school year, and teacher qualifications. Within each school system then are principals of individual schools and each school's faculty (teachers) who set the curriculum.

Herein lies the challenge of implementing school or curriculum reform; specifically, of implementing Chinese language instruction in the early elementary classroom. At some systems, the local school board may be involved; at some school systems, it may fall to the superintendent or principal to make the decision, and within some schools, and change will fall mostly to the teachers within individual schools.

How do we go about influencing some or all of these different levels of control to advocate for changes? There are an array of factors which may serve to influence this change, including:

1) General emotional receptivity;
2) Community wealth;
3) Relative urgency of the problem or issue;
4) Tenacity of traditions;
5) Presence or absence of strong local personalities with an interest in change;
6) Rates of change in the larger cultural community surrounding the local community;
7) Development in that larger cultural community of well-defined and easily transmittable measures to assess change;
8) International influences in the community, including companies with international ties;
9) The relative international composition of the citizens of the community;
10) Local universities with international composition;
11) An involved Confucius Institute.

Finally, it needs to be understood that the differences in the communities being served have a large effect on the attitudes of the pupils and the pedagogic problems of the teachers. In my opinion, to successfully implement Chinese language programs or other similar programs in K-12 education, the group advocating for change must first recognize the structure of US national, state and local control, then understand the change factors within the local school system, and then work to use these factors to their advantage to effect the change.

Implementing changes for the better in K-12 school systems is important to Western Michigan University and we sincerely appreciate the cooperation of the Portage School System, its leaders and teachers. We also sincerely appreciate the support of the Hanban and BLCU and its teachers as we make a positive impact on school children in Michigan.

区域语言教育的本土化需求

[美国] Timothy Greene and Donald McCloud

摘要：全球化的发展需要能够使用多种语言的人才。本文首先概述非西方语言在美国的发展现状。当前，汉语、日语、阿拉伯语等“非西方”语言日益受到西方人的青睐，尤其是国际专业的学生，愈发认识到需要通过学习诸如汉语、日语、阿拉伯语这样的“非西方”语言来提升自己的语言能力。但是，在西方的教学环境中，统一或者“一成不变”的汉语与文化教学方法很难产生应有的效果。本文通过重点介绍美国中小学教育决策的历史沿革和发展现状来阐释出现上述问题的一个原因。在多种族、多民族和多元文化并存的美国，教育决策权曾经高度分散。目前，州政府和地方政府对中小学教育拥有一定程度的自主权，学区和学校的董事会对课程大纲等政策的制定仍拥有较大的影响和控制权。联邦政府教育部通过制定法案和提供财政支持等措施增加对各地教育政策的干预。因此上述因素对孔子学院在中小学系统开展汉语教学会产生一定的影响。本文也分析了西密歇根州许多学区面临的几个经济和社会制约因素。结合西密歇根大学孔子学院在当地中小学成功开展汉语教学的实际，本文建议孔子学院采取非正式或者灵活的方法支持学区开展汉语学习项目。本文最后指出，如果认识到美国中小学教育制度的差异和社区的差别并进行适应性调整，孔子学院的汉语教学将得到良性发展。

关键词：区域语言教育；美国的教育体系；语言项目的实施

Foreign Language Education in Mexico: The Intercultural and Interdisciplinary Foreign Language Curriculum at the Universidad Autónoma Metropolitana Iztapalapa

[Mexico] Javier Vivaldo Lima and Margaret Lee Zoreda

Abstract: The enforcement of guidelines for foreign language teaching and learning at the primary, secondary and tertiary levels of education has become a major priority of the educational system in Mexico. Accordingly, advancements are being made in the establishment of national standards for the evaluation and certification of competences in foreign languages at all major levels of the educational system, aimed at the articulation of academic programs, teaching practices and professional development initiatives. Based on a succinct overview of current endeavors carried out in our country, mainly the issuing of a National Certificate of Foreign Language Competence, an innovative curricular experience recently developed at a campus of one of our major public universities, the Universidad Autónoma Metropolitana, will be described in detail. Among its main characteristics, this Intercultural and Interdisciplinary Foreign Language Program has articulated current national and international standards into a plurilingual and pluricultural educational proposal incorporated into the curricula of all undergraduate programs at two main levels: 1) as a required curricular component (intermediate levels); and 2) as elective curricular courses (upper and advanced levels). The main pedagogical and operational implications of the program are discussed, as well as its relevance for future instructional developments in the country.

Keywords: foreign language education; intercultural education; Mexico

Introduction

The 21st century will undoubtedly be renowned for the global communication revolution that has taken place ever since the turn of the century and for the related challenges that such a revolution entails. Our new global citizens are born into a world where previously traditional physical, cultural, social, and linguistic frontiers increasingly lead to complex, multilingual and multicultural scenarios and encounters at all levels of life. Thus, it is an era that poses major challenges for educational institutions, making it imperative to devise innovative and visionary curricular decision-making. Our new students, the imminent frontier crossers of the new global village, will have to face communication demands never before foreseen. The ultimate aim of education will be to help them develop the talent to communicate and negotiate purposefully and creatively with a myriad of other peoples and cultures, while understanding and valuing both their own particular cultural heritage as well as those of others. As never before, foreign language and culture education (FLCE) becomes an absolute imperative of higher education. In such regard, in a recent analysis of rankings of higher education institutions throughout the world, Abby Chau (2011), in analyzing the role of foreign language education (FLE) as a determinant element of excellence at university level, remarked:

> Modern languages have never been so important. The ever accelerating spread of mobility and internationalization—both in the professional and academic worlds—shows little sign of abating any time soon. At the forefront of these cross-border exchanges of people and skills are a troupe of able and willing multilingual graduates, facilitating progress that would otherwise be rendered impossible by linguistic boundaries (Chau, 2011: p.1).

Foreign Language Education in Mexico

Foreign language education has traditionally been a major concern of public education in Mexico. Ever since the early 70s, FLE, predominantly in English, was introduced as a compulsory subject in both secondary and high schools, with an average of 200 hours of instruction programed at each of those levels. However, the impact of those FLE programs has been inconsistent throughout institutions, mainly due to the diversity of teaching approaches, teachers' academic backgrounds, and to the lack of national policies that could ascertain the articulation of FLE curricula throughout our educational system.

The deep concern about the pervasive low levels of English of students upon entrance to higher education in Mexico, led the National Association of Universities and Higher Education Institutions (ANUIES, Spanish acronym) to commission, at the end of the 1990s, an inter-institutional diagnostic study aimed at the evaluation of the linguistic competence profiles in English of incoming freshmen students in Mexico (González, Vivaldo and Castillo, 2004). Between 2001 and 2002, 4,690 students, selected at random from nine of the most important public and private higher education institutions in Mexico City, were evaluated. According to the results (Figure 1), only 10.6% of the sample achieved a total passing score on the three bands (basic, intermediate, and advanced) of linguistic competence in English evaluated via a standardized international test, while only 23.9% of the students managed to pass its basic level band of linguistic competence. As a whole, the results of the ANUIES study revealed an important deficit in achievement outcomes in FLE in the country, especially considering that the great majority of the students participating had had an average exposure to FLE instruction of at least 400 hours prior to their admission to higher education. Furthermore, the analysis of score distributions by institution showed the existence of significant differences in scores between students entering private and public higher education institutions, with the latter obtaining median scores far below the passing criteria. As depicted in Graph 1, only two institutions, both of them private (COLMEX and ITAM), showed mean scores well above the passing criteria, while the other seven institutions (all of them public, with the exception of the UVM) obtained failing mean scores in the 20-30/100 interval.

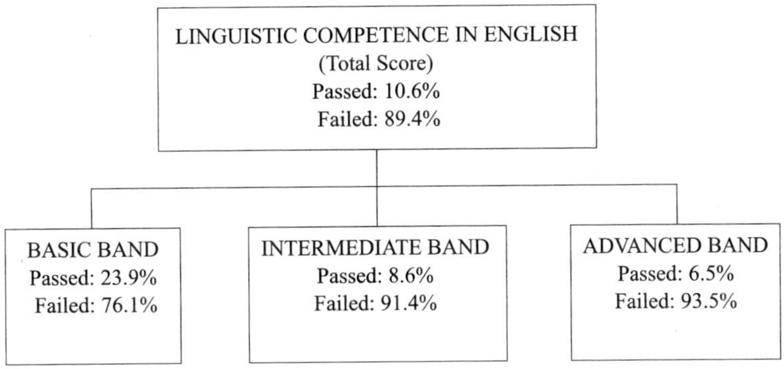

FIGURE 1. Profiles of Linguistic Competence in English in Incoming Freshmen Students (González, Vivaldo and Castilo, 2004)

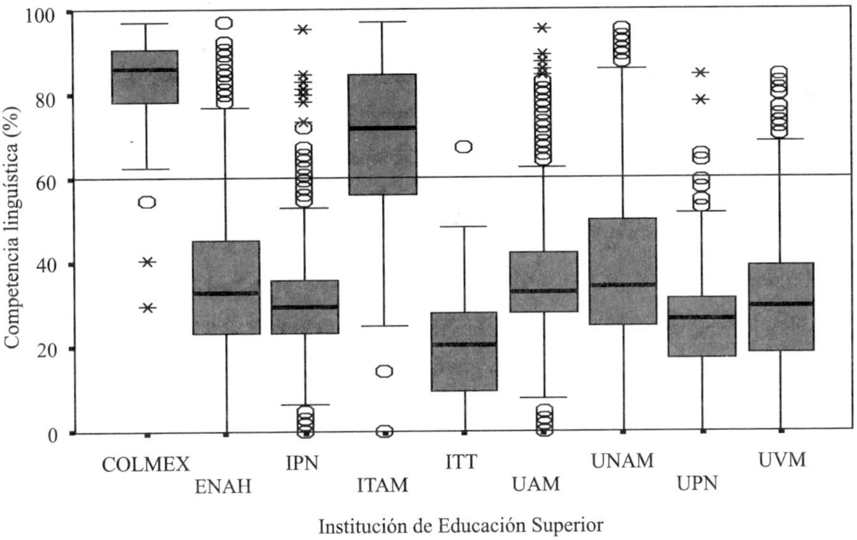

GRAPH 1. Distribution of Linguistic Competence in English Scores by Institution (González, Vivaldo and Castilo, 2004)

Therefore, at the turn of the century, three major initiatives regarding FLE were undertaken by the Secretary of Public Education in Mexico (SEP, Spanish acronym). First, there was the publication of a preliminary scheme of national standards for the development of educational FLE programs and for the certification of teachers and students at all levels of the educational system, based on the general parameters established by the *Common European Framework of Reference* (*CEFR*) (Subsecretaría de Planeación y Coordinación..., 2006). Second, we had the publication in 2008 of an official decree, whereby FLE became integrated as a compulsory subject in the primary education curriculum in all public schools throughout the country. The Program of English Teaching in Primary Education (PEIB, Spanish acronym) is currently being piloted in a sample of 5,000 schools and is expected to be officially launched by the year 2013. Finally, there was issued in 2010 the National Certificate of Foreign Language Competence (CENNI), a document granted by the General Coordination of Studies Revalidations at SEP. This latter document, based on an individual's FLE record of accomplishment, officially certifies the level of competence reached according to the national benchmarks of language competence in FLE. Furthermore, in 2006 Mexico's Secretary of Public Education published a series of recommendations for FLE that placed intercultural education on a par with the development of linguistic abilities:

Recommendation 7. To educate students with humanistic, holistic, and intercultural perspectives developed through linguistic and cultural diversity, by teaching not only foreign languages, but also the general and historical context of the cultures of those languages. (Subsecretaría de Planeación y Coordinación..., 2006, pp. 14-15)[①]

Most recently, in 2011, the SEP decreed an official reform in the definition of standards in FLE to be achieved by each sector of the education system in order to respond to international pressure to raise FLE standards (Figure 2). The reform involved the following national commitments: first, "By 2018, all primary schools in Mexico will have to be teaching English as a compulsory subject;" and second, "The B1 competence level is expected to be reached by the end of the beginning year of secondary education." (López Andrade, 2011)

---

① All translations in this paper are ours.

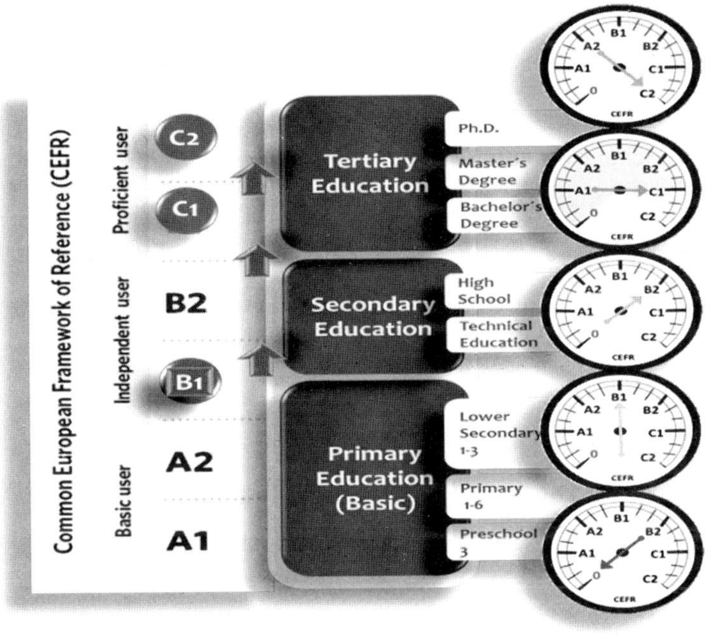

FIGURE 2. Definition of Foreign Language Competence Bechmarks in FL for Mexico – SEP 2011

Among other repercussions, the aforementioned initiatives have had a strong impact on the reconceptualization of the relevance of FLE at all levels of the educational ladder and, most importantly, are gradually leading to a much needed articulation in the definition of pedagogical objectives, evaluation criteria, and certification guidelines at the primary, secondary, and tertiary levels of education. The purpose of this paper is to present, against the framework of national initiatives and regulations for the promotion of foreign language education in our country, our experience at the Universidad Autónoma Metropolitana Iztapalapa in developing a FLCE curriculum that, based on an intercultural and interdisciplinary approach, is aimed at responding to Mexico's national strategy to guarantee equalitarian access to FLCE of excellence for the students of the Mexican public universities.

A Model for FLE at the Tertiary Level of Education in Mexico

The Universidad Autónoma Metropolitana (UAM, Spanish acronym) is one of the youngest and most prominent public universities in Mexico. It was founded in 1974 in response to the impressive demand for higher education in the country as a "... modern, flexible, and solid institution open to the world of ideas, currents of thought, new discoveries, and to the vast diversity of world views, while deeply rooted in our country's cultural heritage" (Universidad Autónoma Metropolitana, 2012a). The UAM is integrated by five academic campuses throughout the Mexico City area. In accordance with its regulatory framework, every campus is functionally and administratively self-regulated under the government of a Board of Rectors (a Rector General and particular Rectors for each campus) (López, González and Casillas, 2001). As to its current student enrollment figures, during 2011, it offered academic programs to 49,508 undergraduate and 861 postgraduate students in the fields of Basic Sciences and Engineering, Social Sciences and Humanities, Biological and Health Sciences, and Arts and Design (Universidad Autónoma Metropolitana, 2011a).

During 1999, and consistent with its foundational motto, *House Open to Time*, the institution underwent an unprecedented process of reflection and critical self-evaluation through the conjoint, decisive participation of academics, students and workers. The process, which amounted to a university congress, led to the redefinition of the institution's educational model for the new millennium. In the words of Dr. José Luis Gázquez Mateos, at that time Rector General for the UAM:

> We did not envision a technical exercise of institutional engineering and neither tried to confront ideological positions. What we did was to establish a serious, ordered, and systematic dialog, in which the whole community could contribute with a common purpose. What we did was to reflect as an academic community... The educational model at UAM, in contraposition to the models of many other higher education institutions, demands to develop in parallel our teaching, research, and cultural promotion activities, all being equally relevant. Our institutional identity derives from the conjunction of these three basic dimensions and requires that all of them revolve around a unique cultural project. (Una reflexi ó n sobre la Universidad..., 2001: 10–11).

Among the most influential byproducts of this visionary process of institutional reflection was the issuance of a set of General Academic Operational

Policies which reoriented the academic life of our university. In such regard, FLCE was granted an outstanding preeminence in the definition of the profile of our university graduates. The mandatory insertion of FLE was expressed in the following terms in our University Legislation under the Articles: "Academic Programs", "Students", and "Basic Competences" (Universidad Autónoma Metropolitana, 2012b):

Academic Programs

3.4 To guarantee that all academic programs incorporate studying and communication strategies focused on reading, oral, and written expression, and on the acquisition of other languages as fundamental elements of university education (emphasis added).

STUDENTS

1.7 To guarantee conditions for the acquisition of at least a second language during the period of education of our students at the University (emphasis added).

BASIC COMPETENCES

3.2 To integrate the study of at least one foreign language as a required curricular subject in all undergraduate academic programs (emphasis added).

In strict accordance with the institutional guidelines derived from the agreements and regulations approved after this process of reflection, in 2003 the Iztapalapa Campus (UAMI, Spanish acronym) launched a thorough process of revision of all its undergraduate and postgraduate academic programs which has led in recent years to the approval of new syllabuses in the fields of Social Sciences and Humanities, Basic Sciences and Engineering, and Biological and Health Sciences. All the new syllabuses now integrate FLE in the form of three required subjects with credits, amounting to one-year of compulsory education either in German, French, English, Italian or Russian at a B1 level of competence. Furthermore, the Institutional Development Plan 2011—2024 from the Rector General has established as a major goal to guarantee the acquisition of the B1 level of the CEFR in at least 40% of our entire undergraduate student population by 2024 (Universidad Autónoma Metropolitana, 2011b).

The Foreign Language Intercultural and Interdisciplinary Program at UAM Iztapalapa②

In 2007, the Academic Council at UAMI approved the *Interdisciplinary and Intercultural Program of Foreign Language and Culture Education* for our campus. This decision led to the official integration of FLCE in English, French, German, Italian, or Russian for credits in all its undergraduate and graduate degree programs (Consejo Académico de la UAM Iztapalapa, 2007, p. 19). Previously, students could take optional courses of languages without credits to meet their degree program requirements in foreign languages, whether for reading comprehension of academic texts or for a general four skills proficiency.

The FLCE program at Iztapalapa is based on the following premises (Consejo Académico de la UAM Iztapalapa, 2007: 20-21):

1) Foreign language education and the certification of competences in foreign language should be based on international standards (Byram, 1997: 29-30; 107-111).
2) The traditional instructional schemes that approach foreign language education mostly as a technical training focused on the instrumental transmission of linguistic knowledge and competences should be overcome (Swaffar, 2006: 248-249; Kramsch, 2006: 250-252; Schultz, 2006: 254; Tucker, 2006: 265-266).
3) The knowledge of the linguistic system of a given language must not be disassociated from the knowledge of the cultures of the peoples who speak such language if learning is to be meaningful and relevant (Kramsch, 1998; 2006).
4) The teaching of a target culture must not be limited to the transmission of isolated cultural facts, but must be based on its critical analysis as well as on the reflection about one's own culture (Byram and Grundy, 2003;

② This curricular program was based on research work related to the doctoral dissertations by Vivaldo (2003) and Lee (2001).

Corbett, 2003; McKay, 2002; Paran, 2006; Wendel, 2003; Hoecherl-Alden, 2006: 244-246; Williams, 2005: 181-183; Lee Zoreda, 2001).

5) The learning of the English language system must be anchored in the linguistic knowledge of the student's first language (grammar, lexis, syntax, etc.), promoting a synergetic comparative reflection on the way both languages operate (Phillips and Gonzalez, 2004: 148-165).
6) The learning of a foreign language in the context of university education should be directly related to the academic objectives and priorities of the student, assuring an authentic connection between the knowledge acquired in the language classroom and the professional and academic demands imposed by the professional contexts in which they will have to participate (Swaffar, 2006: 248-249; Rifkin, 2006: 263; Kasper et al., 2000; Pally, 2000).
7) The practice of competences associated with FLE must go beyond the classroom and thus offer opportunities for the students to apply their knowledge and skills in authentic multicultural and multilingual contexts, thus promoting a life-long learning process (Phillips and Gonzalez, 2004: 108-130).

Curricular Strategy: A Fusion of Local, Regional and International Standards of FLE

The curricular model for foreign language education at the UAMI was conceived as a fusion of local, regional, and international standards into a holistic educational set of policies that define pedagogical objectives, competences to be developed, as well as evaluation, accreditation, and certification criteria for foreign language education. The main objective of our program was to create an academic and instructional environment that could realistically promote the skills, knowledge, and competences required by our students to become successfully integrated into the multicultural and multilingual academic and professional contexts in which they will have to interact as citizens of increasingly global societies.

As was previously mentioned, our point of departure was an integrative curriculum design strategy. Firstly, the definition of the linguistic strand of our FLCE program was set in accordance with the linguistic benchmarks established by the *Common European Framework of Reference* (*CEFR*), (*Common European Framework of Reference for Languages,* 2001). Those benchmarks were translated into specific linguistic instructional objectives for the basic, intermediate, and upper intermediate levels of the program. Secondly, given our interest in providing our students with FLE well beyond the realm of linguistic competence to encompass intercultural and humanistic perspectives and competences, we further based our curricular scheme on the *Standards for Foreign Language Learning* (SFLL) of the United States of America (*Standards for Foreign Language Learning,* 2006). This influential document became the main referent in the conceptualization of our approaches to culture and interculturality, as well as in the delimitation of instructional practices associated with the promotion of contrastive analysis between first and foreign languages and cultures, with the liaison of FL competence with our students' disciplines, and with the extrapolation of competences to scenarios beyond the sphere of the foreign language classroom.

Thirdly, the overall definition of standards of the UAMI's FLCE program was also framed on the guidelines and recommendations proposed by the Secretary of Public Education in Mexico, aiming at the articulation of FLE objectives within the different sub-systems of education in the country. Therefore, the exit requirement for our B.A. programs was set at the B1 level of the CEFR, while the optional upper intermediate and advanced programs were set at the B2 and C1 levels, respectively.

Description of the Curriculum. Following the guidelines advanced by the American SFLL document, our program aims at developing in our students, interpersonal, interpretive, and expository communication competences. The pedagogical scheme has been developed into a curricular framework (Diagrams 1A and 1B) constructed around the following five curricular strands, each one of them receiving an equivalent relative weight of importance within the curriculum:

- Communication: [To] communicate in languages other than their own;

- Cultures: Students gain a knowledge and understanding of the cultures that use that language;
- Comparisons: Students develop insight into the nature of language and the concept of culture and realize that there are multiple ways of viewing the world;
- Connections: Learning languages provides connections to additional bodies of knowledge that may be unavailable to the monolingual English speaker;
- Communities: These elements enable the student of languages to participate in multilingual communities at home and around the world in a variety of contexts and in culturally appropriate ways. (*Standards for Foreign Language Learning*, 2012: 3)

Operationally, the program extends along the twelve trimesters of any of our B.A. programs and is divided into four curricular blocks (each one of them lasting for three trimesters[③]). The first, the propaedeutic stage, is carried out in trimesters 1, 2, and 3. It aims at establishing competences associated to the A1 level of the CEFR and to the Basic Level of the SFLL. The second, the required curricular stage, is compulsory for all students in B.A. programs and corresponds to trimesters 4, 5, and 6, leading to competences associated with the B1 level of the CEFR and to the Intermediate Level of the SFLL. Its accreditation is considered a requirement for graduation in all B.A. programs. The third stage, the elective curricular stage, runs from trimesters 7 to 9 and is focused on the development of skills and competences at the upper intermediate level of competence as established by the B2 level of the CEFR and the Upper Intermediate Level of the SFLL. It is important to note that the upper intermediate level is required for graduation at all postgraduate programs in our institution. Therefore, any student pursuing elective courses during his/her undergraduate studies will have fulfilled such requirements well in advance of obtaining the B.A. degree. Finally, the fourth stage corresponds to a further elective curricular stage with credits. It moves from trimesters 10 to 12 and its objectives are twofold: to improve the students'

③ It is important to emphasize that although this paper focuses on the Intercultural and Interdisciplinary Program in English, equivalent programs have been developed in French, German, Italian, and Russian.

linguistic competences and to promote a deeper immersion in cultural critical analyzes and discussions. Students at this level fulfill standards equivalent to the C1 of the CEFR and the Advanced Level of the SFLL.

As to the contents of each curricular strand, they are programed as follows: First, the Communication strand centers on the development of linguistic competences and focuses on the use of a textbook series (*Touchstone*). Among other criteria, the selection of textbooks is based on the existence of clear referents to the benchmarks of linguistic competence of the CEFR in the delimitation of educational objectives, teaching/learning practices, and evaluation and certification criteria. Second, the Cultures strand introduces the student to the vast diversity of peoples that speak the language they are learning. Each trimester, our students approach the study of a specific Anglophone country through the critical analysis of cultural modules that lead them through the particular cultural perspectives, processes, and products of the country under study. Specifically, for each course the student is involved in the reading of introductory expository texts of the country, and in the aesthetic experience of reading a simplified novel selected from its vast cultural heritage, together with its movie version with English subtitling. Complementary activities are the analyzes of key selections of poetry and songs from each country. With regard to the Comparisons and Connections strands, both permeate along all levels of our curriculum. The former refers to the permanent comparisons established at all times and at all levels between linguistic and cultural contents related to the students, first and foreign language (L1 and L2) as well as their culture (C1) and the foreign culture (C2). The Connections component refers to the constant link between the learning of the foreign language and its use in the acquisition of relevant knowledge related to the students' disciplines and academic interests. Finally, the Communities strand is centered on the development of group projects and activities aiming at promoting experiences in the use of the language in authentic multilingual and multicultural situations outside the context of the classroom (group interviews with speakers of the foreign language, oral academic presentations, attendance at conferences, bibliographic research, Internet collaborative projects, etc.).

DIAGRAM 1 A. The Intercultural and Interdisciplinary FLCE Program at UAMI: English Version (Basic, Intermediate, and Upper Intermediate Levels)

CURRICULAR STRAND	PROPAEDEUTIC STAGE BASIC LEVEL			REQUIRED CURRICULAR STAGE INTERMEDI ATE LEVEL			ELECTIVE CURRICULAR STAGE UPPER INTERMEDIATE LEVEL		
	TRIM. 1	TRIM. 2	TRIM. 3	TRIM. 4	TRIM. 5	TRIM. 6	TRIM. 7	TRIM. 8	TRIM. 9
COMMUNICATION *CEFR*	*Touchstone* 1 Units 1-4	*Touchstone* 1 Units 5- 8	*Touchstone* 1 Units 9-12 **Level A1 / A2 (MCE) SFLL: Basic**	*Touchstone* 2 Units 1-4	*Touchstone* 2 Units 5-8	*Touchstone* 2 Units 9-12 **Level A2 / B1 (*MCE*) SFLL: Intermediate**	*Touchstone* 3 Units 1-4	*Touchstone* 3 Units 5-8	*Touchstone* 3 Units 9-12 **Level B1 / B2 (*MCE*) SFLL: Upper Intermediate**
CULTURES *SFLL*	UNITED STATES	GREAT BRITAIN	UNITED STATES	IRELAND	AUSTRALIA AND NEW ZEALAND	UNITED STATES	GREAT BRITAIN	UNITED STATES	CANADA
	Novel: *Of Mice and Men* (Steinbeck) **Poem:** *Fog* (Sandburg) **Song:** *This Land Is My Land* (Guthrie) **Film:** *Of Mice and Men* (Sinise) **Informative texts**	**Novel:** *King Arthur and the Knights of the Round Table* **Poem:** *The Eagle* (Tennyson) **Song:** *Fairest Isle* (Purcell) **Film:** *Excalibur* (Boorman) **Informative texts**	**Novel:** *Last of the Mohicans* (Cooper) **Poems:** *Wolf Song* (Teton Sioux); *The Death Song of White Antelope* (Cheyenne) **Song:** *Shenandoah* **Film:** *Last of the Mohicans* (Mann) **Informative texts**	**Novel:** *The Picture of Dorian Gray* (Wilde) **Poems:** *The Lake Isle of Innisfree; The Second Coming* (Yeats) **Song:** *Both Sides the Tweed* (Gaughan) **Film:** *Michael Collins* (Jordan) **Complementary films:** *The Secret of Roan Inish; The Boxer* **Informative texts**	**Novel:** *Walkabout* (Marshall) **Poem:** *Old Botany Bay* (Gilmore) **Song:** *Waltzing Matilda* **Film:** *Walkabout* (Roeg) **Complementary films:** *An Angel at my Table; The Piano* **Informative texts**	**Novel:** *Ethan Frome* (Warthon) **Poem:** *Harlem* (L. Hughes) **Songs:** *Amazing Grace; Strange Fruit* (B. Holiday) **Film:** *Ethan Frome* (Madden) **Complementary film:** *Jungle Fever* **Informative texts**	**Novel:** *1984* (Orwell) **Poem:** *If* (Kipling); *Seven Ages of Man* (Shakespeare) **Song:** *The Wall* (Pink Floyd) **Film:** *1984* (Radford) **Complementary film:** *Brazil* (Gilliam) **Informative texts**	**Novel:** *The Mosquito Coast* (Theroux) **Poem:** *America* (Whitman); News Item (Parker); *La Migra* (Mora) **Song:** *Blowin' in the Wind* (Dylan) **Film:** The Mosquito Coast (Weir) **Complementary Films:** *Real Women Have Curves; Matewan* **Informative texts**	**Short-story:** *The Age of Lead* (Atwood) **Essay:** *From Survival: A Thematic Guide to Canadian Literature* (Atwood) **Poem:** *From Brébeuf and His Brethren* (Pratt) **Song:** *Both Sides Now* (Mitchell) **Film:** *Black Robe* (Beresford) **Informative texts**
COMPARISONS *SFLL*	Contrastive analysis of contents of the linguistic (L!/L2) and cultural (C1/C2) strands								
CONNECTIONS *SFLL*	Reading simple expository texts / Brief oral presentations.			Academic bibliographic research related to students' disciplines; brief oral and written presentations of selected topics			Reviews of literature in the discipline / Brief written critical essays		
COMMUNITIES *SFLL*	Group interviews / Internet discussion groups.			Structured interviews to foreign language specialists / Internet discussion groups / Written academic reports.			Internet discussion groups / Oral presentations about Anglophone cultures.		

DIAGRAM 1 B. The Intercultural and Interdisciplinary FLCE Program at UAMI: English Version (Advanced Level)

ELECTIVE CURRICULAR STAGE ADVANCED LEVEL Trimesters 10-12		
ADVANCED ACADEMIC WRITING		**SELECTED TOPICS IN ANGLOPHONE CULTURES I, II, III, IV (Not consecutive)**
I Analysis of Academic Written Discourse	II Scientific Academic Writing Strategies	Otherness in Anglophone Cinema Dupin and Holmes: The Birth of the Modern Detective Movie-Video in English: Breaking Away Classic American Movies I Classic American Movies II Intercultural Encounters in Anglophone Cinema Science Fiction in English I Science Fiction in English II Science Fiction in English III Key Moments of Life in Movie, Poetry, and Literature Ultra-short Science Fiction Stories in English

The Integration of Language and Culture to Our FLCE Curriculum

One of our earliest curricular decisions was to assure the integration of the language/culture binomial into the FLCE curriculum by exposing our students from the very early stages of the program to a critical analysis of the vast diversity of Anglophone cultures to which they would be introduced. Such contents were dealt with mainly in the Cultures and Comparisons strands of the program (the latter focused on the critical comparative analysis between the Anglophone cultures and the students' own culture).

Specifically, the FLCE Program at UAMI seeks to educate students with a holistic perspective centered on the analysis of perspectives, processes, products, and milestone events of Anglophone peoples, thus promoting an understanding and appreciation of both their richness and heterogeneity, while overcoming traditional, biased, and limited views, mostly associated with stereotypes deeply rooted in misinformation (Lee Zoreda, 2001). In such regard, Swaffar and Arens emphasize the importance of incorporating critically cultural elements in the curriculum of FL education:

> Recognizing significant moments in foreign countries and cultures involves first knowing how to read texts to identify that culture's expectations at any given time or place in its history (the dominant practices and speech acts of the day) and to assess how those expectations have been challenged or renegotiated by alternative discourses. (Swaffar and Arens, 2005: 5)

The curricular proposal is anchored on a structured interdisciplinary approach. During each trimester, the students are immersed into the critical study of a specific Anglophone country through their exposure to a cultural module that introduces them to the country's literature (graded readers with audio versions), poetry, cinematography, and music (both popular and canonical), which are complemented with the study of expository texts offering historical, geographical, educational, and social background information about the particular country. At the current stage of curricular development of our program, the cultural strand centering on the analysis of what Kachru has been referred to as the "Inner Circle", that is, "countries in which English is the mother tongue: Canada, the United States of America, Great Britain, Ireland, Australia and New Zealand" (Kachru, 1992: 356). This curricular decision is associated to current limitations in published materials and texts related to the "Outer Circle" (graded literary readers, relevant cinematographic versions with English subtitling, graded expository texts introducing specific countries, etc.). However, we have made an effort to include oppositional discourses within the "Inner Circle" countries. It is our interest, though, to broaden the scope of the program in the future by developing cultural modules relevant to countries in the outer circle as more simplified readers dealing with postcolonial Anglophone topics get published.

As to the design of our cultural models, it is based on Vygotsky's educational metaphor of "scaffolding." This comes from a social constructivist conception of learning in which the teacher creates an affective and pedagogical support (including materials, experiences, peer interaction, and teacher-student interaction) through activities of increasing difficulty, which systematically present a challenge for the student, but achievable given his level of experience, in his "zone of proximal development" (McMahon, 1996, p. 60). On describing the scaffolding notion in the context of FLCE, Foley emphasizes that the teacher:

> By using contexts that are extremely familiar and routinized ...can facilitate learning....[S]caffolding is provided by leading or probing questions to extend or elaborate knowledge the learner already possesses. Rather than evaluating the learner's answers, the teacher is supporting, encouraging, and providing additional props. As the learner's competence grows, so the scaffolding is gradually reduced until the learner is able to function autonomously in that task and generalize to similar circumstances. (Foley in "Key concept: Scaffolding", 2005, p. 1)

Such a learning environment goes far beyond just merely getting "right" answers, and is centered on a teacher "confident enough to depart from the book and structure the classroom around the learners, following up interesting comments or questions which arise" (Morrow in "Key concept: Scaffolding", 2005, p. 3). Thus, we consider it as a fundamental part of the scaffolding for the graded class reader which, according to Prowse, can function as a "springboard into language use" (2002, p. 144), and as a gateway into critical thinking, movie appreciation, and intercultural reflection.

What we sought in the design of each of our pedagogical modules was the interdisciplinary synergetic merging of simplified texts and original texts in various media, all thematically related to an aesthetic Anglophone product, a literary classic or provocative narrative (Lee and Vivaldo, 2008). Such a teaching unit could easily be classified in current EFL terminology as a form of sustained content-based instruction. In other words, it deals with the deep exploration of only one content theme in a course, dealing complementarily with the linguistic and discursive aspects related to the given content.

This approach, in which the student can acquire holistically and thematically related vocabulary, concepts, and knowledge, together with an improvement in the English language, has shown to be successful in American and Canadian university programs for foreign students or immigrants. In such regard, it has been of utmost pre-eminence in our curriculum design strategy to acknowledge the potential for education that comes from being exposed to literature and other imaginative cultural texts, as is the case of movies. On this point, the reader can refer to Lee (2005) for the rationale to include aesthetic experiences in the teaching-learning process of FLCE. In brief, it means that active participation in an aesthetic encounter can become an educative experience that sharpens our perception of the everyday world, opens new possibilities to us, and gets us "out of our own skin" as we enter into distinct worlds than ours and establish an empathetic relation with that otherness.

Conceptualization of Culture and Interculturality in the Design of Cultural Modules. In developing our Culture strand, the term "culture" has been conceptualized as the attitudes, behaviors, and products (both tangible and intangible) shared and revealed in any society; that is, both "culture" as well as "Culture." Claire Kramsch has further enhanced that definition to include an imagined social space:

> [C]ulture can be defined as membership in a discourse community that shares a common social space and history, and common imaginings... [T]his diachronic view of culture focuses on the way in which a social group represents itself and others through its material productions over time—its technological achievements, its monuments, its works of art, its popular culture—that punctuate the development of its historical identity. (Kramsch in Scott and Huntington, 2002: 622–623)

In the specific case of FLCE, such an intensification of awareness and sense of otherness is manifested in two dimensions when students are simultaneously exposed both to art and Anglophone cultures. It is important to note that we believe in the concept of culture in its most ample sense, as proposed by Kramsch:

> Culture consists of precisely that historical dimension in a group's identity. This diachronic view of culture focuses on the way in which a social group represents itself and others through its material production over time—its technological achievements, its monuments, its works of art, its popular culture—that punctuate the development of its historical identity. (1998: 7–8)

Stimulating the student's imagination, principally through narrative, in any of its artistic manifestations of the experience of a particular social group, can become "an important corrective for the dehumanizing effects of abstract theory or generalization (Srebrnik, 2002, p.108)". In other words, "our real life experiences are complemented and enriched by the 'borrowed' experience gained through reading (Sharman, 2002, p.99)". Through such complex experiences, students can develop both critical thinking understood as "reflective scepticism" as well as "an increased awareness of self and others [with] deep cognitive processing skills (Schultz, 2002, pp. 10, 13)".

Another related ability that we want our students to develop with cultural, narrative, and aesthetic encounters is that of acting and thinking interculturally, where a person can place himself at a critical distance from both the foreign culture as well as from his own culture (Byram, 1997; Kramsch, 1993). Establishing this as an educational objective would definitely broaden the scope of EFL programs. Sercu has remarked that "becoming an interculturally competent user of a foreign language not only involves the acquisition of communicative competence in that language, it also involves the acquisition of particular skills, attitudes, values, knowledge items and ways at looking at the world (as cited in Shelley & Baumann, 2005, pp. 121–122)". Such an educational target profile becomes a real shift in FLCE curricula, moving away from the use of cultural capsules (if they were ever present) toward programs that sustain that "the true content of the foreign language course is not the grammar and the vocabulary of the language, but the cultures expressed that language (*Standards for Foreign Language Learning⋯*, 2006: 47–48)".

Conclusion

One of the major goals of the curriculum at UAMI is to expose the students of the Mexican public universities to the beauty of the humanities whereby the peculiarities and the universalities of the human condition can be experienced in diverse cultures. Instead of merely teaching the predominant survival English (whatever that is), the student is immersed, through language, in intercultural encounters at intellectual, emotional, memorable, and pleasurable levels. By vicariously entering into and understanding other cultures, that is, their imaginary, collective consciousness, iconic symbolic figures, and master narratives, our students develop an understanding of other cultural historical identities and memories as well as their envisioned futures. However, it is important to note here that in no way does this mean that students are expected to accept uncritically foreign cultures, but to develop sensitivity and respect toward difference while simultaneously developing a critical distance to their native culture.

At the same time as they become intercultural, by entering into master narratives, literatures, history, and the arts, this will stimulate, enhance and encourage our students to use their imagination in the process of broadening their horizons. In such regard, we are convinced that our future world citizens will have to develop as never before a higher capacity of empathetic imagination in order to think of and project novel possibilities in ever-changing situations, which is what our world desperately needs. Isn't this a major expression of creativity?

What we propose here is nothing new but has been disregarded in favor of technical efficiency teaching and learning. We can go back one hundred years to the thinking of one of the world's most famous and continually pertinent educational philosophers, John Dewey. He always championed the widening of the born condition of each student, that is, the expansion of his or her spatial and temporal boundaries from primary school onward, so that "each individual gets an opportunity to escape from the limitations of the social group in which he was born, and to come into living contact with a broader environment" (Dewey, 1966: 20). At the same time, based on the need to educate for democracy, he felt that mere tolerance was insufficient. On the contrary, he believed that schools must try to promote the formation of a socialized mind, social intelligence, which he defined as "the power to understand things in terms of the use made of them; a socialized mind is the power to understand them in terms of the use to which they are turned in joint or shared situations (Dewey in Lee, 2001: 33)".

To conclude, it is our hope that our Intercultural and Interdisciplinary Foreign Language Program will soon make a marked difference for Mexican public university students in that they will have an enhanced formation as intercultural, imaginative and visionary global citizens opening up the possibility in all domains to create a better world.

References:

[1] Byram, Michael. (1997). *Teaching and Assessing Intercultural Communicative Competence*. Clevedon: Multilingual Matters Ltd.

[2] Byram, Michael, and Peter Grundy (eds). (2003). *Context and Culture in Language Teaching and Learning*. Clevedon: Multilingual Matters Ltd.

[3] Chau, Abby. (2011). *The World's Best Language Courses*. http://qsiu.wordpress.com/2011/06/27/the-worlds-best-modern-languages-courses (July 5, 2012).

[4] *Common European Framework of Reference for Languages: Learning, Teaching, Assessment*. (2001). Cambridge: Cambridge University Press.

[5] Consejo Académico de la Unidad Iztapalapa. (2007). Programa de Enseñanza de Lenguas Extranjeras: Un Curriculum, Interdisciplinario e Intercultural. Universidad Autónoma Metropolitana, Unidad Iztapalapa. http://www.izt.uam.mx/conacad/doc_relevantes/programas/Programa_de_Ensenanza_de_LEx.pdf (August 1, 2012)

[6] Corbett, John. (2003). *An Intercultural Approach to English Language Teaching*. Clevedon: Multilingual Matters Ltd.

[7] Dewey, John. 1966 (1916). *Democracy in Education*. New York, NY: Macmillan.

[8] González Robles, Rosa Obdulia, Javier Vivaldo Lima and Alberto Castillo Morales. (2004). *Competencia lingüística en inglés de estudiantes de primer ingreso a instituciones de educación superior del área metropolitana de la Ciudad de México*. Mexico, D.F.: ANUIES/UAM.

[9] Gordon, David and Alexander, Gad. (2005). The Education of Story Lovers: Do Computers Undermine Narrative Sensibility? *Curriculum Inquiry*, 35 (2), 133-159.

[10] Hoecherl-Alden, Gisela. (2006). Connecting Language to Content: Second Language Literature Instruction at the Intermediate Level. *Foreign Language Annals*, 39 (2): 244-254.

[11] Kachru, Braj. (1992). Teaching World Englishes. Braj Kachru (ed.). *The Other Tongue: English across Cultures* (second edition). Urbana, IL: University of Illinois Press.

[12] Kasper, Loretta, et al. (2000). *Content-Based College ESL Instruction*. Mahwah, NJ: Lawrence Erlbaum.

[13] Oxford Teachers' Club. (2005). *Key Concept: Scaffolding*. http://www.oup.com/elt/teachersclub/articles/scaffolding?cc=global (April 26, 2005).

[14] Kramsch, Claire. (1993). *Context and Culture in Language Teaching*. Oxford: Oxford University Press.

[15] Kramsch, Claire. (1998). *Language and Culture*. Oxford: Oxford University Press.

[16] Kramsch, Claire. (2006). From Communicative Competence to Symbolic Competence. *The Modern Language Journal*, 90 (2), 249-252.

[17] Lee Zoreda, Margaret. (2001). *Valoración y propuesta de la enseñanza de inglés como lengua extranjera a la luz de John Dewey.* Unpublished doctoral dissertation. Mexico, D. F.: Universidad La Salle.

[18] Lee Zoreda, Margaret. (2005). Artes e imaginación en la enseñanza-aprendizaje del inglés. In G. Cortés & G. Novoa (Eds.), *Memorias del cuarto coloquio de lenguas extranjeras*. México, DF: Universidad Autónoma Metropolitana Azcapotzalco.

[19] Lee Zoreda, Margaret and Javier Vivaldo Lima. (2008). Scaffolding Linguistic and Intercultural Goals in EFL with Simplified Novels and Their Movie Adaptations. *English Teaching Forum*, 46, (3), 22-29.

[20] López Andrade, Guillermo Pablo. (2011). *English in Modeling Global Universities: Challenges for Tertiary Sector Institutions of Mexico as they Respond to Demand for English*. Unpublished paper presented at the 4th International Conference of ALTE. July 8, 2011. Kraków, Poland.

[21] López Zarate, Romualdo; Oscar M. González Cueva, and Miguel Ángel Casillas Alvarado. (2000). *Una Historia de la UAM: Sus Primeros 25 Años*. México: Universidad Autónoma Metropolitana.

[22] McKay, Sandra Lee. (2002). *Teaching English as an International Language*. Oxford: Oxford University Press.

[23] McMahon, Susan. (1996). Book club: The Influence of a Vygotskian Perspective on a Literature-Based Reading Program. In L. Dixon-Krauss (ed.), *Vygotsky in the Classroom: Mediated Literacy Instruction and Assessment*. White Plains, NY: Longman. pp. 59-76.

[24] Pally, Marcia (ed.). (2000). *Sustained Content Teaching in Academic ESL/EFL*. Boston: Houghton Mifflin.

[25] Paran, Amos (ed.). (2006). *Literature in Language Teaching and Learning*. Alexandria, VA: TESOL.

[26] Phillips, Alison and Mike Gonzalez. (2004). *Modern Languages: Learning and Teaching in an Intercultural Field*. London: Sage.

[27] Prowse, P. (2002). Top Ten Principles for Teaching Extensive Reading: A Response. *Reading in a Foreign Language,* 14 (2), 142-145. http://nflrc.hawaii.edu/rfl (February 23, 2005).

[28] Rifkin, Benjamin. (2006). A Ceiling Effect for Communicative Language Teaching. *The Modern Language Journal,* 90 (2), 262-264.

[29] Scott, Virginia and Julie Huntington. (2002). Reading Culture: Using Literature to Develop C2 Competence. *Foreign Language Annals,* 35(6), 622-631.

[30] Schultz, Jean Marie. (2002). The Gordian Knot: Language, Literature, and Critical Thinking. In V. Scott & H. Tucker (eds.). *SLA and the Literature Classroom: Fostering Dialogs*. Boston, MA: Heinle & Heinle. pp. 3-31.

[31] Schultz, Renate. (2006). Reevaluating Communicative Competence as a Major Goal in Postsecondary Language Requirement Courses. *The Modern Language Journal,* 90 (2), 252-255.

[32] Sharman, Gundula M. (2002). Literature in the Modern Language Syllabus. *Academic Exchange Quarterly*, 6 (4), 98-103. Expanded Academic ASAP Database, http://infotrac.galegroup.com.../purl=rcl_EAIM_0_A97725099&dyn=3!ar_fmt?sw_aep=ua (March 4, 2003).

[33] Shelley, Monica and Baumann, Uwe. (2005). Assessing Intercultural Competence Gain in a German Distance Learning Course. In B. Holmberg, M. Shelley, and C. White. (eds.), *Distance Education and Languages: Evolution and Change*. Clevedon: Multicultural Matters Ltd. pp. 119-139.

[34] Srebrnik, Henry. (2002). Literature, Politics and Pedagogy. *Academic Exchange Quarterly*, 6 (4),108-113. Expanded Academic ASAP Database. http://infotrac.galegroup.com.../purl=rcl_EAIM_0_A97725099&dyn=15!ar_fmt?sw_aep=ua (March 4, 2003).

[35] *Standards for Foreign Language Learning: Preparing for the* 21st *Century*. (2012). http://www.actfl.org/files/public/StandardsforFLLexecsumm_rev.pdf (August 12, 2012).

[36] *Standards for Foreign Language Learning: Preparing for the* 21st *Century*. 2006 (third edition). National Standards in Foreign Language Education Project. Lawrence, KS: Allen Press.

[37] Subsecretaría de Planeación y Coordinación, Dirección General de Acreditación, Incorporación y Revalidación, Recomendación No. DGAIR/_/2006. (2006).

Estándares internacionales que en materia de acreditación de conocimientos y docencia de lenguas extranjeras, recomienda la Dirección General de Acreditación, Incorporación y Revalidación. Mexico, D. F.: Secretaría de Educación Pública. http://www.sep.gob.mx/wb2/sep/sep_0826_04.

[38] Swaffar, Janet and Catherine Arens. (2005). *Remapping the Foreign Language Curriculum: An Approach through Multiple Literacies*. New York, N.Y.: Modern Language Association.

[39] Swaffar, Janet. (2006). Terminology and Its Discontents: Some Caveats about Communicative Competence. *The Modern Language Journal,* 90 (2), 246-249.

[40] Tucker, Holly. (2006). Communicative Collaboration: Language, Literature, and Communicative Competence Redefined. *The Modern Language Journal,* 90 (2), 264-266.

[41] Una Reflexión sobre la Universidad desde la Docencia. (2001). Mexico, D.F.: Universidad Autónoma Metropolitana.

[42] Universidad Autónoma Metropolitana. (2011a). *Anuario Estadístico*. http://www.uam.mx/transparencia/inforganos/anuarios/anuario2011/anuario_estadistico_2011.pdf (August 12, 2012).

[43] Universidad Autónoma Metropolitana. (2011b). *Plan de Desarrollo Institucional*. http://www.uam.mx/pdi/pdi/pdi_2011_2024/assets/downloads/PDI_2011-2024.pdf (August 12, 2012).

[44] Universidad Autónoma Metropolitana. (2012a). UAM: Presente y Pasado. http://www.uam.mx/sah/pre-pa/indice.html (August 13, 2012).

[45] Universidad Autónoma Metropolitana. (2012b). *Legislación Universitaria*. http://www.uam.mx/legislacion/ (August 13, 2012).

[46] Vivaldo Lima, Javier. (2003). *Understanding Differential Academic Reading Comprehension of Good vs. Poor Readers in English as a Foreign Language*. Unpublished doctoral dissertation. London, UK: Institute of Education.

[47] Wendel, Reinhold. (2003). Teaching India in the EFL-Classroom: A Cultural or an Intercultural Approach? Michael Byram and Peter Grundy (eds.). *Context and Culture in Language Teaching and Learning*. Clevedon: Multilingual Matters Ltd. Pp. 72-80.

[48] Williams, Kevin. (2005). *The Limits of Aesthetic Separatism*. The Routledge Falmer Reader in Philosophy of Education. London: Routledge. pp. 174-184.

墨西哥的外语教育：墨西哥城自治都市大学跨文化和跨学科的外语课程

[墨西哥] Javier Vivaldo Lima and Margaret Lee Zoreda

摘要：在初等、中等及高等教育中贯彻外语教学的方针政策现已成为墨西哥教育的首要任务。相应地，在教育系统的主要层面上建立国家标准来评估和认证外语能力的工作正在取得进展。上述工作的目的是要建立起外语学术项目、教学实践以及学科或者专业发展之间的联系。本文首先概述墨西哥近年来在外语能力国家认证方面所做的工作，并详细描述墨西哥一所主要公立大学——墨西哥城自治都市大学进行创新性教学的经验。该大学开展的这一跨文化、跨学科的外语教学项目具有“多语言和多元文化”的特点。它整合了国际和国内标准，按照两个级别进入该大学所有本科专业的课程体系，一个是中级水平，属于必修课；另一个是中高和高级水平，属于选修课。本文最后讨论这一项目在教学法和实际操作方面的意义及其与未来墨西哥教学可持续性发展之间的关系。

关键词：外语教育；跨文化；墨西哥

Promoting the Language Standard of College Graduates: The Implementation and Pedagogical Implications of an English Graduation Benchmark

[Chinese Taipei]

Li-Jiuan Tsay, Pey-Chewn Duo, Min-Hsun Su, and Hsiang-I Chen

Abstract: As the quality of language learning becomes a shared concern around the world and with the rapid development of globalization, English language learning has been catapulted into a widely spread "fever" in Asia for many learners and parents (Krashen, 2003). Two key components ensuring the success of learning are the quality of teachers and evaluation of student achievement outcomes. In order to promote the standards of language education, the APEC economies have launched several projects starting from 2004. A summit held in 2004 in Beijing gathered educational policy makers and researchers to look closely into the areas of instructional methods and curriculums, which have led to some educational reforms in many regions. A research project conducted in 2007 by the APEC Education Network on language standards and related assessments offered a comprehensive and resourceful database on current practices in the setting and assessing of foreign language standards for teachers and learners in the APEC regions (Chen, Sinclair, Huang and Eyerman, 2008).

To further reinforce the standards in language education, Chinese Taipei has carried out a series of projects to promote language standards. One project, the Schweitzer Program, integrates available resources from different levels of schools and universities to help underprivileged students, particularly in primary and secondary schools in remote areas. For those who are gifted in languages, the English Talents Learning Program is carefully planned to sharpen students' achievements even further. Moreover, in higher education, in order to promote college graduates' competitiveness and meet the demands of the workforce after graduating from universities, Chinese Taipei began encouraging universities to establish graduation benchmarks for English proficiency in 2002. A considerable amount of related research was subsequently conducted. According to the data, in 2006, 53 universities set up graduation benchmarks, and by 2008, the number had gone up to 67. In 2011, there were more than 100 schools implementing English proficiency tests as a graduation benchmark (Lin, 2011). The establishment of a graduation benchmark involves three aspects of modification and consideration: curriculum alignment, teachers' teaching and students' learning. Research related to teachers' and students' attitudes can be found in the existing literature (e.g., Su, 2005; Su, 2009; Lin, 2010; Chu, 2009). However, studies on related policies for curriculum design and the pedagogical implications have not been prolific. Can a tailored curriculum help improve students' language proficiency? Hence, the purposes of this paper are to provide some insight on the implementation and possible pedagogical implications for the improvement of language education through the establishment of an English graduation benchmark.

Keywords: graduation benchmark; washback effect; students' attitude; standardized assessment; language education standard

Introduction

With the advent of globalization, English has become a basic ability to possess for the global citizens in many non-English speaking countries and regions. In order to promote the standards of language education, the APEC economies have launched several projects starting from 2004. To further reinforce the standards in language education, Chinese Taipei has carried out a series of projects to promote language standards, such as the carefully planned Schweitzer Program and the English Talents Learning Program, to improve and sharpen students' achievements based on their different proficiencies. In 2002, the MOE also began to encourage colleges and universities to establish English proficiency graduation benchmarks in an attempt to enhance college students' competitiveness and prepare them for the demands of the workforce after graduating from schools.

The establishment of a graduation benchmark involves three aspects of modification and consideration: curriculum alignment, teachers' teaching and students' learning. Research related to teachers' and students' attitudes can be found in the existing literature (e.g., Su, 2005; Su, 2009; Lin, 2010; Chu, 2009). However, studies on related policies for the make-up measure regarding the curriculum alignment and the pedagogical implications have not been prolific.

Hence, in the following sections, the implementation and the pedagogical implication of the English graduation benchmark are discussed.

The Implementations of the English Graduation Benchmark

Ever since the encouragement, a considerable amount of related research was subsequently conducted. According to the data, in 2006, 53 universities set up graduation benchmarks, and by 2008, the number had gone up to 67. In 2011, there were more than 100 schools implementing English proficiency tests as a graduation benchmark (Lin, 2011). The MOE's *2005—2008 Administration Guidelines* has specified that college students should achieve a 50% passing rate at intermediate GEPT level and students in the vocational ones should reach a 50% passing rate at the elementary level by the year 2007. As a result, a lot of attention has been centerd on the assessment of students' English proficiency as well as the establishment of the graduation benchmarks. In Su's (2005) research, more and more institutes have set up English proficiency graduation benchmarks in face of the trends and needs in society as well as job industry. For students majoring in English and other related fields, certainly, they are expected to reach a higher English graduation threshold set by their departments.

Standardized Assessments

After the implementation of the English graduation benchmark, students are required to pass certain standardized proficiency tests and achieve a satisfactory score. Some universities have developed their self-designated proficiency test in order to assess their students easily and more cost-effectively, while many of them prefer standardized tests. Take Ming Chuan University as an example. The Department of Applied English has created a test bank for assessing students' progress of English proficiency in an attempt to monitor students' learning and help them achieve their graduation benchmark; however, when it comes to reaching the graduation benchmark, students of Ming Chuan University still need to take a standardized test, such as GEPT/TOEIC/IELTS or the equivalent to get a satisfactory score to be able to graduate.

Remedial Courses on the Aligned Curriculum

The main purpose of establishing an English graduation benchmark is to promote students' language proficiency, not to keep them from graduating. Along with the implementation of the benchmark policy, the aligned curriculum design is provided by most universities. When students cannot achieve a satisfactory score for graduation, they are required to take some remedial English courses to make up the proficiency deficiency. Only if they passed those courses, can they graduate from universities.

Therefore the impact of the implementation has been an impetus to students' learning. In a survey conducted by Su (2005), more than half of the college students agreed on the policy of setting up a graduation benchmark, for it can enhance their competitiveness as long as the goals are attainable. Similar results were also found in Duo, Chen, Su and Tsay (2012), Yen and Hsin (2006), and Chu's (2009) studies. However, while some held a positive attitude, other students regarded the graduation benchmark as redundant to their learning. Liauh (2010), for example, surveyed 311 students from 7 universities of technology and found that many held a negative attitude toward the implementation of the exit English examination as well as the English curriculum alignment, teaching materials and teaching methods.

Nevertheless, the passing rate of GEPT or other equivalent standardized tests have substantially increased due to the benchmark policy set forth by universities. Take Ming Chuan University as an example. After establishing the graduation benchmark in 2005, the students' passing rate of GEPT has been improved progressively. Similar results were found at other universities.

The Pedagogical Implications

After more and more universities and colleges have set up the English graduation benchmark, some pedagogical implications are offered here.

Two streams of universities are shaped to accommodate students with different needs and expectations for their future career. Students who study at technical universities focus more on their training in professional skills and the knowledge of English for Specific Purpose (ESP), while those who study at general universities tend to have higher competency and confidence in English performance (Huang, 1998; Lo, 2000). Questions therefore arise here. What are the considerations for the alignment of the curriculum to accommodate the implementation of the English graduation benchmark? What is the students' attitude toward the English proficiency graduation benchmark?

Attitude toward the Policy

Some policymakers and educators believing in Pygmalion Effect may decide to set up a higher standard of the benchmark, while others do it based on their understanding of the recruited students' English proficiency. Nevertheless,

Vice Minister of Education, Lin, stated (2011) that it was important for the universities to make the regulation for the graduation benchmark clear right before students enter the universities.

Since the implementation of the graduation proficiency benchmark, research on students' attitude toward this policy has been found positive and supportive (Duo, Chen, Su and Tsay, 2012; Tsai and Tsou, 2009; Shen, 2004; Chen, 2004). A study conducted by Huang et al. (2006) stated that 57% of the students from universities of technology, 64% of the students from academic universities, and 76% of the teachers from universities of technology showed a positive attitude and supported the implementation of the English proficiency graduation benchmark policy. Nevertheless, a negative attitude was also reported and found from different surveys (Chen, 2006).

In Liauh's study (2010), it was found that the graduation benchmark seemed to have influenced the students with lower achievement more than those with higher English proficiency. A similar result was found in Duo et al. (2012).

Washback Effects

"Washback", known as the effect of testing on teaching and learning (Hughes, 1989; Bailey, 1993) is a neutral term, which has the potential to become either positive or negative (Alderson and Wall, 1993; Bailey, 1996; Hamp-Lyons, 1997; Hughes, 2003; Lin, 2010). Tests will somehow control the design of the curriculum (Spolsky, 1994) and have impacts on teaching methods and students' learning strategies (Biggs, 1995). Cheng (2005) indicated that washback was an intended or accidental direction and function of curriculum change in aspects of teaching and learning through a change of public examinations.

Two dimensions of washback effects of the English graduation benchmark have been investigated in some research. Chu (2009) indicated that washback on teaching was limited only to teaching of test-taking strategies in order to help students pass the requirement. And the washback on learning was not positive, because most of the participants found that the benchmark requirement was too high to achieve while it was not helpful to the high achievers (Chu, 2009). Hence, Chu (2009) concluded that washback was likely to be generated positively if students' language needs were taken into consideration. Some educators indicated that various professions required different language abilities, and not all graduates from universities should possess the same proficiency (Lin, 2009).

Conclusion

It has been almost a decade since the first establishment of the English proficiency graduation benchmark. Although positive results have shown that the majority was in favor of the establishment of the policy, the average performance of current students at universities and institutes of technology is behind what was expected from the MOE (LTTC, 2004; MOE, 2008).

As many studies have evidenced, the setting of the English graduation benchmark has given positive impacts upon the learning of students, especially on their extrinsic motivation once their attitude is set right. However, as many educators have pointed out, students with intrinsic motivation tend to be more persistent in their learning process and it is more important to activate students' autonomy in learning for the ultimate goal of language education.

Nunan's (2003, p.589) survey of the impact of English language on educational policies and practices in the Asia-Pacific region revealed "significant problems regarding a disjunction between curriculum rhetoric and pedagogical reality". Cheng (2007) also indicated that setting a graduation threshold was not the key to improve students' overall English competence. Reforming the English curriculum at the university level to increase students' interest and motivation is the fundamental solution to this problem (Hung, 2011). The research conducted has grounded some bases for the improvement of the implementation. Recommendation on further research should be focused on whether the curriculum alignment meets the students' needs and whether washback effect overwhelms the learning performance.

References:

[1] Alderson, C., and Wall. D. (1993). Does Washback Exist? *Applied Linguistics*, 14,115-129.

[2] Biggs, J. B. (1995). Assumptions Underlying New Approaches to Assessment. *Curriculum Forum*, 4, 1-22.

[3] Chen, H., Sinclair, P., Huang, S. Y., and Eyerman, L. (2008). APEC EDNET Project Seminar on Language Standards and Their Assessment, Chinese Taipei.

[4] Cheng, L. (2005). *Changing Language Teaching Through Language Testing: A Washback Study*. Cambridge: Cambridge University Press.

[5] Chu, H. Y. (2009). *Stakes, Needs and Washback: An Investigation of the English Benchmark Policy for Graduation and EFL Education at Two Technological Universities in Taiwan.* Unpublished Dissertation. NTNU, Chinese Taipei.

[6] Duo, P.C., Chen, H. I., Su, M. S. and Tsay, L. J. (2012). *English Proficiency Graduation Benchmark: Challenges and Concerns.* Paper presented at 2012 Chung Yuan Christian University Conference of Applied Linguistics.

[7] Hamp-Lyons, L. (1997). Washback, Impact and Validity: Ethical Concerns. *Language Testing*, 14, 295-303.

[8] Hughes, A. (1989). *Testing for Language Teachers*. Cambridge: Cambridge University Press.

[9] Liauh, Y. H. (2010). A Preliminary Study of Students' Attitudes toward the Exit English Examination in Technological and Vocational Higher Education in Taiwan. *Journal of National Huwei University of Science & Technology,* 29, 41-60.

[10] Lin, Y. T. (2010). *A Study on the Washback Effect of the Basic Competence English Test on Junior High School Students in Northern Taiwan.* Chinese Taipei, MA: NCCU dissertation.

[11] Ministry of Education. (2002). *Challenge 2008: National Developmental Plan.* Chinese Taipei: Ministry of Education.

[12] Nunan, D. (2003). The Impact of English as a Global Language on Educational Policies and Practices in the Asia-Pacific Region. *TESOL Quarterly*, 37, 589-613.

[13] Spolsky, B. (1994). The Examination of Classroom Backwash Cycle: Some Historical Cases, in Nunan, D., Berry, V. and Berry, R. (eds.) *Bringing about Change in Language Education,* Hong Kong: University of Hong Kong, Department of Curriculum Studies, 55-56.

[14] Su, S.W. (2005). A Study on the Needs for the Related Regulations of Exit English Exam in Taiwan. *Educational Review of the Kaohsiung Normal University in Taiwan*, 24, 47-66.

[15] Su, S.W. (2009). A Study of Graduation Threshold of English Competency from the Perspective of EFL Teachers of Technological Institutions in Southern Taiwan. *Kaohsiung Normal University Journal,* 27, 37-60.

[16] Tsai, Y., and Tsou, C. H. (2009). A Standardized English Language Proficiency Test as the Graduation Benchmark: Student Perspectives on Its Application in Higher Education. *Assessment in Education: Principles, Policy & Practice*, 16, 319-330.

[17] Yen, S. C., and Hsin, C. A. (2006). *Taiwanese Undergraduate Students' Attitude toward Graduation English Language Proficiency Benchmark: A Pilot Study*. Paper presented at the meeting of the Kaohsiung Taiwan, R.O.C. Air Force Academy, the Department of Foreign Languages.

[18] 陈江麟（2006）毕业门砍六成大学生排斥英检、沦为待宰羔羊！外语学院七成一反对，文化一周新闻网，http://jou.pccu.edu.tw/weekly/survey123/survey13.html(2009-12-15).

[19] 洪佳儒（2011）不符大学教育内涵　何万顺主张应废止英语毕业门坎，政治大学，http://www.nccu.edu.tw/news/detail.php?news_id=2874(2012-5-26).

[20] 林志成（2011）毕业怕卡到“英”大学生疯考多益，http://tw.news.yahoo.com (2011-4-5).

[21] 张武昌（2007）提升台湾大学英语文能力的政策与策略,《教育资料与研究专刊》第 12 期：157-174。

促进高校毕业生的语言水平：英语毕业基准的实施和教学的启示

[中国台北] Li-Jiuan Tsay, Pey-Chewn Duo, Min-Hsun Su, and Hsiang-I Chen

摘要： 本文主要介绍大学英语毕业的基准在台湾的实施过程。随着国际化的迅猛发展，在亚洲，英语学习在很多学生和家长中间已经形成了一种热潮。为确保学习的效果，必须抓住两个关键因素，即教师的素质和学生学习成绩的评测。为了进一步强化语言教育的标准，亚太经合组织各经济体从 2004 年开展了各种项目。北京 2004 年峰会就聚集了众多的语言决策者和研究者，峰会深入研讨教育方法和课程设置，促进了很多地区的教育改革。2007 年，教育网络委员会关于语言能力标准和相关测评的研究项目为亚太经合组织内各成员制定与评估外语能力的标准提供了全面而丰富的数据和信息。

为了进一步强化语言教育的标准，台湾教育主管部门实施“斯威策项目”和“英语天才学习项目”等系列项目。“斯威策项目”融合了现有的学校资源来帮助贫困学生，尤其是偏远地区的中小学校的学生。“英语天才学习项目”对有语言天赋的学生进行精心规划，使其能取得更大的成绩。本文重点介绍了在大学里实施英语毕业基准项目的过程和现状。台湾教育主管部门于 2002 年开始鼓励高校设立大学毕业生的英语基准，其目标是要提升高校大学生的竞争力，满足社会对劳动力的需求。截止到 2011 年，超过 100 所大学把测试英语熟练程度作为毕业生的基准。该基准的设立涉及审议和修订大纲、教师的教学及学生的学习三个方面。本文最后提出在实施英语毕业基准过程中可能采用的一些教学方法。

关键词： 毕业基准；后效作用；学生态度；标准化评估；语言教育标准

Towards Cross-Regional Language Education Cooperation for High-End Talent Training: Perspectives from a Thai University Context

[Thailand] Neungreudee Lohapon

Abstract: This paper presents an overview of the learning and teaching of Western languages, especially of Italian at Chulalongkorn University, Thailand. It begins with a brief history of Western languages instruction in Thailand, focusing on the development of teaching and learning of Western languages throughout the last 20 years. The paper further explores the role of Western languages instruction in the Thai context, deliberating particular areas, namely the needs of stakeholders, challenges of improving language instruction in the way of both instructor training and approaches to dealing with curriculum reviews and strategic curriculum updating. Whereas in the past, the traditional goal of learning the language for communication and literature appreciation was stressed as the main objective of language learning; at present, despite difficulties, movement is seen towards more emphasis on higher-order thinking skills in the classroom. This shift, a direct response to the university educational policy, is a radical change that has stimulated the implementation of positive professional development activities for our language instructors that are complementary and compatible with the aim to develop our students.

In addition, for this process of training students to be effective, it is critical that joint cooperation be made across regions, so as to provide our learners with the exposure necessary for them to become high-end talented citizens and in the meantime to promote networking across regions.

Keywords: Western languages instruction in Thailand; objective of language learning; educational policy; networking across regions

A brief history of Western language instruction in Thailand

The instruction of Western languages at higher-education level in Thailand was first established in 1917 with the foundation of Chulalongkorn University, starting with courses of English and French offered in the undergraduate program. In 1920, German was introduced, followed by Spanish in 1967 and Italian in 1974. In 1977, approval was given to teaching Italian as another language. The Department of Western Languages from then on took the responsibility of teaching the above-mentioned languages as major subjects at the undergraduate level, in addition to English, which was and still is under the Department of English. French and German were launched as graduate courses in 1942 and in 1974 respectively. The Portuguese and Russian languages were later on included, firstly as elective courses, but now as minor courses. By 2013, Russian had been promoted as a new major subject, and Portuguese will be so by 2016.

In terms of content and language training, the courses have been designed and updated to cover not only the study area of language, but also students' opportunity to expand their learning towards a deeper understanding of culture through literature, music and art history. Teaching and learning concentrate on practical and professional usage of language and applied language with emphasis on developing task-based skills, from communication skills to translation and other communication skills for specific purposes.

The Department of Western Languages at Chulalongkorn Unviersity, in particular, has been continuously developing teaching and learning strategies to better serve the needs of main stakeholders in the Thai society and beyond. Especially focusing on the development of teaching and learning of Western languages over the last 20 years, we have delivered the needs of both state and private sectors, maintaining high quality and standards as our major concern. In a rapidly changing environment of higher education, the courses and curriculum have been revised and updated respectively in 1995, 2003, 2008, 2009 and 2012.

Role and Challenges of Western Languages Instruction in a Thai University Context

By listing numerous foreign language training centers in Thailand today, we can understand and foresee a significant demand for foreign language acquisition among the public in general. With regard to high-end language training in Thailand, however, we may be encountering a challenging phase of how to join education policy and implementation. At the Department of Western Languages of Chulalongkorn University, this is one of our main focuses—to develop high-end talent training according to the quality and standards of the current updated curriculum which focuses on new learning outcomes.

Whereas in the past, the traditional goal of learning the language for communication and literature appreciation was stressed as the main objective of language learning; at present, despite difficulties, movement is seen towards more emphasis on higher-order thinking skills in the classroom, as well as in extracurricular activities. This shift, a direct response to the university educational policy, is a radical change that has stimulated the implementation of positive professional development activities for our language instructors that are complementary and compatible with the aim to develop our students.

Referring to the Thai Qualifications Framework for Higher Education① and Chulalongkorn University learning outcomes②, in the last three years, the Department of Western Languages has emphasized a cooperative team work among our faculty staff through a self-study process moving toward outcome-based curriculum updating and strategic improvement of teaching and learning. Thanks to Chulalongkorn University resources, particularly to knowledge, technical and financial support, we have been able to invest time and energy to deepen our working capacity, including faculty staff idea-sharing sessions, specific-purpose

① *Thai Qualifications Framework for Higher Education*, 2009, http://www.mua.go.th/users/tqf-hed/news/FilesNews/FilesNews3/News328072552.pdf.

② *Desirable Characteristics of Chulalongkorn University Graduates 2010*, http://www.academic.chula.ac.th/CU_CAS/Desirable_Charac_2010FINAL.pdf.

staff trainings, meetings, seminars, workshops, cross-regional field trips, the study of course evaluations, course revisions and certainly updating of our French, German, Spanish, Italian, Portuguese and Russian curriculums. As one of the main stakeholders, instructors require continuous training and preparation of different kinds in order to deal with major curriculum revision. Inevitably, instructors are now facing high expectations to meet the challenging standards of outcomes aimed at expanding wider learning opportunities for students and fostering other high-order skills.

In response to the Thai Qualifications Framework for Higher Education and Chulalongkorn University policy, our department has integrated courses of language and other content-based courses with tasks that aim to instill higher-order skills, such as critical thinking skills, problem-solving skills and creative thinking skills. In addition, there has been an intradepartmental working process in progress, which is strongly oriented towards innovative development and improvement of teaching and learning, starting with our self-study and cooperative learning sessions among the department staff. This is to better respond to the mentioned requirements of both national and university outcome standards. Comments and needs of main stakeholders, including students, alumni, employers and public expectation towards AEC (ASEAN Economic Community) have all enhanced the course revision and curriculum updating.

Language Education Networking across Regions for High-End Talent Training

Under such an evolving curriculum offered at our Department of Western Languages, our graduates have been well embraced into both professional and academic careers with a wide range of fields beyond those of language, literature and culture. However, looking ahead, for high-end talent training to be effective, it is critical that joint cooperation be made across regions, so as to provide our learners with the exposure necessary for them to become high-end talented citizens and in the meantime to promote networking across regions.

Our main mission of teaching and learning in the last 20 years dealt with the languages of French, German, Spanish and Italian. Only recently were Portuguese and Russian introduced as minor courses. International cooperation we have, therefore, is mostly related to bilateral agreements between our institution or our government with European institutions or governments. In the last four years, our international cooperation plan have been aiming to broaden sustainable networking towards other institutions where Western languages were instructed as foreign languages. Firstly, thanks to our main sponsorship of H.R.H. Princess Maha Chakri Sirindhorn, we had a fruitful chance to open a roundtable meeting with colleagues at Peking University. Secondly, Chulalongkorn University Council has recently approved to invest more on AEC regional and international mobility with a series of support measures, which include guest professorship for short-term and long-term visits, as well as mobility of students, researchers and faculty staff for the purpose of regional and cross-regional cooperation, research and academic interests. Over the last four years, the Department of Western Languages has developed cross-regional cooperation following this strategic plan, starting from ASEAN and Asian countries and regions.

To construct and strengthen an efficient and friendly cooperation across regions, we aim to promote and support cooperation platforms (networking), where we could share more common interests than strictly promoting our own objectives, so that such a cross-regional cooperation could be a more coherent, coordinated and result-oriented one, and one that would yield well-rounded high-end talents that also possess cross-cultural awareness and adaptability in a global world that is becoming more interdependent.

为高端语言人才培养进行跨区域的语言教育合作
——以泰国大学为视角

[泰国] Neungreudee Lohapon

摘要：本文概述了泰国朱拉隆功国立大学的西方语言，尤其是意大利语的教学情况。首先梳理泰国西方语言教学的简史，并指出西方语言教育的日趋兴盛对语言教学提出了新的要求：语言教学的内容和培训由单一语言知识拓展到了对文化的深度理解；教学重点转变为语言的实用性和专业性。本文以朱拉隆功大学为例进一步探讨在泰语语境下西方语言教学的作用，详细探究某些教学改革领域面临的挑战，如语言教育接受者对西方语言的学习需求、教师培训、课程评价方式以及从战略角度对课程大纲的更新。传统语言学习的主要目标在于交流和文学欣赏。尽管存在诸多困难，人们现在更加重视在课堂上培养学生的高端思维能力。语言教学目标的这一转变是对语言教育政策的直接回应，它激励语言教师投身于与学生培养目标一致并具有互补性的职业发展活动中。本文最后指出跨区域合作在培养学生语言能力方面的重要作用和显著效果。比如通过跨区域的语言教育合作平台，学生得以在真实的语言环境中迅速成长为高端语言人才。

关键词：泰国的西方语言教学；语言学习目标；教育政策；跨区域合作

Teaching Languages for Dialog

[The United Kingdom] Michael Byram

Abstract: The notion of "dialog" has become a key element of policy as economic globalization has to be accompanied by communication across national boundaries and the creation of new communities. As a result, in the context of community, the combination of the words "dialog" and "respect" is becoming important. Dialog in such a kind of context is explicitly intercultural, and is defined as an open and respectful exchange of views between individuals and groups with different backgrounds and heritage. Dialog requires communication through language, and though there is a tendency to assume that a universal or world language such as English will remove barriers to communication, it is equally true that intercultural awareness is not implemented in curricula and classrooms. This lecture briefly discusses why this problem happened and what people should notice to solve it.

Keywords: economic globalization; dialog; exchange of views; intercultural awareness

My experience of language teaching has been influenced by my work over the last ten years or more as an adviser to the Language Policy Division of the Council of Europe. In the most recent years at the Council of Europe and in the European Union—two separate bodies which nonetheless co-operate on cultural and educational policy—the notion of "dialog" has become a key element of policy. It is interesting but not surprising that the same word appears in APEC activities—not surprising because in both cases, the emphasis on dialog is a consequence of globalization, both economic and cultural, and the increase in mobility of all kinds.

Let me begin with a quotation from the APEC website:

APEC is the only intergovernmental grouping in the world operating on the basis of non-binding commitments, open dialog and equal respect for the views of all participants. Unlike the WTO or other multilateral trade bodies, APEC has no treaty obligations required of its participants. Decisions made within APEC are reached by consensus and commitments are undertaken on a voluntary basis.

APEC was established in 1989 to further enhance economic growth and prosperity for the region and to strengthen the Asia-Pacific community. (http://www.apec.org/About-Us/About-APEC.aspx)

"Dialog" has always been important and the etymology of the word can be traced back to ancient Greek, where it meant a conversation among two *or more* people; it is often assumed that it refers only to conversation between two people. However, dialog is increasingly important as the world becomes an open market-place. Economic globalization has to be accompanied by communication across national boundaries and—as is said in this text—the creation of new communities.

The word "community" is also important because it refers to the kind of social context in which dialog may take place, a context of cooperation, and community was distinguished from society by the sociologist Ferdinand Tönnies in the late 19th century. In the context of community, the combination of the words "dialog" and "respect"—together with consensus—is also important and the effect of these keywords is to create a discourse of cooperation which in the APEC case is focused on economic matters.

The combination of "dialog" and "respect" is also presented in the Council of Europe's White Paper from 2008 on "Intercultural Dialog". The need for dialog in APEC is linked to economic prosperity; the need for dialog in the 47 member states of the Council of Europe is linked to social cohesion. Many of those states have multiple, long-existing and indigenous ethnic groups within their boundaries, and many of them also have new groups living as immigrants who have become mobile in search of better economic conditions for their lives and those of their children. Dialog in this kind of context is therefore explicitly intercultural and is defined as:

an open and respectful exchange of views between individuals and groups with different ethnic, cultural, religious and linguistic backgrounds and heritage, on the basis of mutual understanding and respect. (http://www.coe.int/t/dg4/intercultural/whitepaper_EN.asp, p. 5)

Dialog also requires a favorable environment, as the White Paper makes clear:

The universal values upheld by the Council of Europe are a condition for intercultural dialog. No dialog can take place in the absence of respect for the equal dignity of all human beings, human rights, the rule of law and democratic principles.

What I have emphazised in the last line are the three principles or "pillars" on which all Council of Europe work is constructed and which are the condition for a state being a member state of the Council of Europe. Furthermore, the environmental conditions for dialog also include equal access to the means of holding a conversation, i.e. to the language or languages which are used. The role of language experts within organizations such as APEC and the Council of Europe is to make explicit to others the power-relations which are inherent in communication and in the degree of language competence of the participants.

This is where the focus of this APEC forum at BLCU is important. Dialog requires communication through language, and though there is a tendency to assume that a universal or world language such as English will remove barriers to communication, this is in fact not the case. It may not be obvious to non-specialists, but it is clear to language teaching experts in organizations such as APEC or the Council of Europe, and I have read with interest the work of APEC on language teaching.

It is clear for several reasons:

First, it is necessary in dialog to have a thorough knowledge of a language, its grammar, its phonology—superficial knowledge of English or any other international language leads to breakdowns in dialog because of grammatical misunderstanding; that at least is well understood by everyone, whether language experts or not.

Second, research shows that when two people speak a common foreign language—for example, a Russian and a Japanese speaking English—then they bring to the communication the semantic connotations of words translated from their own languages. They do not share the depth of meaning that even apparently simple words have; communication takes place, but without full understanding—the semantics of languages is crucial here, but this is less well understood by many people.

Third, we know that communication is not only verbal, but also non-verbal, and the same difficulties of a lack of shared connotations in non-verbal communication arise; this is now recognized on a superficial level by many training courses for business people, but these often do not go beyond recipes, superficial rules, generalizations and stereotypes which can often cause more harm than good.

There is therefore a need for a more refined teaching of languages than is often the case and my own research and publications for the last 30 years have been focused on "intercultural communicative competence". This phrase describes the competence in language-and-culture that is necessary for successful dialog. The hyphens in that phrase are there to show the integration of language and culture. It refers to linguistic competence—to knowledge and skills in using the language itself—but it also refers to "something else". For it is perfectly possible for someone to have excellent language skills, but still be misunderstood or misunderstand what is being said. That "something else" is knowledge about other people's cultures, but not just knowledge. For there are cultural skills and attitudes which are crucial to dialog, too.

It might appear at first glance that language teaching inevitably aims to create in learners the competence they need for dialog. It is indeed true that many language teaching policy statements—such as those collected on the APEC website—refer to that "something else" with phrases such as "intercultural awareness". However, it is equally true that intercultural awareness is not implemented in curricula and classrooms. There are two reasons for this:

First, most teachers of languages in most countries have no training in how to teach intercultural awareness or competence—and this is a weakness which needs to be corrected quickly.

Second, there are few if any attempts to assess intercultural competence in examinations and this means that teachers pay less attention to it because examination results have become more important than ever—not least through international comparisons of education systems.

There is not enough space here to discuss in technical details what the problems are and how we should address them. Let me put the points in simplified form regarding what we need and what we have:

1. We need definitions and descriptions of intercultural competence and its components;

We DO have many definitions already produced for many different contexts;

2. We need definitions and descriptions of the link between intercultural competence and linguistic competence, both because this is crucial for dialog and because it will help language teachers to teach linguistic competence and intercultural competence in a systematic way.

We do NOT have this except in some preliminary work on semantics and on teaching the meanings of words and phrases in detailed and enriched methods—not just using the dictionary to find an equivalent.

3. We need teacher training and a systematic teaching methodology which takes into consideration not just how languages are learnt, but how intercultural competence is learnt, i.e. the attitudes, skills and knowledge which are necessary in addition to language.

We do NOT have systematic answers to this problem although there are many imaginative examples of good ideas which could be the basis for a proper methodology.

4. We need a systematic approach to assessment of intercultural competence so that it can be tested in examinations and then taken seriously by teachers and learners—the Washback Effect.

We do NOT have assessment which is suitable for education and examination systems although we do have many psychological tests of intercultural awareness which are not suitable for examinations in education systems.

At the Council of Europe, we have worked on some of these problems and tried to make them accessible for teachers as a first step in teacher training. Here are two references which might be of interest:

Developing the Intercultural Dimension in Language Teaching. A Practical Introduction for Teachers.

http://www.coe.int/t/dg4/linguistic/Source/Guide_dimintercult_EN.pdf

Young People Facing Difference

http://www.coe.int/t/dg4/linguistic/Source/youngpeople_difference_EN.pdf

I would like to finish by giving a web reference to the Autobiography of Intercultural Encounters which is a tool for self-assessment:

http://www.coe.int/t/dg4/autobiography/default_EN.asp. There is however still much to do and the sooner the better for the sake of dialog whether in APEC or elsewhere.

对话——语言教学的目的

[英国] Michael Byram

摘要：“对话”作为概念已经成为共同体语言教育政策中的一个重要成分。本文首先讨论“对话”和“尊重”两个概念在跨境沟通中的作用。在经济全球化的进程中，跨境沟通并产生新的共同体是大势所趋。在共同体的语境下，“对话”与“尊重”两个概念变得空前重要。本文重点阐述“对话”的定义和性质。这里的“对话”明确具有跨文化的性质，其定义是在生活背景和文化传统存在差异的个人和群体之间坦率而礼貌地交换双方的观点和意见。“对话”需要借助语言来完成，虽然有一种倾向认为像英语这种通用语或者世界语会去除人际沟通的障碍，但实际情况并非如此。本文还指出“对话”出现障碍的原因。很多时候人们很难在课内外的沟通和交流中表现出足够的跨文化意识，导致沟通受阻。本文对造成这一问题的原因，以及如何将语言训练与跨文化交际能力有机地结合起来——进行了分析。

关键词：经济全球化；对话；观念交流；跨文化意识

Teaching English in Peruvian Schools

[Peru] Maria Elisa Lidia de la Vega Polanco

Abstract: *Teaching English in Peruvian Public Schools* has to deal with the reduced number of teachers who teach English as a second language, two hours weekly to teach English in the study plan, shortage of training programs for English teachers, not very much importance of English as an international language, and the challenge of teaching English in rural zones where they do not even have basic facilities. The 26 regions in Peru are conscious of that and have proposed a regional study plan, in which English is considered as a challenge to be achieved. The Callao Region is an example and pioneer in teaching English from pre-primary to first grades of primary.

Keywords: teaching English; Peruvian public schools; regional study plan

The National Curricular Design is a document containing all the study plans for every single Peruvian student and it is a must. It also makes sure that the education must be equal nationwide. This document provides the guidelines to improve the pedagogical work in class and it is distributed to all the 26 Peruvian regions.

All the Peruvian public schools used to follow these given guidelines, but now every region creates their own Regional Curricular Design according to their students' needs and interests. Every region proposes the learning which focuses on their own development, having into consideration their own culture, tourist development, their own natural resources, trading with bordering countries, etc.

Every region knows that it is a must for our Peruvian students to learn English to become part of this modern world. One of the purposes of the Regular Basic Education is:

To master English as an international language

Within the bounds of globalization, learning English as an international language will contribute to strengthening students' communicative competence in terms of coming into contact with English speakers in all types of settings, theirs included.

Schools should give students the chance to learn a language that can open doors to new knowledge and new information on the latest advances in science and technology from a variety of sources (the Internet, printed material, etc.); in other words, students need to develop their oral and written communication as well as reading skills in English.

Knowledge of English will help them get information that comes from scientific, technological, and cultural research and innovation. It also simplifies interculturality with other realities and contexts.

Apart from English, each sub-national political region may choose teaching a second foreign language, if deemed necessary. It must be clear that every region must teach English first.

To achieve a grasp of the language, the National Curriculum Design lists some competences to be achieved at the end of Cycle VI, including the 1st and 2nd, and Cycle VII, including the 3rd, 4th and 5th grades at the secondary level. These competences are as follows:

Oral Comprehension and Expression for Cycle VI:

- Every student can express his ideas about themselves and immediate surroundings employing an adequate intonation and pronunciation, showing respect for other classmates' opinions during the interactive process.
- Every student can understand their interlocutor's message and ask for information when necessary.

Oral Comprehension and Expression for Cycle VII:

- Every student can express ideas, opinions, and sentiments about topics of social interest for a fluid interaction with their native interlocutor, during their communicative process.
- Every student can understand their interlocutor's message, expressing their points of view.

Understand Written Comprehesion for Cycle VI:

• Every student can understand texts related to themselves, their family and immediate surroundings.

Understand Written Comprehesion for Cycle VII:

• Every student can understand different texts with a higher level of difficulty, related to real topics expressed in a common language.

Written Production:

• Every student can produce different texts with adaptation and coherence, related to themselves and their immediate surroundings, employing linguistic and non-linguistic elements.

Having all this into consideration, the Callao Region took the National Curriculum Design as a reference and elaborated a project that applies teaching English at the first level, that is, kindergartens and Primary 1st and 2nd grades.

The Callao Region is the pioneer nationwide in teaching English in public schools. They wanted to bring forward and spread the teaching of English in the second cycle of pre-primary, and the third cycle of primary level education. This project was in charge of the Mg. Ofelia Sàntos Jimènez.

To develop this project, they had to train all the teachers of kindergartens, and the first and second cycles of primary level education in the performance of the teaching / learning process of English in the classrooms, using a communicative, participative and integrated methodology, which allowed all the students to become familiar with this new process.

Also, teacher participants should develop skills and knowledge of grammar, reading comprehension, writing, vocabulary, listening comprehension, pronunciation, all of which focus on real situations and are developed at the elemental level.

The question is why to teach English in the early years.

It is because children earily learn a new linguistic code. Besides, it is easy for them to pronounce the new code correctly and they are not ashamed when they speak a different language.

If they have a good experience learning the language at this age, that will be a significant learning experience and they will remember it all their lives.

What is the purpose of this program?

It is to implement an integral program of teaching English as a second language according to the grade that the teachers are teaching, so at the end of their training program, they will be able to satisfy their students' (of pre-primary 1st and 2nd of the primary levels) needs.

What will be the benefits for the teachers?

There will be pedagogical consultancy for every teacher involved in this project. Every teacher will be evaluated and also be part of an "Introductory Course". They will receive training in the methods and didactics of use of materials for children in the classroom. This training program includes methodology and didactics as well as consultancy in class during all the years. Teachers and students will also improve their English language skills in class.

Workshops improve the use of techniques and strategies in this project and also they will learn to elaborate materials for class.

What will be the teachers' duties?

Teachers will also have some duties when participating in this project:

- The beneficiary teacher must take an exam to establish his / her right placement;
- The beneficiary teacher will have to attend every given workshop of improvement and methodological strategies of teaching English to guarantee the teaching / learning process according to the level and class during the school years;
- The teachers will form groups and every single group of teacher participants will have a formative teacher who will be in charge of these training activities;
- The teachers who fulfill the two previous requirements will receive a monthly bonus during the entire program. This bonus is given based on time dedicated to the training and their students' achievement;
- Every participating teacher will receive the training materials which include methodology and didactics of the teaching and learning process given by the center;

• The enter will carry out workshops about the use of these materials in class, such as: workbooks, CDs, music, games, flashcards, etc.;

• Every children will receive the materials and their parents will be responsible for it.

It is a mandatory requirement in this program about the coordination and collaboration of the directors of the selected 90 educational institutions to ensure the good results of the project.

The Region of Callao also has "a School for the Talented", which only students with high performance can attend.

The Lima Region has some projects to improve the English language, such as:

• English workshop which is given after regular daily classes in some key schools. Since August 2012, this English workshop has been given in eight key schools. The objective of the workshop is to develop oral skills and teachers have been trained for this. It is given after regular school classes. During the regular classes, it was not easy to develop oral skills, because of the number of students per class (more than 35) and the methodology used. That is why this workshop was set up.

• English program for the 4th and 5th grades in School for the Talented of the Callao Region.

• Major School President of Peru (MSPP) in Lima. It is only for students who have good academic performance and they are from different regions of Peru. To study in this special school, students must take an entrance exam and pass with the required score. Most of the students from this school participate in different national and international contests, and at the end of the secondary level, they enter the best universities in Peru.

• Bilingual Schools in the Callao Region. It is another project in the Callao Region to improve students' English proficiency.

• English program for public school teachers. Peru also works with the American Embassy to provide training for Peruvian public school teachers. Some of them travel to the United States for a certain period to improve their knowledge of the language. These teachers will become trainers for other teachers.

- Participation in the international event "You Think Green" as climate ambassdors. In this year, some students traveled to Germany to participate in this contest.
- Participation in the United World Colleges.

Teaching English in Peru has many challenges to overcome:

- There is a limited number of people who speak English as a second language;
- The number of hours to teach English in a compulsory way in public schools is minimal, just two hours weekly;
- There are few programs to develop teachers in foreign languages;
- The educational system does not give relevance to the English area;
- Heterogeneous geography: a challenge in the rural zones (the grasp of the native and aborigines languages);
- Too many areas in the national curriculum, which means there are too many contents to study;
- Not enough teachers to cover all the public schools;
- Not very well-qualified teachers.

Improving students' English proficiency in public schools is a challenge and in the near future we will overcome it.

秘鲁中小学的英语教学

[秘鲁] Maria Elisa Lidia de la Vega Polanco

摘要： 本文首先介绍了秘鲁国家英语教学大纲的基本内容。公立学校以前必须依照全国统一的国家教学大纲开展教学，而现在每个地区都可以根据学生的需要和兴趣制定本地区的教学大纲。各地区都认识到秘鲁学生必须掌握英语才能成为当代世界的一分子。各地在开设英语课程后，可以依据需要开设第二外语。为了掌握语言能力，国家教学大纲规定了第六（中学一、二年级）和第七学习阶段（中学三、四、五年级）需要掌握的各种英语技能，包括口语表达和理解能力、书面阅读和写作能力。本文重点介绍了卡亚俄区的英语教学情况。作为英语教学的范例，卡亚俄区率先在幼儿园和小学 1—2 年级开展英语教学。该校参照国家教学大纲开发教师培训项目，训练幼儿园和小学教师重视英语教学过程，在课堂上运用交际法、活动参与和综合教学法进行教学。本文最后指出秘鲁公立学校英语教学面临的困难和问题，如作为第二语言的英语教学师资缺乏、教学大纲规定的周学时数只有两个学时、英语教师培训项目极少、农村地区英语教学缺乏基本设施等，同时指出全秘鲁 26 个地区都意识到了这些问题，并且通过制订区域性教学计划来应对这些挑战。

关键词： 英语教学；秘鲁公立学校；区域学习计划

语言教师的职业发展

Professional Development for Language Teachers

Types of Education, Innovation in Language Teaching and Training Models

[Brunei Darussalam] Hajah Lena binti Mohammad Hassan

Abstract: This paper will focus on the language education and talent cultivation in Brunei Darussalam. In the beginning, I will introduce the languages and related facts of language education in Brunei. Then, I will discuss teachers' education and professional qualification in Brunei, including the methods of training teachers, the competency they will get and the Role of Teachers' Training and Development Unit of the Department of Schools. In conclusion, I will propose a framework for Innovation in Language Teaching and Training Models. To help local teachers in their teaching career, Continuous Professional Development (CPD) trainings and 100 hours' Civil Service Training are provided. The training is coordinated by the Department of Schools and the Human Resource Department under the Ministry of Education. In addition, full-time and short courses both locally and overseas are also provided to enhance teachers' performance. The full-time courses allow teachers to improve or get promoted to the next level of qualification, for example, Diploma, First Degree, Master's Degree and Doctor's Degree, whereby full in-service training is the norm. Teachers are also allowed to do part-time courses or online courses, and take unpaid leave or study leave in order to pursue further studies locally or overseas.

Keywords: language education in Brunei; talent cultivation; teachers training methods

Introduction

Brunei Darussalam is a relatively small and peaceful country with a population of 408,786 (July 2011 estimate), made up of 7 ethnic races (Brunei Malay, Kedayan, Tutong, Dusun, Belait, Bisaya, and Murut). It is rich in linguistic diversity. Malay is the official language. English is the medium of instruction in schools and is widely used in business.

Education

Free education is provided to Brunei citizens. Pre-schools and lower primary schools are taught in both the Malay and English languages. Upper primary schools, secondary schools, higher institutions and tertiary education are also taught in English; while religious schools are taught both in the Malay and Arabic languages, while English is taught as an additional subject. In addition, in Chinese schools, which are usually private schools, the medium of instruction is Chinese, and Malay and English are taught as additional subjects.

Language

Brunei Malay is widely used and standard Malay is used in teaching in schools. English language is the second, third and can be the fourth language for many Bruneians. The English language is the medium of instruction in most of the primary, secondary schools and tertiary institutions. Therefore, language teaching can be very challenging to teachers. Malay and English are compulsory subjects in all the schools, while these two subjects are equally important in education and business.

Teachers' Education and Professional Qualifications

Our presentation is based on the information of the government primary and secondary schools under the Ministry of Education, Negara Brunei Darussalam. There are more than 70,000 students and more than 7,000 teachers. There are 120 government primary schools and 34 secondary schools which include the fifth or sixth level. The English language teaching force is made up of 400 locals, 24 contract-based teachers and 260 teachers supplied by the Center for British Teachers (CfBT).

The majority of the 400 local teachers are trained in English language either locally at the Universiti Brunei Darussalam or well-known universities in the United Kingdom. There are also about 500 teachers in the primary schools who teach English language besides other subjects. The contract-based teachers are well qualified and very experienced in their countries of origin, such as Malaysia, the UK, Australia, New Zealand and India. On the other hand, teachers of the Center for British Teachers are fully qualified and graduated from universities in the UK, Australia, New Zealand, Canada or Ireland. Many have extra qualifications and experience which compliment the new 21st Century National Education System's assessments and resource development.

Teachers' Competency

The Department of Schools, in collaboration with Human Resource Department, Department of Examinations, Department of Curriculum Development and Department of Inspectorate, has taken a lot of initiatives in providing professional support to local teachers at both the primary and the secondary levels. This initiative will raise the teachers' level of competency in their teaching.

On the other hand, the CfBT teachers and managers also provide a range of capacity building inputs for both CfBT and Bruneian teachers. In addition, customized in-country SEAMEO-RELC (Regional English Language Center) workshops for at least 30 primary school teachers and 30 secondary school teachers respectively are run at one time in the country. This is cost-effective, and more teachers can attend the workshop in one go. In the past, only four teachers (2 primary, 2 secondary) were nominated to attend a similar workshop in Singapore. Such a speed of giving training to every teacher was time-consuming. In addition, other departments in the Ministry of Education also provide training for English language teachers to enhance their teaching. The Department of Schools in cooperation with these departments will run training programs locally or overseas so as to keep abreast with the new approaches in language teaching.

Networking amongst English language teachers is encouraged. Resources and teaching materials are available free for teachers to use. These resources are usually prepared by Special Interest Groups (SIGs) and through this, teachers are always kept up-to-date with their colleagues in other schools in Brunei. In this way, the teachers can improve their teaching. The Internet access and the use of ICT help to teach English language (computers are available in schools provided by the government).

Professional and skill enhancement workshops and training programs include the following for primary and secondary school teachers:

1) Professional Development Workshops for Local English Language Teachers (10 sessions) since 1999;

2) SCOPE (Senior Cambridge O-Level Public Examination);

3) IGCSE Workshops (up to 8 sessions);

4) LSERP (Lower Secondary English Reading Program);

5) Customized RELC Teaching Reading Workshop for 30 primary and 30 secondary teachers in 2008;

6) Customized RELC Teaching Writing Workshop for 30 primary and 30 secondary teachers in 2009;

7) Customized RELC Teaching Listening and Oral Communication Skills Workshop for 30 primary and 30 secondary school teachers in 2010;

8) Customized RELC Language Curriculum and Materials Development Workshop in 2011;

9) Customized RELC Action Research on Writing Skills in 2012;

10) Drama workshops (ongoing);

11) School-Based Assessment for Learning (SBAfL) for primary and secondary school teachers (ongoing);

12) Several courses and workshops are also available for primary school teachers carried out in-house by the Department of Schools and the Ministry of Education in various topics.

Customized courses available for teachers are based on the discussions made between facilitators and the officers in the Ministry of Education. Priorities are given to topics that are in dire need in order to improve teaching and learning in English language. Hence these training programs have contributed to the increase in public examination results.

Role of Teachers' Training and Development Unit of the Department of Schools

The role of the unit is to evaluate the training needs for improvement and enhancement, based on reports by school inspectorates, Department of Examination, school heads, heads of Departments, appraisals, dialogs, School-Based Committee, surveys and questionnaires.

The coordinate training programs are provided in schools or at training centers. The unit will coordinate and monitor the training programs. The most important thing is the Post Training Evaluations. The unit will compile reports and feedback from teachers, school heads, senior masters, heads of departments' reports and/or observations and students' performance. The monitoring can be a short-term or long-term process (3 months, 6 months or one year), and teachers will go back to school and apply what they have learnt. They will come back and meet again after 1—3 months of application in the classroom and share what they have done and its impact on or achievement in their teaching and students' performance.

The unit designs training programs or courses either coordinated or facilitated by local teachers at the Ministry of Education, Universiti Brunei Darussalam or by overseas experts. In order to evaluate the teachers' competencies, during the training programs, the facilitators are also required to provide rubrics to assess the teachers' capabilities in the specific topics covered in the training programs. The training programs also evaluate the teachers' abilities to relay the knowledge they have acquired during the training programs.

The language training programs are not restricted only for English language teachers, but also extended to other teachers' teaching of other English subjects, such as Social Studies, Business Studies, Sciences, Mathematics and Technical Studies. The course is designed for teachers to improve their English language for specific purposes.

Innovation in Language Teaching and Training Models

The Department of Schools, in collaboration with the Human Resource Department, Department of Examination, Department of Curriculum Development and Department of School Inspectorate under the Ministry of Education, has taken a lot of initiatives in providing professional support to local teachers in both primary and secondary education to raise their level of competencies in teaching. Short courses and Continuous Professional Development (CPD) help local teachers in their teaching career and enhance teachers' performance, which also serve as incentives.

CfBT teachers and managers also provide a range of capacity building inputs for CfBT and Bruneian teachers, in line with CfBT's contract with the MoE. Customized SEAMEO-RELC (Regional English Language Center) workshops are run locally and cost-effectively for at least 30 teachers from primary and 30 secondary schools at one time. Workshops are customized according to Brunei's needs. Moreover, these teachers in turn become facilitators for cascading sharing sessions. As a result, more teachers are able to enhance their knowledge in different areas.

Therefore, constant discussions and dialogs with the school heads, English language heads of department through the Subject-Based Committee and also relevant authorities help both the unit of trainings and section of the Ministry of Education to provide trainings for the teachers.

100 Hours of Training

In Brunei, it is a requirement that every civil servant fulfill 100 hours of training. The training is annually analyzed through individual's performance appraisal to ensure improvement in their teaching. Teachers usually receive more than 100 hours of training as there are a lot of initiatives by individuals, schools, departments and the Ministry of Education to provide training. This serves as a platform for teachers to achieve the 100 hours of improvement training and updates their knowledge and enhancement in teaching so as to produce quality teachers as a result of the courses attended. Based on the Department of Schools' annual report, teachers have received more than 100 hours of training and have acquired the knowledge sought.

In-Service Full-Time Training

The Ministry of Education also offers in-service full-time courses for teachers who wish to further their studies and upgrade their level of qualifications (Diplomas, First degrees, Master's degrees and Doctor's degrees). The teachers can apply for further studies, but approval depends on the availability of the relevant courses either locally or overseas. Those who are unable to meet the requirements can take part-time courses, unpaid leave or do online courses as long as the courses are accredited by the National Accredited Section of the Ministry of Education.

Other Programs

- Brunei-Singapore Joint Working Group—School Twinning Program (Work Attachment in Singapore) since 2006. 10 teachers annually do a three-week work attachment at Singapore's primary or secondary schools to teach English language. They not only gained experience from peer teaching, individual teaching and observations of the classroom teaching in Singapore, but were also able to learn other expertise, for example, the role of head teachers, senior masters, assistant school heads, and other activities implemented in the schools.

- Brunei-Malaysia Joint Working Group—Malaysian Training Cooperation Program (MTCP) trains teachers in English language teaching and provides training for trainers. Annually, selected ASEAN teachers attend training for three weeks in Malaysia.

- Brunei-US Projects—Training programs (in the country and overseas) and attachment (In ASEAN countries). It's a five-year project between Brunei and the US for English language teachers. 10 selected local Brunei English language teachers plus teachers from ASEAN countries attended 11 weeks' training programs locally as well as in Hawaii, US, which started in September 2012. Another group of Brunei English language teachers will be sent to ASEAN countries to teach English language for 10 months under US mentors.

- Southeast Asian Ministers of Education Organization Regional language Center (SEAMEO RELC) in Singapore provides trainings annually for ASEAN English language teachers. Several local English language teachers have attended various courses at the center since 1990. The Ministry of Education in cooperation with RELC has designed and implemented in the country various topics in English language for Brunei teachers.

- Networking and cooperation between other countries through English language teachers' associations, such as BELTA and MELTA, discuss the latest updates on teaching and learning in English language. Conferences and forums between the associations help teachers to keep abreast with the new approaches and best practices to enhance and improve language teaching and learning.

教育类型、语言教学创新与教师培训模式

[文莱] Hajah Lena binti Mohammad Hassan

摘要： 本文围绕文莱达鲁萨兰国的语言教育与人才培养展开讨论，首先介绍文莱多种语言共存的社会背景和语言教育的现状，然后讨论文莱的教师专业资质，包括教师培训的方法、教师从教学中获得的能力以及学校司师资培训与发展处的作用等，最后提出一个创新语言教学和教师培训模式的框架。为了帮助教师获得较好的职业生涯，国家提供持续性职业培训和 100 小时的公职人员培训。这些培训由学校下属的学校司和人力资源司协调组织。此外，为提高教师的教学能力，国家还提供国内外的全日制短期课程。全日制课程属全日制在职培训，有助于教师提升教学能力或取得更高级别的专业资质，如毕业文凭、学士学位、硕士学位、博士学位等。教师们还可选择业余课程和网络课程，也可申请停薪假或进修假，以便在国内或国外学习和进修。

关键词： 文莱的语言教育；人才培养；教师培训方法

English Teaching and Professional Development for English Teachers in Vietnam

[Vietnam] Dang Thuy Chi

Abstract: It is recognizable that language education is of great importance in strengthening APEC economies and connecting people coming from different countries and regions. Vietnam's language education has been paid much attention to in order to help young people to acquire global knowledge and create opportunities for them to learn from international friends; however, English is considered as the dominant language in terms of foreign languages taugh in Vietnam, including English, French, Russian, and Chinese. This writing focuses on the change of English teaching in Vietnam and the trend of English usage of primary and secondary curriculums. It will point out that English teachers who were in the progress of the English project from 2011 to 2012 were seen as a fundamental factor contributing to English teaching and learning improvement, as it was big progress for young people. The first stage of the English language project will be described to help the readers understand the real context of English teaching in Vietnam. Moreover, it will discuss that keeping the balance between different languages not only is beneficial, but also essential in Vietnam because young Vietnamese people will have more opportunities to participate in exchange programs among APEC economies. In short, improving language teaching is an important thing in language education, and that is the link to the development of APEC economies.

Keywords: Vietnam; language education; English teaching; English teachers' professional development

Introduction

In some countries around the world, language teaching has changed rapidly in the last twenty years; but in Vietnam, the teaching of English has been far from satisfactory. For quite a long time, there have not been any contact with the teaching and learning of English outside Vietnam, and only recently, some groups of teachers have been sent abroad to study. Thanks to the aid of some international organizations and countries, the teaching of English has improved, but chiefly at universities and colleges where English is taught by foreign lecturers. At schools, the situation remains unchanged, for different reasons, including unsuitable textbooks, inadequate teaching and learning facilities, but one of the most important factors is unqualified teaching staff.

Background

In recent years, professional development has been one of the issues concerning not only educational leaders, educators, and teachers, but also the community as well as parents and children in most countries. This means education in general, and teaching and learning quality in particular, have been regarded as one of the most important factors in Vietnamese society. In Vietnam, English has been taught for quite a long time, and it is now one of the compulsory subjects in all universities, colleges, and almost all upper and lower secondary schools, and even in some primary schools. Vietnamese students have been spending much time learning English and each year a number of them who come from big cities may achieve high results in the exams, and their level of English is accepted in some international universities. However, the real situation of teaching and learning English is a topic of discussion in the educational domain, and more particularly, English teachers' competence with their different levels of knowledge has been a controversial issue for years.

Most teachers, whose pre-training is often inadequate, are unable to carry on even a simple conversation in English because during their teaching process, they are dependent on textbooks that are the major source for their teaching. Do (Cam, 2005) commented that English teachers in Vietnam seemed to like speaking Vietnamese all the time, which has resulted in students' poor English speaking and listening skills. Do also indicated that the teaching and learning materials discouraged learning, and this, combined with the poor quality of teaching staff, was the main reason leading to the low quality of English teaching and learning in Vietnam. He also claimed that it was necessary to review English teaching in secondary and high schools in Vietnam in terms of teacher training and retraining in order to cater to the requirements of regional and global integration.

The Current Project Relating to English Teachers' Professional Development

In order to develop English teachers' profession and enhance young people in Vietnam to use English more effectively, the Vietnam government has decided to carry out a big project entitled Teaching and Learning Foreign Languages in the National Education System, Period 2008—2020. The aim of the project is:

> ...by 2020, most Vietnamese students graduating from secondary, vocational schools, colleges and universities will be able to use a foreign language confidently in their daily communication, their study and work in an integrated, multi-cultural and multi-lingual environment, making foreign languages a comparative advantage of development for Vietnamese people in the cause of industrialization and modernization for the country.

The tasks of the project are:

1) To establish Vietnamese people's language proficiency framework consisting of 6 levels compatible with the *Common European Framework of Reference for Languages: Learning, Teaching, Assessment;*

2) To implement new intensive English programs at colleges and universities at Level 3 (B1);

3) To teach math and science in English at high schools;

4) To teach the senior class university courses in English: ICT, Engineering, Tourism, Business, Nursing, etc.;

5) To renovate tests and exams to cover all the four language skills;

6) To apply ICT in language teaching and learning.

The current project offers opportunities for Vietnam because it can help a massive group of teachers and young people be aware of the importance of English for career and professional development. In Vietnam, English is understood as the official language of ASEAN Community: after Vietnam joined the WTO, English helped Vietnam with strong international cooperation and partnership with international organizations (scholarships, teacher development and training, specialists). Moreover, it offers a new investment in Regional Teacher Development Centers, teacher training colleges and universities.

Some solutions are given according to the careful steps:

Teachers' development is considered as the key to the success of the project; therefore, teachers will be retrained according to the following steps:

1) Develop "Language Teachers, Competency Framework";

2) Develop Regional Teacher Development Centers and invest in teacher training colleges and universities;

3) Renovate Teacher Training Programs at all teacher training colleges and universities;

4) Run teacher development programs;

5) Train ELT overseas: PhD, Postgraduate Diploma, M.A, short-term training.

Secondly, there will be curriculum changes:

1) Primary and secondary schools will apply new textbooks;

2) Pre-service and in-service teacher training curriculum renovation;

3) Evaluate outcome/quality of English language teacher training colleges;

4) Blended solutions and the use of ICT application in language teaching and learning.

International cooperation is said to be one of the most effective solutions for the success of the project:

1) More foreign investment into the teaching and learning of foreign languages will be mobilized;

2) Encouraging education institutions to establish international partnership with foreign institutions and set up exchange programs for teachers and students;

3) Developing policies to promote international cooperation to attract overseas Vietnamese teachers and foreign experts to teach in Vietnam;

4) Promoting educational exchanges and scholarship programs for both teachers and students.

Incentives and policies are also evaluated:

1) Review, amend, revise the mechanism, regulations and the policy to encourage the teaching and learning of foreign languages in the national education system;

2) Revise policies on investment for language training institutions;

3) Create incentives for language teachers;

4) Issue regulations on teaching and learning, testing and evaluation, and language certification and degrees; encourage the establishment of qualified foreign language training centers and institutions.

The project has been applied throughout the country, at least at the first stage which is assessing English teachers according to European standards; however, some problems have emerged.

A low result of most English teachers' language proficiency has caused several unanswerable issues.

Firstly, European standards applied in assessment seem not to be linked with the teachers' ability.

Secondly, there should be a careful consideration about universities and institutions where English teachers were trained in terms of curriculum and models of teaching and learning.

Thirdly, there is no English environment in and outside schools in almost all the provinces in Vietnam. That is the reason why teachers cannot practice their subject even in front of their colleagues at schools.

Next, the overall aim of the project is too high.

Suggestions Balancing the Impossibility in the Real Context

Based on my personal experience, I would like to give some suggestions in order to balance the situation and help the teachers to enjoy more effective professional development:

First, teachers should be encouraged to participate in non-assessed teaching and learning activities, such as peer group assistance in a secure, trustful and helpful atmosphere.

Second, textbooks should be taught carefully, accompanied by proper teaching and learning equipment.

Third, teachers should be sent to English-speaking countries to learn short-term courses because only in this way may they have more opportunities to practice speaking and listening skills.

Next, MoET and provincial departments of education and training should connect non-governmental organizations and volunteers to have foreign teachers work at schools. This seems more effective in terms of the cost and benefit, and suitable for both the government and MoET.

Being an insider of Vietnamese education in general and the English project for teachers in particular, I would like international colleagues from APEC economies to think and discuss the above ideas.

I hope, with the contribution from APEC friends, Vietnamese English teachers will be encouraged and enhanced in effective professional development activities.

越南的英语教学和教师的职业发展

[越南] Dang Thuy Chi

摘要： 语言教育在促进东盟经济发展和各国人民之间的联系方面发挥着巨大作用。本文首先概述越南英语教学的现存问题。在过去 20 年里，越南英语教学发展缓慢，与外界交流甚少。近年来，在一些国家和国际组织的帮助下，大学英语教学取得了一些进步，但是中小学英语教学依然不容乐观。其原因包括不合适的教材和匮乏的教学设施，但是缺乏合格的外语教师是最重要的问题。本文着重介绍现阶段越南英语教学的变化以及中小学教学大纲有关语言使用方面的发展趋势。为了促进英语教师的职业发展，提高年轻人更加有效地使用英语的能力，越南政府制订了《国民教育计划（2008—2020）》之“外语教学计划”。该计划的目标为，到 2020 年，大部分中学、职业学校、大中专的毕业生在日常交流、在融合多元文化和多种语言的场所学习和工作时能够自如地使用一门外语，且外语能力要达到有助于个人职业发展、有助于越南工业化和现代化建设的水平。此外，本文还详细介绍和分析了越南政府为实现该计划制定的具体任务和措施。针对当前越南英语教学的现状，本文最后提出了几点关于教师职业发展的建议。

关键词： 越南；语言教育；英语教学；英语教师的职业发展

Preparing and Supporting Language Teachers Throughout Their Professional Life Cycle

[The United States] Shuhan C. Wang

Abstract: In May 2012, the APEC Education Ministers convened a meeting on the theme of *Future Challenges and Educational Responses: Fostering Global, Innovative and Cooperative Education* in Gyeongju, Republic of Korea. In response to the recommendations made by the Education Network (EDNET) Committee, the ministers agreed that it is important to "support foreign language education throughout students' academic careers and [develop] a system to nurture and train highly qualified language education teachers who also reflect cultural diversity" (Joint Statement, Section 10.3). In particular, the ministers "recognize the importance of teachers, and teacher quality as the most important factor determining students' success" (Joint Statement, Section 12).

In this paper, focusing on this call to prepare and support world language teachers, I will discuss a few major initiatives in the United States (US). I will discuss lessons learned from STARTALK, a multi-year, multi-million dollar federal initiative on developing and supporting prospective and practicing teachers of ten critical languages (Arabic, Chinese, Dari, Hindi, Persian, Portuguese, Russian, Swahili, Turkish, and Urdu). Drawing upon recognized teacher standards and teacher development projects in the US, I will outline the knowledge, skills, perspectives, and experiences world language teachers must possess in order to help students develop 21st century skills and global competency. In closing, I will propose a framework for preparing and supporting teachers throughout their professional life cycle, which ranges from recruitment, preparation, and induction, to mentoring and coaching, retention, and advancement. It is only with high-quality and effective teachers that a society is able to achieve the goal of preparing multi-lingual global citizens.

Keywords: Future Challenges and Educational Responses; teacher development projects in the US; multilingual global citizens

Introduction

In May 2012, the APEC Education Ministers convened a meeting on the theme of *Future Challenges and Educational Responses: Fostering Global, Innovative and Cooperative Education* in Gyeongju, Republic of Korea. In response to the recommendations made by the Education Network (EDNET) Committee, the ministers agreed that it is important to "support foreign language education throughout students' academic careers and [develop] a system to nurture and train highly qualified language education teachers who also reflect cultural diversity" (Joint Statement, Section 10.3). In particular, the ministers "recognize the importance of teachers, and teacher quality as the most important factor determining students' success" (Joint Statement, Section 12).

In this paper, focusing on this call to prepare and support world language teachers, I will discuss a few major initiatives in the United States (US). I will discuss lessons learned from STARTALK, a multi-year, multi-million dollar federal initiative on student learning and teacher development for ten critical languages (Arabic, Chinese, Dari, Hindi, Persian, Portuguese, Russian, Swahili, Turkish, and Urdu) during the summer. Drawing upon recognized teacher standards and teacher development projects in the US, I will outline the knowledge, skills, perspectives, and experiences world language teachers must possess in order to help students develop 21st century skills and global competency. In closing, I will propose a framework for preparing and supporting teachers throughout their professional life cycle, which ranges from recruitment, preparation, and induction, to mentoring and coaching, retention, and advancement. It is only with high-quality and effective teachers that a society is able to achieve the goal of preparing multi-lingual global citizens.

In this paper, I will use the term "world languages" instead of "foreign languages" when I refer to languages other than English in the US. This is to reflect that in the US, there is an increasing awareness of the existence of numerous heritage language learners in the educational system. For these students, a language that they study in a foreign language classroom may not be "foreign". This use of "world languages" is especially prevalent in K-12 schools.

STARTALK's Efforts in Expanding World Language Teacher Education Capacity in the US

In 2006, former President George Bush signed the National Security Language Initiative (NSLI) (US Department of State, 2006). Programs under the NSLI umbrella include Title VI/Fulbright Hays Programs of the US Department of Education, the Language Flagship Programs sponsored by the National Security Education Program, and Study Abroad and Exchange Programs of the US Department of State. As explained on its website, STARTALK is the newest of the component programs of the initiative, seeking to expand and improve the teaching and learning of strategically important critical languages that are not commonly taught in the US (http://www.startalk.umd.edu).

One feature that distinguishes STARTALK from all other federal projects is its mission to provide learning opportunities for teachers of these critical languages in K-12, higher education, and heritage community schools, in addition to increasing the number of American students learning these languages. Teacher education programs that seek STARTALK funding must provide teachers of these languages with creative and engaging summer experiences that strive to exemplify best practices in language education and in language teacher development. From 2007 to 2011, STARTALK has provided training to almost 6,000 teachers and formed extensive communities of practice, as shown in Table 1 below.

Table 1: STARTALK Programs at a Glance: 2007—2011

Year	Combination Programs[①]	Student Programs		Teacher Programs	
	Number of Programs	Number of Programs	Number of Participants	Number of Programs	Number of Participants
2007	12	21	874	25	448
2008	11	52	2608	40	1038
2009	9	77	4455	48	1193
2010	8	83	5489	59	1451
2011	25	108	7672	73	1583
Total	65	341	21098	245	5713

STARTALK was implemented nationwide, however, it became apparent that the current world language teacher education capacity in the US is inadequate to produce the numbers and types of world language teachers needed to meet an increasing and changing demand. According to a 2009 US Department of Education report, thirty-six states and the District of Columbia have identified foreign languages, world languages, or languages other than English as teacher shortage areas. As documented in a white paper entitled *The Teachers We Need: Transforming World Language Education in the United States* (Ingold and Wang, 2010), US K-12 schools have experienced trends that urgently call for attention to teacher education capacity and states' certification policies: (1) there are more demands for elementary school immersion and early language learning programs (traditionally, world languages have been taught in high schools); (2) critical languages have been added to the world language offerings in addition to commonly taught languages such as French, German, Italian, Latin, or Spanish; (3) students are expected to develop and demonstrate language proficiency based on their study of a world language—no longer is the language taught just for

① Combination programs include both student and teacher components. The numbers of combination programs have been incorporated into the student and teacher programs. The numbers of student participants are from all student programs, including the student component of combination programs. Similarly, the numbers of teacher participants are from all teacher programs, including the teacher component of combination programs.

exploration or a taste of different cultures; (4) expanded delivery systems and technology in the classroom are becoming more common than ever. Because today's students have grown up in the digital age, the traditional face-to-face and textbook-driven language learning cannot match the diverse learning styles and interests of students in the current system. The US world language teacher supply system was built for the past era, and it must be modernized to become more effective and responsive (Ingold and Wang, 2010).

Driven by the question of how to expand and reform the teacher supply system, the National Foreign Language Center at the University of Maryland, the national administrator of STARTALK, convened two national meetings of twenty-five states and the District of Columbia, teacher education programs, national professional organizations, and federal government representatives to dialog and look for answers. The results of these two meetings appear in the white paper previously mentioned, co-authored by Dr. Catherine Ingold and myself. The paper captures the essence of rigorous discussions and incorporates extensive data from STARTALK. A wide range of information and resources was collected and analyzed, in addition to a national survey of states and the District of Columbia about their respective world language educational policies and practices, research findings pertinent to the US world language teacher shortage, comparisons of US and international world language education policies, and alternative routes to certification.

This paper makes a strong case for the need to expand the US world language capacity, and it suggests ways to design a teacher supply system that will produce the kinds of world language teachers that expanded capacity demands. "An Additive Language Policy for All Students" is the vision that the white paper proposed. Such a policy is particularly relevant for the US as a nation of immigrants. This vision is also in line with that of the 2012 APEC Educational Ministerial Meeting Statement (APEC, 2012) and of the Council of Europe Language Education Policy (Council of Europe, n.d.). As the world becomes increasingly interconnected at an unprecedented rate, migration of people from one nation/state to another has become a common phenomenon. Such a vision acknowledges the home language background of children while ensuring that they will also be proficient and literate in the majority language of a given society.

Five goals are identified as critical in setting an agenda for transforming world language education in the US: (1) To increase the number and effectiveness of language education programs; (2) To expand the range of languages offered; (3) To begin language instruction at a younger age and continue through a longer, articulated sequence; (4) To establish clear expectations for students' language learning outcomes; and (5) To expand access and opportunity to learn via both traditional and innovative delivery systems (Ingold and Wang, 2010).

To meet the demands, the white paper makes it clear that the US needs:

- Effective teachers for all languages;
- Elementary and immersion world language teachers;
- Teachers of emerging world languages/critical languages;
- Teachers with technological literacies, who can teach distance learning, online, and in blended learning environments.

Because world language education has not been assessed nationally or by the states in the same way as the content areas of English, Reading, Writing, and Math, issues related to world language teacher supply have not had the same priority as other areas. A surface problem exposed by the efforts of STARTALK is the shortage of teachers, particularly in the critical languages. A deeper structural problem is the limited availability of teacher training faculty and the small number of institutions of higher education that are able and willing to offer rigorous yet flexible teacher education programs capable of servicing the needs of diverse teacher candidates. Interest in providing programs is further limited by the absence or complexity of state teacher certification or licensure requirements. This is a national problem that will require a concerted effort from national professional organizations working with multiple states. The lack of teacher education capacity in the face of outdated teacher certification / licensure requirements must be addressed urgently if the goal is to expand world language and critical language capacity. Furthermore, there must be clear expectations outlining the knowledge, skills, disposition, and experiences required for an effective world language teacher for the global age.

World Language Teacher Competencies

There is already an emerging consensus about the competencies that effective world language teachers must possess. They must acquire and demonstrate adequate proficiency in the language they will teach, an understanding of the structure of the language and the culture(s) where the language is spoken, knowledge of second language acquisition and learner development, and pedagogical skills appropriate to the setting in which they will be teaching.

In 2010, under the auspices of STARTALK, NFLC formed a task force of national experts and began to examine various nationally recognized teacher standards in order to develop its own framework for teacher development for all teacher programs supported by STARTALK. In order to make sure the product would be aligned with what is being used for teachers in other content areas across the nation, the STARTALK task force consulted Charlotte Danielson's seminal work, *Enhancing Professional Practice: A Framework for Teaching* (2008). The Association for Supervision and Curriculum Development used Danielson's framework as a foundation for their Teacher Effectiveness resources, widely used for teacher preparation and evaluation of teaching practice in all content areas (ASCD, 2012). The framework categorizes the activity of teaching into four major domains of practice: Planning and Preparation, the Classroom Environment, Instruction, and Professional Responsibilities. Under each domain, Danielson also develops components describing what the competencies are within that domain.

Subsequently, the STARTALK task force analyzed several sets of nationally-recognized world language teacher standards that define the body of knowledge, skills, disposition, and experience that a prospective teacher must acquire and demonstrate. They included teacher standards developed by the Interstate Teacher Assessment and Support Consortium (INTASC) (CCSSO, 2010), the National Board for Professional Teaching Standards (NBPTS) (NBPTS, n.d.), and the National Council for Accreditation of Teacher Education (NCATE), in cooperation with ACTFL (NCATE and ACTFL, 2002). These standards address different stages of teacher development and align well with one another. The ACTFL/NCATE

Standards for accrediting teacher education programs detail what the graduates of their programs should know and be able to do; the INTASC Principles apply to beginning teachers who are in their first to third years of teaching; and the NBPTS Core Propositions target at experienced and effective teachers in various content areas. The following tables compare Danielson's framework with ACTFL/NCATE Standards, INTASC Principles, and NBPTS Core Propositions, organized by domains. References are provided so that readers may review each of the standards for more details.

Alignment of Danielson's Components with World Language Teacher Standards by Domains

Table 2: Domain 1: Planning and Preparation

DANIELSON	NBPTS	ACTFL/NCATE	INTASC
1. Demonstrating knowledge of content and pedagogy	2. Knowledge of language	1a. Language proficiency 1b. Understanding linguistics 1c. Language comparisons	1. Content knowledge
2. Demonstrating knowledge of content and pedagogy	3. Knowledge of culture	2a. Cultural understandings 2b. Literary, cultural texts and traditions	1. Content knowledge
3. Demonstrating knowledge of content and pedagogy		2c. Integrating other disciplines in instruction 4b. Integrating standards in instruction	
4. Demonstrating knowledge of content and pedagogy	4. Knowledge of language acquisition	3a. Language acquisition	1. Content knowledge
5. Demonstrating knowledge of content and pedagogy	4. Knowledge of language acquisition		
6. Setting instructional outcomes		4a. Standards-based planning 4b. Standards-based instruction	
7. Demonstrating knowledge of students	1. Knowledge of students		2. Learner development 3. Diversity of learners

DANIELSON	NBPTS	ACTFL/NCATE	INTASC
8. Setting instructional outcomes	7. Assessment	2c. Integrating other disciplines in instruction 3b. Instructional practices, language outcomes and learner diversity 4a. Standards-based planning	7. Planning for instruction
9. Demonstrating knowledge of resources		4c. Selection and developing materials	
10. Designing coherent instruction	6. Designing curriculum and planning instruction	3b. Instructional practices, language outcomes and learner diversity 4a. Standards-based planning 4b. Standards-based instruction 4c. Selection and developing materials	7. Planning for instruction
11. Designing student assessments	7. Assessment	5a. Knowing and using assessment 5b. Reflecting on assessment 5c. Reporting assessment results	8. Assessment

Table 3: Domain 2: The Classroom Environment

DANIELSON	NBPTS	ACTFL/NCATE	INTASC
1. Creating an environment of respect and support	5. Fair and equitable learning environment	3b. Instructional practices, language outcomes and learner diversity	3. Diversity of learners 5. Learning environment
2. Establishing a culture for learning	5. Fair and equitable learning environment		5. Learning environment
3. Managing classroom procedures	5. Fair and equitable learning environment 6. Designing curriculum and planning instruction		5. Learning environment
4. Managing student behavior	5. Fair and equitable learning environment		5. Learning environment
5. Organizing physical space	5. Fair and equitable learning environment		5. Learning environment

Table 4: Domain 3: Instruction

DANIELSON	NBPTS	ACTFL/NCATE	INTASC
1. Communicating with students	6. Designing curriculum and planning instruction	3b. Instructional practices, language outcomes and learner diversity 4b. Standards-based instruction	4. Instructional strategies
2. Using questioning and discussion techniques	6. Designing curriculum and planning instruction		4. Instructional strategies
3. Engaging students in learning	6. Designing curriculum and planning instruction		4. Instructional strategies
4. Using assessment in instruction	6. Designing curriculum and planning instruction 7. Assessment	5. A knowing and using assessment 5b. Reflecting on assessment 5c. Reporting assessment results	8. Assessment
5. Demonstrating flexibility and re-sponsiveness	5. Fair and equitable learning environment 6. Designing curriculum and planning instruction 7. Assessment		

Table 5: Domain 4: Professional Responsibilities

DANIELSON	NBPTS	ACTFL/NCATE	INTASC
1. Reflecting on teaching	8. Reflection		9. Reflective practice & professional development
2. Maintaining accurate records	8. Reflection		
3. Communicating with families	9. Professionalism		6. Communication
4. Participating in a professional community	9. Professionalism	6a. Professional development	10. Community
5. Growing and developing professionally	9. Professionalism	6a. Professional development	9. Reflective practice & professional development
6. Showing professionalism	9. Professionalism	6a. Professional development 6b. Advocacy for foreign language learning	

In addition, the language teaching community has developed a body of empirically-based knowledge and expertise that can be used to define and measure teacher competencies. Available tools include nationally-recognized standards for student learning, teachers, and teacher preparation programs; language proficiency scales and assessment tools; and assessment tools to measure teachers' subject matter knowledge and pedagogical skills. What follows are some examples that are available in the US.

Foreign Language Content Standards for Students

World language teachers must know and be able to implement standards-based instruction for their students. ACTFL's *Standards for Foreign Language Learning: Preparing for the* 21st *Century*,② first published in 1996, defines five-goal areas for student outcomes, known as the "5 Cs": Communication, Cultures, Connections, Comparisons, and Communities (ACTFL, et al., 2006). These goal areas are supported by eleven standards. Currently, standards exist for Arabic, Chinese, Classics (Latin and Greek), French, German, Hindi, Italian, Japanese, Portuguese, Russian, and Spanish, with initiatives underway for other languages. As of 2007, over thirty state and regional foreign language professional organizations had endorsed these standards.

In recent years, state leaders have launched the Common Core State Standards Initiative③ to define the knowledge and skills that all K-12 students should obtain in preparation for college or work. To date, forty-seven states and the District of Columbia have adopted these standards for mathematics and English language arts (NGA Center and CCSSO, n.d., Common Core State Standards for English Language). The alignment of world languages with the Common Core State Standards should reinforce the importance of developing students' bilingualism and biliteracy as part of a world-class education.

② For more information on ACTFL National Standards For Foreign Language Education, see ACTFL, et al., (n. d.), National Standards (http://www.actfl.org/i4a/pages/index.cfm?pageid=3392).

③ To learn more about the Common Core Standards Initiative, visit http://www.corestandards.org.

Language Proficiency Scales

Language proficiency has been defined as "the ability of an individual to carry out in appropriate ways communicative tasks which are typically encountered in cultures where the language is natively spoken (Egan, 1999)". It is important that world language teachers understand the language proficiency scale so they can facilitate students' acquisition of real-life communication skills that enable them to function in another culture where the language is used.

Although language study is generally a marginalized subject in US schools, the federal government has invested heavily in developing an infrastructure for producing the language-competent professionals that the government needs. One important product of this investment is the nationally and internationally recognized language proficiency scale established by the federal government's Interagency Language Roundtable (http://www.govtilr.org/). ACTFL subsequently developed its Proficiency Guidelines for Academic Purposes based on the ILR scale. Both the ILR scale and the ACTFL Guidelines (ACTFL, 2012) contain detailed descriptions of the base levels in the four component skills included in language proficiency—listening, reading, speaking, and writing (Herzog, 2004). These scales, along with the *Common European Framework of Reference for Languages: Learning, Teaching, Assessing* (Council of Europe, n.d., Common European Framework), provide a solid basis for meaningful assessment of learner outcomes.

Language Proficiency Assessment Tools

Ensuring that prospective teachers attain the level of language proficiency needed for effectiveness in the classroom is a major concern for teacher preparation, particularly in the most difficult languages for English speakers to learn. ACTFL has pointed out that world language teachers need to be able to teach students of diverse backgrounds and levels and can carry out specific instructional tasks in the target language. They must be able to use language for real-life purposes and model the language for students, with the end result of moving them to higher levels of proficiency (Hamlyn, 2009). In dual language and immersion environments, teachers must also be able to teach the content of the assigned school curriculum in the foreign language, a task that requires a high level of proficiency.

Nationally recognized assessments to measure language proficiency are currently available. For example, the Oral Proficiency Interview (OPI) and the Writing Proficiency Test (WPT) developed by ACTFL can be used as measures of a teacher candidate's competency in the language of his or her choice. The PRAXIS series of tests developed by Educational Testing Service (ETS) offers another assessment tool for language proficiency and cultural knowledge for prospective French, German, and Spanish teachers (Hamlyn, 2009).

One major task related to setting a required proficiency level or passing score for teacher candidates is to determine a level of proficiency that is fair and equitable for prospective teachers across languages. Different languages require varying amounts of time and efforts to reach the same proficiency level because of the linguistic and cultural differences between the target language and English. The Foreign Service Institute (FSI) of the US Department of State has established three categories of languages to differentiate the amount of time required to reach a defined level of proficiency. Category I languages, such as French, German, and Spanish, are the closest to English and comparatively faster for native English speakers to learn. Category II languages, such as Hindi, Pashto, and Russian, have significant linguistic and cultural differences from English and require more time to learn; whereas Category III languages like Arabic, Chinese, and Korean are the most different from English and consequently require the most time to learn, especially reading and writing skills.

Traditionally, most states have required teacher candidates to show credit hours in language study as evidence of language proficiency. In recent years, an increasing number of states have begun to allow teacher candidates to use test scores to demonstrate that they have the language proficiency required. To date, sixteen states allow teacher candidates to take the ACTFL OPI and WPT to provide evidence of their language proficiency. Although there is no uniformly accepted minimum score, the emerging consensus in the field is that all language teachers should attain, at a minimum, Advanced Low proficiency on the ACTFL rating scale in speaking. In writing, teachers should attain Advanced Low proficiency for FSI Category I languages and Intermediate High for FSI Category II or III languages. For those languages that have PRAXIS tests, each state works with ETS to set its own passing scores for each language.④ Some other states, such as California and Georgia, have also developed their own tests of language proficiency.

Assessment Tools for Subject Matter Competence

Some states have standards related to subject matter competence and pedagogical competence for all teachers, including world language teachers. For instance, California has defined subject matter competence for world language teachers in five key areas: general linguistics, linguistics of the target language, literary and cultural texts and traditions, cultural analysis and comparisons, and integrated target language skills (Jacobson, 2009). A prospective teacher's subject matter knowledge in all five areas is assessed through the California Subject Examination for Teachers.

Assessment Tools for Pedagogical Competence

To date, many states continue to require a certain number of credits for coursework in education and methods courses that teacher candidates must show as proof of their competencies. Some more progressive states have developed other methods to assess a prospective teacher's pedagogical competence. California has a comprehensive set of standards for beginning teachers, known as the Teaching Performance Expectations, and a portfolio system of assessment (Jacobson, 2009). The State of Washington requires prospective language teachers to take the Washington Educator Skills Test. Competency expectations include child and adolescent development, individuality and diversity, language and culture,

---

④ For more information about the PRAXIS language tests, see http://www.ets.org/praxis.

language acquisition and teaching, learning environment, assessment, language competency and proficiency, and professional development.[5] A number of other states require world language teacher candidates to take the ETS PRAXIS test in pedagogy as proof of competency. Detailed information on this topic can be found in the *Resource Guide to Developing Linguistic and Cultural Competency in the United States* (Wang, Jackson, Mana, Liau and Evans, 2010) and in annual state reports available on the NCSSFL website (www.ncssfl.org).

So far, there has not been much discussion about the technological skills that a world language teacher should possess and demonstrate. The International Association for K-12 Online Learning recently published the National Standards for Quality Online Teaching that can serve as a reference and a tool for measuring the effectiveness of online teachers (INACOL, 2011).

World Language Teachers' Professional Life Cycle: A Framework for Systematically Changing Teachers' Development as a Continuum

In order to redesign the world language teacher supply system to align with the demands of an expanded and responsive world language education system, and to ensure teachers can acquire and demonstrate the types of competencies outlined in the previous section, it is essential to envision what the system should look like. Aspects of development and support for teachers might be imagined as a continuum along a teacher's career path, i.e., aspiring teachers, teacher apprentices/candidates, novice teachers, practicing teachers, master teachers and teacher developers. This continuum aligns beautifully with a professional life cycle of a teacher, which begins with recruitment, preparation, certification, licensure, induction, mentoring, professional development, and reflection and lifelong learning, as shown in Figure 1 below:

---

⑤ For more information about Washington's teacher assessment, go to http://www.k12.wa.us/certification/teacher/teachertesting.aspx.

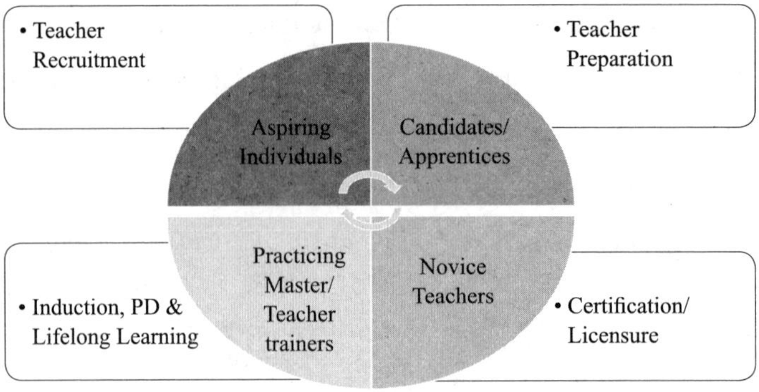

Figure 1. Continuum of Teacher Development & Life Cycle of a World Language Teacher

Using the backward design model (Wiggins and McTighe, 2005), it is necessary to outline the desired output of the system, i.e., the competencies, experiences, and other qualities of world language teachers that the system must produce. Additional critical factors that influence the teacher supply system include the available pools of teacher candidates, the content and process of teacher preparation, clinical experiences ranging from classroom observations to student teaching under a skilled teacher, the means of assessing teacher candidates and certifying their credentials, and the evaluation of the efficacy of the system via data collection on teacher performance. It is also important to consider ways to leverage resources so they can be shared across schools, school districts, states, and nations. While the task of transforming the world language teacher supply system is daunting, it might be helpful to consider the notion of the professional life cycle of a teacher as a framework for teacher development. Because each nation has its own system of recruiting, preparing, licensing, and supporting its own teachers, I will not labor to delineate how to support teachers in each cycle of their development and professional life. For more details, please see the white paper (Ingold and Wang, 2010).

Conclusion: A Systemic Approach for Preparing and Supporting World Language Teachers

So far, I have described some federal efforts in expanding world language capacity in the United States, namely, the National Security Language Initiatives (NSLI). Among the NSLI initiatives, the most significant large-scale effort in preparing and supporting world language teachers is STARTALK. In addition to sharing program data from STARTALK, I have discussed insights gained from promoting its designated ten critical languages. Building upon issues emerged from changing demands for world language programs, teacher quality and supply became an urgent task that STARTALK and states may tackle together. A resulting white paper produced by two national meetings on expanding and reforming teacher capacity issues was published by the National Foreign Language Center, the University of Maryland (Ingold and Wang, 2010). I highlighted key points of the white paper, which includes the new vision and goals for a world language education in the global age. I also listed in detail what teacher competencies are expected. At the end, I proposed a framework of viewing teacher development as a continuum that coincides with a professional life cycle of a teacher.

Leaders of all professional organizations and governmental and non-governmental agencies must engage in high-level dialogs and coordinate efforts and funding priorities. It is time for stakeholders to unite in order to undertake the larger task of developing global competence and transnational communicative competence, and prepare students for this increasingly interconnected world. Such collaboration must be purposeful and intentional, with a clear goal for all stakeholders.

There is a critical need for developing more robust mechanisms to recruit, prepare, certify, and support a larger cadre of effective world language teachers. There must be a mechanism to help teacher candidates find positions and to provide ongoing mentorship and professional development. In the end, the issue at hand is how to address the disparity between the rapidly growing interest in the world languages and the severe lack of infrastructure to sustain high quality programs for many of the new emerging world languages that are being taught in schools. Expansion of capacity for these will require innovations and investments similar to those in other fields deemed important to a nation, such as science, math, and technology. Today's economic competitiveness and global security challenges mandate a larger pool of highly proficient speakers of a wider range of world languages. We need to develop an effective teacher who SPEAKS with students—one who possesses Skills to communicate and solve problems, one who understands and instills multiple Perspectives in students, one who provides meaningful Experiences for all students, one who serves as an Agent for change, one who has Knowledge of the languages and of the pedagogy for teaching language and content, and one who equips students with Strategies to seek answers in the journey of lifelong learning. The time is right for language investments to focus on teachers.

References:

[1] American Council on the Teaching of Foreign Languages (ACTFL), American Association of Teachers of French (AATF), et al. (n.d.). National Standards for Foreign Language Education: A Collaborative Project of ACTFL, AATF, AATG, AATI, AATSP, ACL, ACTR, CLASS and NCJLT-ATJ. http://www.actfl.org/i4a/pages/index.cfm?pageid=3392.

[2] ACTFL, AATF, et al. (2006). *Standards for Foreign Language Learning: Preparing for the 21st Century*. (3rd ed.). Lawrence, KS: Allen Press.

[3] ACTFL. (2012). *ACTFL Proficiency Guidelines*. Arlington, VA: ACTFL. http://www.actfl.org/files/public/ACTFLProficiencyGuidelines2012_FINAL.pdf.

[4] Asia Society. (2006). Preparing Chinese Language Teachers Initiative, Funded by the Freeman Foundation. http://asiasociety.org/arts/preparing-chinese-language-teachers-initiative.

[5] Asia Society & College Board. (2008). *Chinese in 2008: An Expanding Field*. http://www.askasia.org/chinese/announcements/nclc.htm. (January 16, 2008).

[6] Asia-Pacific Economic Cooperation (APEC). (2012). *Envisioning Together for the Future and Hope*. Joint Statement. Gyeongju, Korea: 2012 5th APEC Education Ministerial Meeting. http://www.apec.org/Meeting-Papers/Ministerial-Statements/Education/2012_education.aspx. (May 23,2012).

[7] Association for Supervision and Curriculum Development (ASCD). (2012). The Charlotte Danielson Library of Professional Development Resources. http://www.ascd.org/professional-development/teacher-effectiveness-suite.aspx.

[8] The College Board (2008). *Chinese Language and Culture Programs in the United States: National Data*. Unpublished study.

[9] Council of Chief State School Officers (CCSSO). (2010). Interstate Teacher Assessment and Support Consortium (InTASC). *Model Core Teaching Standards: A Resource for State Dialog (Draft for Public Comment)*. Washington, DC: CCSSO. http://www.ccsso.org/Resources/Publications/Model_Core_Teaching_Standards.html.

[10] Council of Europe. (n.d.). *Council of Europe Language Education Policy.* http://www.coe.int/t/dg4/linguistic/Division_en.asp.

[11] Danielson, C. (2008). *Enhancing Professional Practice: A Framework for Teaching.* (2nd edition). Alexandria, VA: Association for Supervision and Curriculum Development.

[12] Educational Testing Service (ETS). (n.d.). The PRAXIS Series. http://www.ets.org/praxis.

[13] Egan, K. (1999). Speaking: A Critical Skill and a Challenge. *CALICO Journal 6*(3). https://www.calico.org/a-615-Speaking%20A%20Critical%20Skill%20and%20a%20Challenge%20.html.

[14] Hamlyn, H. (2009). *The Use of ACTFL Proficiency Assessments for Teacher Certification.* Presentation given at the National World Language Teacher Certification Summit, Arlington, VA. http://startalk.umd.edu/2009/meetings/certification/.

[15] Herzog, M. (2004). *An Overview of the History of the ILR Language Proficiency Skill Level Descriptions and Scale.* Interagency Language Roundtable website: http://www.govtilr.org/Skills/IRL%20Scale%20History.htm.

[16] Ingold, C. W., & Wang, S. C. (2010). *The Teachers We Need: Transforming World Language Education in the United States.* College Park, MD: National Foreign Language Center at the University of Maryland. http://www.nflc.org/publications/the_teachers_we_need.pdf.

[17] International Association for K-12 Online Learning (INACOL). (2011). *National Standards for Quality Online Teaching.* Vienna, VA: INACOL. http://www.inacol.org/research/nationalstandards/NACOL%20Standards%20Quality%20Online%20Teaching.pdf.

[18] Jacobson, P. (2009). *Moving from Effective Input to Successful Output.* Presentation given at the National World Language Teacher Certification Summit, Arlington, VA. http://startalk.umd.edu/2009/meetings/certification/.

[19] National Board for Professional Teaching Standards (NBPTS). (n.d.). *NBPTS Standards and Five Core Propositions.* http://www.nbpts.org/the_standards.

[20] National Council for Accreditation of Teacher Education (NCATE) & American Council on the Teaching of Foreign Languages (ACTFL). (2002). *ACTFL/ NCATE Program Standards for the Preparation of Foreign Language Teachers.* Available:http://www.actfl.org/i4a/pages/index.cfm?pageID=3384.

[21] National Council of State Supervisors for Languages (NCSSFL). (n.d.). *NCSSFL State Reports.* http://ncssfl.org/reports2/index.php?reports_index.

[22] National Governors Association Center for Best Practices (NGA Center) & the Council of Chief State School Officers (CCSSO). (n.d.). *Common Core State Standards Initiative.* Available:www.corestandards.org.

[23] NGA Center & CCSSO. (n.d.). *Common Core State Standards for English Language Arts & Literacy in History/Social Studies, Science, and Technical Subjects.* http://www.corestandards.org/the-standards/english-language-arts-standards.

[24] NGA Center & CCSSO. (n.d.). *Common Core State Standards for Mathematics.* http://www.corestandards.org./assets/CCSSI_Math%20Standards.pdf.

[25] State of Washington, Office of Superintendent of Public Instruction. (n.d.) *Teacher Assessments.* http://www.k12.wa.us/certification/teacher/teachertesting.aspx.

[26] U.S. Department of State, Bureau of Educational and Cultural Affairs. (2006). *National Security Language Initiative* (NSLI). http://web.archive.org/web/20080929044930/http://exchanges.state.gov/NSLI/.

[27] Wang, S. C. (2009). Preparing and Supporting Teachers of Less Commonly Taught Languages. *The Modern Language Journal,* 93(2), 282-287.

[28] Wang, S. C., Jackson, F. H., Mana, M., Liau, R., & Evans, B. (2010). *Resource Guide to Developing Linguistic and Cultural Competency in the United States.* College Park, MD: National Foreign Language Center at the University of Maryland. http://www.nflc.org/publications/the_teachers_we_need_Resource_Guide.pdf.

[29] Wiggins, G.P., and McTighe, J. (2005). *Understanding by Design.* (2nd ed.). Alexandria, VA: Association for Supervision and Curriculum Development.

语言教师生涯的准备和扶持

[美国] 王周淑涵

摘要：2012 年 5 月，亚太经合组织（APEC）各成员体的教育部长在韩国庆州召开了以“未来的挑战及教育对策”为主题的会议。与会部长一致认为：当前的一个重要任务是“在学校教育阶段向学生提供外语教育，同时开发一种能培养出既具有很高语言教学水平又能深度理解文化多样性的语言教师的体系”。更值得一提的是，部长们认识到教师质量是决定学生成功与否的最重要的因素。为了回应各成员体教育部长对培养和扶持世界语言教师的提议，本文将概述美国有关教师职业发展的几项主要举措，还将分享“星谈（STARTALK）计划”实施以来获得的经验和教训。“星谈计划”是美国联邦政府的一项实行多年、预算逾千万的项目，该项目致力于培养十种关键语言的潜在教师和在职教师，这十种关键语言包括汉语、阿拉伯语、俄语、乌尔都语、波斯语、土耳其语、葡萄牙语、斯瓦西里语、达里语和印度语。本文还将根据美国学界认可的教师标准和教师培训计划，概述为帮助学生掌握 21 世纪相关技能、提高全球竞争力，世界语言教师必须具备的知识、技能、视角和经验。本文最后提出了一个旨在培养潜在语言教师、支持在职语言教师职业发展的框架。该框架涵盖教师的录用、培养、就职、导师制度、辅导培训、留任和晋升等诸多方面。要实现培养具有多语能力世界公民的目标，拥有优质高效的师资队伍是成功的关键。

关键词：未来的挑战及教育对策；美国教师发展项目；具有多语能力的世界公民

Becoming a Mindful Teacher: Reflective Teaching Practices

[The United States] Alice Murray

Abstract: To some degree, most teachers are consciously aware of what goes on in their classrooms, but "mindful" teachers go a step further and systematically contemplate their teaching situations and are attune to their students. Teachers do not automatically acquire knowledge about how they teach just from teaching. Combining the teaching experience along with structured reflective practices enables us to learn about ourselves at a professional level and can lead us to becoming more successful and mindful language teachers. This plenary will offer some examples of reflective practices in the hopes that we can begin a discussion on how we each examine, question, and reflect on our beliefs and approaches to classroom teaching.

Keywords: mindful; language teachers; structured reflective practices; US

I just want to share this quote that I found from the famous American educator, John Dewey. Dewey defined reflective thought as "active, persistent, and careful consideration of any belief or supposed form of knowledge in the light of the grounds that support it and the further conclusions to which it tends" (Dewey 1933: 118).

If we had time, I would ask you to take a moment and talk to the person sitting next to you or behind you and share what you believe reflective practice is. Most educators believe that some form of reflection or reflective practice is desirable, but few can agree what it is, and what form it is. There are many words that have been used over the past two decades to describe reflective practice.

What does it mean to you? Now, I am not going to tell you what I think reflective practice is yet. Instead, I want to ask you a second question:

How would you recognize a reflective practitioner if you saw one? It might be someone, a teacher, looking at him or herself in a mirror. Maybe it's someone sitting in a corner, being quiet, thinking deeply. Or possibly it's someone like this action hero figure. Does that make him/her or me a reflective practitioner? Possibly, it's hard to know. For me, a reflective practitioner is someone who asks the following questions:

What Do I Do/How Do I Do It = Method/Technique

Why Do I Do It = Reason

What Is the Result = Result

What Changes = Justification

What and How are kinds of descriptive reflections and this is where most people start. Why is more conceptual. Now what is not covered in this list but something we will want to consider is Critical Reflection, which emphasizes the ethics and morals of what we do. Back to the list—What Is the Result—many teachers forget what they do sometimes, they focus too much on how they do—we are trying to teach the students something, in this case, EFL. So we need to figure out how/what you do in the classroom to promote language learning.

This first stage, Reflection-in-Action, is when reflection occurs on the spot, dealing with issues as they occur. OK, let's try this—think about when your class falls flat, the lesson just isn't going in the direction you wanted/expected. Even experienced teachers find it difficult to recognize what is going on in the classroom while it is going on. What teachers think they do and what they actually do are very, very different. Reflection-in-Action is a learned process as is reflective practice. If experienced teachers find it difficult, imagine how it is for new teachers. Novice teachers think that they have to stick to the lesson plan no matter how badly the class is going—the students are dying, running out of the classroom screaming, pulling their hair out, but the lesson plan is the key to everything. Why do novice teachers do this? Mainly because they don't have the schema of our teaching experiences to call upon while they are teaching.

Reflection-on-Action is probably the most utilized of the three as it happened once the teaching was in the past. There are so many kinds of reflective tools you can use to accomplish this.

Ideally, Reflection-for-Action is a result of the first two. It happens before you go into class. Many of us forget that you can reflect before you teach. What we need to remember about reflective practice is that it is a CIRCULAR process. If we had time, I would ask each of you to describe a recent teaching moment that you felt it was a success or one that didn't go as well as you hoped. A question for you to think about is How Did You Know It Went Well Or Not—Can You Tell Your Neighbor? Let's consider the analogy of going to the doctor because you have been having migraines. The doctor says "OK, take two of these purple pills every six hours and come back next week." And your only response is "OK". Now, if you had had the courage to ask Why Should I—why do we never ask a doctor, who we all know has a medical degree, who knows everything and who is never wrong... OK, this time you ask why should I take them, and the doctor responds, "Well. I know purple is your favorite color and I feel it will be good for you". Well, what would you do? If the doctor responded that the medication would help expand your constricted neurological impulses, which were causing your headaches. In other words, we need to consider the evidence. An important element of reflective practice is discovering the evidence. Reflective teachers don't pull evidence out of thin air; they use the evidence they have collected to make informed decisions about their teaching.

I want to expand on another area that can lead to reflective practice and that is mindful teaching. Now you may be wondering what in the world is she talking about? Mindful teaching? Becoming a mindful teacher? "Mindful" is an unusual word. How would you define it? OK, now think about it in the context of reflection/reflective practice.

Elizabeth MacDonald, an elementary teacher in the Boston Public School System, and Dennis Shirley, a professor at the Lynch School of Education at Boston College, founded a series of seminars geared towards urban teachers in response to alienated teaching. The seminar entitled "The Mindful Teacher" is an opportunity for teachers to participate in collaborations, inquiries, formal meditations, and discussions about research. MacDonald and Shirley (2009) define alienated teaching as "instructional processes in which teachers neglect teaching practices that they believe are best suited for their pupils and instead comply with externally imposed mandates out of a sense of deference to authority." The three areas listed on the slide are often why teachers feel overwhelmed and undervalued, unable to find a way to find a balance between their teaching principles and the expectations of the system they work within.

Mindful teaching is not a textbook or a software program you can buy or even a template of how-to-steps. Instead, mindful teaching is something that evolves from sharing your experiences and asking questions with colleagues who also want to question the hows and whys of their teaching processes in order to become better teachers. It is a form of teaching that develops from contemplative practices and teacher inquiry, enabling teachers to interrupt their hectic and often stressful lives and take time to participate in a collegial, mutual community of inquiry and practice. Mindful teaching also allows us to address certain aspects of our classroom teaching and students' learning that might be overlooked in the everyday routines. Mindful teaching practices are a means to ignite and expand a discussion about mindfulness and its relevance and value to education.

Synergy can mean interaction/cooperation/collaboration, a combined effect, or a concerted effort. Dewey's entire philosophy of education is based upon how such oppositions and dualisms can be overcome, with the intent to establish a harmony and balance in education as well as to develop new capacities and competencies. The seven synergies provide important principles for developing and improving teaching. However, it would be misleading to think that these seven collaborative principles come close to providing a template for pedagogical decision making. They depend on each other to reach a more productive outcome, reminding us how to adjust our own behaviors in order to attain our objectives, in this case, successful language learning and teaching.

References:

[1] Farrell, T.S.C. (2008). *Reflective Language Teaching: From Research to Practice.* London: Continuum Publishers.

[2] MacDonald, E. & Shirley, D. (2009). *The Mindful Teacher*. New York: Teachers College Press.

[3] Pennington, M. (1992). Reflecting on Teaching and Learning: A Developmental Focus for the Second Language Classroom. In J. Flowerdew, M. Brock and S. Hsia (eds.), *Perspectives on Second Language Teacher Education.* Hong Kong: City Polytechnic.

[4] Richards, J. C., and Lockhart, C. (1994). *Reflective Teaching in Second Language Classrooms*. Cambridge: Cambridge University Press.

[5] Schoeberlein, D. and Sheth, S. (2009). *Mindful Teaching: A Guide for Anyone Who Teaches Anything*. Marblehead, MA: Wisdom Publishers.

[6] Wallace, M. J. (1991). *Training Foreign Language Teachers: A Reflective Approach*. Cambridge: Cambridge University Press.

成为一名善于思考的英语教师：反思教学

[美国] Alice Murray

摘要： 大多数教师在某种程度上都能够意识到课堂教学的进展情况，而“善于思考的教师”却能够进一步系统地审视自己的教学情境，并随时调整教学方法以便和学生的思维保持同步。一般来说，教师在教学过程中无法自动获得有关教学法的知识，他们必须把教学经验和系统的反思结合起来，才能从专业的角度了解自己，将自己培养成为更加善于思考、更加成功的语言教师。本文首先分析三组概念的区别及其在教学实践中的应用，包括“行动中反思”“对行动的反思”和“为行动反思”；继而指出“善于思考的教师”开展反思教学的形态和步骤，即教师在教学实践中应该经常回想“为何教”和“如何教”。要做到这一点，必须避免僵化思维和对权威的盲从，代之以积极的经验交流和细致的观察思考。本文还提供了几个反思教学的案例，以便清楚地呈现反思教学的具体内容，同时期待大家探讨如何审视、质疑和反思个人对课堂教学所持有的观念和采用的方法。

关键词： 善于思考；语言教师；结构化的教学实践；美国

Cross-Cultural Challenges: When Chinese Teachers Face Their Foreign Students

[People's Republic of China] Cheng Long

Abstract: Due to the considerable differences between Chinese and foreign cultures, Chinese teachers are facing great challenges in teaching Chinese as a second language and promoting Chinese culture to foreign students. On the basis of the investigations and case studies of Chinese teachers and their classes, the speaker discusses the following three issues on the top of cross-cultural challenges: 1. authority: loss and regain; 2. knowledge structure: far from overlapping; 3. emotional and rational. The traditional education system under which most Chinese teachers are trained and educated can hardly offer any solutions to these challenges. Here the speaker tries to propose to the teachers several suggestions, some of which are conducted in the training programs which the speaker involves.

Keywords: teaching Chinese as a second language; cross-cultural challenges; authority; knowledge structure

On the basis of the investigations and case studies of Chinese teachers and their classes, I single out some examples in the top of cross-cultural challenges for Chinese teachers. Since the traditional education system under which most Chinese teachers are trained and educated can hardly offer any solutions to these challenges, here I want to discuss how to deal with them.

As China's economy keeps booming since the turn of the century, more and more foreigners come here to further their studies, mostly in the fields of Chinese language, culture, history, business and international relation. Statistics indicate foreign students doubled in four years from 110,000 in 2004 to 220,000 in 2008.

Last year, the number reached 290,000 and apparently it is expected to surpass 300,000 by the end of 2012. At the present time, the number of foreign students at BLCU stands at 6,000, while Chinese students only account for two-thirds of this number.

With foreign students' enrollment increasing, the need for Chinese teachers is urgent. Therefore, many young graduate students with a major in teaching Chinese as a second language become teachers, white many elderly teachers who used to teach Chinese students foreign languages now switch to teach foreign students Chinese language, because it is believed their proficiency of English, French, German or Japanese may greatly help the beginners. However, both the young "professional" and elderly "amateur" teachers run into cross-cultural problems in their classes, which they have never encountered before. These troublesome problems, from the view of cultural studies, are also interesting, so is the process of finding their solutions.

I think it must be the first time, for some of you, to come to China, and you must have noticed the big differences China has presented to you, even in a short stay of several days. Chinese culture is so unique that, almost in every aspect, Chinese culture differs from culture of other countries. 170 years ago, an Englishman, who spent two years in China during the Sino-British War of 1840—1842, wrote in his account of the stay: "China is cast in a different mould from all other nations". I bet some of you have the same opinion even today.

Major differences between China and foreign countries include language, geography, history, religion, political and economic systems. All these lead to cultural differences. Cultural differences may be interesting to tourists and students, but sometimes they are impediments of communication, not only in daily life, but also in classes. With the strong cultural disparities, differences in approaches to teaching and learning styles of Chinese and foreign students would be also expected. Due to the considerable differences between Chinese and foreign cultures, Chinese teachers are facing great challenges in teaching Chinese as a second language and promoting Chinese culture to foreign students.

The first problem Chinese teachers face is that their knowledge structure does not have too much overlap with the foreign students', particularly with regard to knowledge of Chinese culture. You can find someone who is a zero beginner of Chinese language, but you can hardly find a person who knows nothing about Chinese culture. Nowadays, the Chinese are making tremendous efforts to learn foreign languages, especially English and Japanese, if we just focus on the languages used in the Asia-Pacific. Through the languages, Chinese teachers know more and more about Western culture; however, they have few ideas of how the Westerners see the Chinese people and their culture.

The images of Chinese culture in our teachers' minds are Four Great Inventions (compass, paper, printing, powder) and many brilliant achievements ascribed to China, which were frequently talked about at their primary schools, high schools to colleges. However, what is in the foreign students' (especially Western students) minds is foot-binding. In fact, Chinese teachers have little information about this historical phenomenon; regarding foot-binding, there is only one sentence in the middle school history textbook, which says "some bad customs like foot-binding were abandoned after the imperial Qing Dynasty was overthrown in 1911." However, foot-binding seems to be the favorite topic when foreigners study Chinese culture, not only in history, but also today. George Stanton, who came to China in 1793 with a British embassy, described foot-binding with curiosity and gave a picture to Western readers. From then on, foot-binding continued to be an interesting topic for Westerners for more than 200 years. In Western countries, textbooks for young students link China with foot-binding very often and thus make foot-binding the strongest image about Chinese culture.

Then, we can easily imagine the clashes between great inventions and foot-binding. Chinese teachers feel embarrassed when asked about it, but they only know this is one of the dark sides of Chinese culture; they do not want to talk about it and actually they do not know about it. They do not know how to respond to the students; they want to defend, but don't know how. The teachers' response to the topic, avoiding or switching to another topic, on the other hand, reinforces the foreign students' bad image about Chinese culture.

In my training program for Chinese teachers, I tell them not to defend. Sometimes we need to admit that we are not perfect, no one is. Foot-binding was really, really a bad thing in Chinese culture. It brought great pain to Chinese women, both physically and mentally. This is the first step. Secondly, we need to communicate with foreign students, and respond to them, instead of merely answering "yes, it is bad." We need to go to something beneath the surface. We do not defend it; we uncover the essence and make the students aware that we have something in common; all human beings have something in common, only with various manifestations.

Foot-binding was a result of Confucianism, which set a woman's role in society as a housewife. A woman could not get a job, inherit her father's property or be assigned as an heiress to the throne. A woman was subordinated to her husband and later her son. Foot-binding helped to fulfill this role by confining a woman to her home. Another reason was that the foot was associated with sexuality. In ancient China, no man except her husband could touch a woman's feet. We can see in the world that the people would like to bear physical pain to some extent to satisfy a cultural or psychological need. Like high heels, women wear them even though they know it is harmful to health and that is proved by medical science. Other examples are tattoos and piecing. In 18th century's Europe, women wore a corset. The exaggerated hourglass figure required that waist be laced in so tightly that some women died from the strain. If we compare all these, we will find the similarity in them: Chinese culture and Western culture have something in common; the only difference is that in China, it was foot-binding, while in the West and many other places, they were corset/tattoo/piecing...

I try to tell Chinese teachers to deal with the problem like this. After the comparison, foreign students begin to understand Chinese culture, not only just criticize it. And the comparison may even trigger further reflection on about their own culture or various other cultures around the world.

Another problem Chinese teachers complain about is that their authority in class is challenged, their opinions are questioned, and their superiority bestowed by traditional Chinese culture on the profession as a teacher is undermined.

Chinese culture emphasizes the respect for the elderly, teachers, parents or anyone whose age, post, or social status is higher. An argument with the teacher is not encouraged; instead, "being obedient" is what a student should do. A student who challenges his / her teacher may be considered aggressive or trying to boast about himself in class. There is an old Chinese saying, "One day as a teacher, a lifetime as a father". In traditional culture, the teacher equals the father. Today, although Chinese people do not abide by the doctrine seriously any more, they still consider respect for their teachers' authority a virtue. That can partly explain why some Chinese students lack creativity and are not good at expressing their own opinions. They are told to follow their teachers, not to deviate from the course. Western students, like Americans, on the other hand, are independent and individualistic, stressing the dignity, rights and achievements of the individual, and space and freedom of the individual. The Americans emphasize verbal skills. Children are trained to participate in the schools during their childhood, taught to present their ideas, and encouraged to persuade others (even adults) to accept their points of view. In classes, American students make oral presentations without any paper in their hands; and if they have the paper, they try not to read it. The Chinese, on the other hand, are accustomed to making their speeches from written pages, as I am doing now.

When foreign students show their disagreements with Chinese teachers, the latter feel they lose their authority. Some of them try to regain the authority by arguing, and some choose to switch to another issue to avoid the confrontation, leaving the problem unsettled.

So, in a training program that I was involved in, I proposed to our teachers that they should learn to be accustomed to disagreements. It is normal that an argument happens between teachers and students. Lower you to the position of the students, and communicate with them equally. The principle is simple and easy to understand, but sometimes hard for Chinese teachers to apply.

By the way, today is Teachers' Day, the time that students show special respect for and say thanks to their teachers by giving them presents, flowers and greeting cards. Both the Chinese mainland and Chinese Taiwan have such a teachers' day, but the festival in Taiwan is on September 28, which is believed to be the birthday of Confucius.

Differences need to be recognized before they can be understood. Only when we begin to understand the differences can we change our ways, adjust our teaching practices to accommodate the differences, and finally communicate with our foreign students / friends in a mutually understandable manner. Recognizing differences is the first step in reducing difficulties in dealing with disparate cultures, and toward understanding and then accommodating the differences. One of the ways to bridge these gaps is to find the things in common behind the cultural differences.

跨文化挑战：当中国老师遇到外国学生

[中国] 程　龙

摘要：由于中外文化之间的巨大差异，很多中国教师在向外国学生教授汉语并传播中国文化的过程中都面临着巨大的挑战。在对中国教师及其课堂进行调查和案例研究的基础上，本文探讨以下三个跨文化挑战的问题：一是教师权威得与失的问题，二是教师知识结构的欠缺问题，三是情感与理智的问题。面对这些挑战，中国传统教育模式下教育和训练出来的教师通常很难找出恰当的解决之道。本文试图向这些教师提出一些建议。其中的一些建议已被运用到作者参与的一些教师培训项目中。

关键词：把汉语作为第二语言教学；跨文化挑战；权威；知识结构

信息技术与语言教育项目

Information Technology and Language Education Project

A Balanced-Bilingual Strategy for Supporting Acquisition of English by Chinese Toddlers

[The United States] Robert Calfee

Abstract: By two years of age, children are "language sponges"; if placed in a natural and engaging environment, they quickly and effortlessly acquire a second language without needing formal instruction. This paper presents an approach for supporting English acquisition by Chinese children from 18 to 36 months of age. The approach builds on a balanced-bilingual strategy that provides English-language experiences (L2) for toddlers that parallel ongoing developments in Chinese (L1). The strategy depends in part on the extent to which vocabulary development in the two languages is comparable at these young ages: (1) the rate of acquisition, (2) the words that children learn, and (3) the concepts that they acquire. Findings from the Communicative Development Inventory (Fenson, et al., 1993) supports the following assumptions: (1) the rate of growth in the two lexicons is comparable for both receptive and productive vocabulary, (2) differences in noun-verb ratios are artifactual, and (3) conceptual structures are quite similar. Based on these findings, the balanced-bilingual strategy offers a viable foundation in designing an English language acquisition program for young Chinese children. The paper describes the practical application of this strategy using a hybrid paperware-webware platform.

Keywords: English acquisition; vocabulary development; Chinese children; a balanced-bilingual strategy

Living in a flat world. Learning a second language can be easy or difficult, depending on circumstances. For a two-year-old playing with other children in a multi-lingual preschool, language learning appears natural and effortless. For adults, in contrast, based on their travels to other countries, classes in high school and college, or time spent with Rosetta Stone language learning software, language learning is a challenge. Communication in a "flat-world" future (Friedman, 2007; Darling-Hammond, 2010) will depend on discovering new strategies for helping the upcoming generations become proficient in learning new languages with the apparent ease of preschool toddlers. What are the secrets of their successes, and how might these serve in the design of programs that support and sustain second language learning?

Most people agree about the importance of universal literacy for the coming generations. Equally important may be the acquisition of multiple languages—in the not-too-distant future, every citizen of the world may need to become fluent in two (or more) languages. The United States has struggled for decades to ensure that every child leaves high school with fluency in English—spoken and written. In China, a similar effort has been underway since Nixon's visit in 1972. From third grade onward, English is part of the school curriculum for Chinese students. Preparations for the *Gaokao* or the National College Entrance Examination, TOEFL and TOEIC are major endeavors for large numbers of young adults. Various sources report that 300 million Chinese are "studying English," but relatively few appear to acquire fluency in speaking and communicating (Economic Voice, Feb 2012). Chinese parents are eager for their children to learn English, to enhance their prospects for a productive and satisfying future life. Some families can afford to place their young children in learning centers to get a head start and to support the efforts of the public schools. But centers are costly, and do not necessarily ensure high levels of competence. English is included in the public school curriculum from third grade onward, but students' performance depends on the teachers' familiarity with English, which can be limited.

This paper explores a strategy for acquiring English as a second language that builds on the idea of early home-based exposure using a combination of technologies—paper and digital—as the learning platform. The scenario is the Chinese mainland, but it could be situated almost anywhere in the world. The strategy makes several assumptions: (1) early experiences with English can have a substantial impact on toddlers; (2) a combination of paperware and webware offers a cost-effective means for home-based experiences with English; and (3) connecting English with Chinese for both social and academic purposes will be especially beneficial.

As a point of reference for the rest of the paper, imagine a program in which, beginning around two years of age, children spend time daily with storybooks that are linked to a website that engages them in exciting adventures and experiences, where all activities are presented in parallel in both Chinese and English. By the time they enter third grade, the graduates of the program will be able to participate in conversations in English, and to read and write. They have participated for several years in a variety of entertaining events, including excursions into science, history and geography, technical subjects, and children's literature, all in both Chinese and English. They are well on their way to becoming citizens of the world.

Background Considerations. Learning a second language (L2) presupposes that a first language (L1) has been learned and is in place. L2 learning is then a transfer task, and depends on the match between the two languages and the conditions of learning. If the two languages are similar, if the learning demands are simple, and if the learner has support, then the task should go relatively smoothly. A mismatch in any of these conditions can lead to challenges. For example, Spanish and Italian are close (learning is relatively easy), compared with Spanish and English (learning is more difficult). A large number of English words have Spanish cognates, but this will help the Spanish speaker only if these relations are made transparent. For the Chinese speaker learning English, the overall match is small across the board, increasing the difficulty of the task.

The age of the learner influences the opportunities for transfer. The situations are quite different for the two-year-old, the twelve-year-old, and the twenty-year-old. The young adult is more experienced and may know a lot about learning to learn. On the other hand, this person has an extensive base for language usage, and the amount that needs to be transferred is substantial. The two-year-old is still studying, and has much less to "talk about" than older individuals. The twelve-year-old has a large repertoire of experiences, but may be less patient than the twenty-year-old. For all the three individuals, motivation is an important consideration—Why go to all the trouble to learn a second language anyway?

Partly related to age is the level of language use. The two-year-old can get along with a limited repertoire of ideas and activities, enough to cover the basic needs of life in a daycare or pre-school setting. The twelve-year-old taking Beginning Spanish in a middle school can apply the learning only in decontextualized academic tasks. The twenty-year-old traveling from Los Angeles to spend a month with a Mexican family must deal with a broad array of situations, from daily routines to dinnertime conversations about the state of the economy.

The conditions for language learning vary widely, from classroom instruction to more casual experiences. Classroom instruction is presumably well planned to support learning, but can be problematic, depending on the skills and facility of the teacher, the curriculum, and the range of language awareness and motivation of students in the class. Participation in a study-abroad program has a romantic feel—imagine travelling to a new country with a companion who introduces you to the language. In contrast, consider the beleaguered individual making his or her way around a crowded airport, rushing to catch a flight, and no one understands anything he or she says.

Several instructional principles are supported by current research (Howard, Sugarman and Christian, 2003; Soderman and Oshio, 2008):

- Focus from the beginning on meaningful communication rather than rote associations;
- Start with "formulaic expressions" (tourist phrases), and then introduce grammatical principles;
- Offer rich language experiences from the beginning; avoid over-simplification;
- Provide ongoing opportunities for interaction and production;
- Maximize motivation and minimize anxiety.

These principles are straightforward from one perspective, but they can present challenges for instructional design, where it is important to balance the implicit and explicit learning, the more casual with the more formal aspects of language.

Finally, the goals of language learning need to be taken into account. It is one thing to acquire a collection of tourist phrases for a two-week vacation trip, where the goal is to be able to order dinner using a few local phrases, assuming that the waiter can fill in any missing pieces. The situation is quite different for a high school student planning to attend university abroad where the language of instruction is unfamiliar and quite different from his first language. An especially important consideration is the degree to which the learning goal is competence in "academic language," in the language of schooling and the professions, in the capacity to read and write in L2. In middle-class homes, almost from the day of birth, parents are providing language experiences that prepare their child for schooling and beyond. They intuitively follow many of the principles for supporting development of the native language (L1) that are also effective for learning a second language. Classroom instruction, in contrast, often goes against these principles, emphasizing grammar and using simplistic phrases, with limited attention to communication and richness of experience.

This paper explores the proposition that the design of a bilingual program should take into account learners' entry levels in both L1 and L2, along with the learning goals for both languages, in shaping the conditions of learning, the variable most directly controllable for both practice and policy. This proposition leads to program designs that are quite different from many in current practice. For example, bilingual programs serving Hispanic students in the US generally assume that learners' goals are to participate in mainstream English language schooling, with little attention paid to students' home language of Spanish. The results appear to be low levels of learner motivation and little development of academic Spanish, and in many cases, limited mastery of academic English.

A Target Scenario: English for Toddlers in the Chinese mainland. Most Chinese families take steps to ensure that their children learn English; they buy storybooks and enroll their pre-schoolers in learning centers. English is a significant part of the curriculum from third grade through high school, but appears to have limited usage outside of school settings, although objective evidence on this point is rather limited (Gil and Adamson, 2011). There seems to be a clear market niche for a program that supports the development of English, especially if the program is effective and self-sustaining, and if it serves conversational, educational, and professional purposes. This paper explores the design of a home-based approach to the acquisition of English for children from 1:6 and 9:0 years of age, with a focus on the toddler span—18 to 48 months. Assuming a hybrid program incorporating both paperware and webware components, how might a program be designed and implemented that attends to the proposition laid out earlier, with special attention paid to entry levels and learning goals?

With regard to entry levels, L1, the oral language of most toddlers in the Chinese mainland, is Mandarin (Putonghua), which differs in several ways from the target L2 language for the present project, US English, phonetically, morphologically, and syntactically (Hao, Xing, and Li, 2008). It is also important in describing entry level to consider the age level of the target clientele. Toddlers are in the early stages of language acquisition, and for practical purposes, the most important consideration is likely to be vocabulary size. Several studies have investigated vocabulary growth for both English and Mandarin using the Communicative Development Inventory (CDI; Fenson, et al., 1993). The CDI relies on parent reports (primarily mothers), but has been validated for accuracy. Important features in the assessment of vocabulary development include the rate for receptive (number of different words that are understood) vs. expressive (number of different words that are produced) vocabulary, characteristics of the actual "words" in addition to the simple count, and words vs. sentences.

Several patterns emerge from the CDI findings. First, for both English and Chinese, vocabulary development reflects parent input, which can vary considerably (Hart and Risley, 1995; Tardif, Gelman, and Xu, 1999; Tardif, Fletcher, Liang, and kaciroti, 2009). Second, expressive vocabulary (the number of words that a child produces) is relatively limited (10—20 words) until about 18 months, when a substantial "spurt" occurs, reflecting in part the arrival of motor skills that are requisites for articulating speech sounds. By the time a child reaches 36 months of age, the expressive vocabulary has grown to several hundred words, and the child produces three to four word sentences (CDI, n.d.). Nouns and verbs appear with roughly equal frequency. To emphasize the point made earlier, vocabulary growth patterns are quite similar across English and Mandarin. For example, Tardif, Shatz, and Naigles (1997) found that English and Mandarin children used words for books and toys equally often. The significance of these findings is that, for the vocabulary domain, the entry level for Chinese mainland toddlers is virtually equivalent to that of US English toddlers. The languages may be quite dissimilar at the surface level, but conceptually and pragmatically, the two groups have much in common to talk about, a finding with implications for program design.

Next, how should one describe "exit" levels for toddlers for L1 and L2? What are the expectations, more generally, for the language development of Chinese children when they enter third grade, at which point they begin to receive formal instruction in English? With regard to L1, these children have spent two to three years acquiring *academic language* (Schleppegrell, 2012; Cummins and Man, 2007), the formal register used in schooling, but also in dealing with social institutions in the modern world (Goody and Watt, 1968; Olson, 1977; Calfee, 1982). In particular, they have learned to read and write both Chinese characters and *pinyin* (Chinese phonetic alphabet). Children in the US have also spent three years in school settings, learning to read and write English, with an emphasis on phonics and spelling. Both populations are shifting from "learning to read" to "reading to learn"; they are being introduced to the academic disciplines—math, science, history, and geography—in preparation for entry to secondary education and beyond. The Chinese third-grader presently begins English several years behind the comparable American third grader; the Chinese student must learn to speak English, then learn to read English, and then begin to learn about academic topics in English. "Catching up" is clearly a challenge.

The entry points for Chinese mainland children also reflect their preschool environments, which vary considerably. For example, some parents are more educated than others, and are better able to support their children's learning. For a home-based program like that being described, most adopters will be from middle-class homes, where parents are eager and able to support their children. But in

China, many of these parents will not be fully fluent in English, and will need backup support in Mandarin to be able to help their children. Even then, they will not be able to provide models of spoken English for their children. For parents with less education, the program will need to operate completely in a stand-alone mode. On a related point, "environmental English" is relatively scarce in China, and so children cannot rely on what they see and hear incidentally for models of the English language. The bottom line is that Chinese children are unlikely to find support for English outside of the program, and will have limited opportunities for the development of academic language (including literacy), other than from English learning centers.

A balanced-bilingual strategy. The guiding hypothesis for the design sketched in the rest of this paper is that a critical ingredient for an English bilingual program is the connection of English language learning to Chinese language learning, by developing parallel experiences in both languages, with support for acquisition of an academic register in Chinese as well as English, all of which is from the earliest stages of language learning. Chinese parents clearly support their children's readiness for school in a variety of ways, including storybook reading, watching educational television, and spending time in museums and similar institutions. These activities, conducted in Chinese, undoubtedly have positive influences on children's preparation for school, but they are in most instances informal and unplanned. The proposal here is to develop a learning path stretching from 18 months of age (children begin to use language to communicate, with a large spurt in vocabulary about to emerge) through nine years of age (the age when a child moves to third grade and to subject matter learning). The path provides systematic guidance for learning academic language, including connections to the primary disciplines, science, history and geography, and literature, where literacy (reading and writing) provides an essential tool for the entire progression. The learning path not only supports the work of the school, but also provides a link between the ongoing acquisition of Chinese and the introduction of English. The progression is balanced for the two languages—the learning experience provides ongoing links between L1 and L2, much as happens in the playground setting described at the beginning of the paper—but is slightly offset—each episode begins with an activity in L1 (Chinese), and is then followed by an interaction in L2 (English). The child who enters the program at eighteen months of age has a relatively small number of experiences to deal with, and so discourse in the program can be limited to a small number of short, simple words in both languages. As the child develops, the discourse becomes more complex, but the balanced design continues to provide equal coverage of new situations in both languages.

Let us turn next to program specifics. We start with a hybrid platform, which includes both paperware and webware. Practically speaking, the family receives a monthly package of stories and work pages (paperware), along with access to a website that provides games, songs, and activities (webware). The first series of packages are picturebooks, with two-page spreads each laying out a colorful and engaging image, along with short captions in both Chinese and English. One book displays a succession of toys, a second book moves through a series of meals, while a third takes the reader through the rooms of a house. The parent reads the Chinese captions to the child (and the English captions as well, if comfortable with this task). The paperware also provides an invitation to open up the website for the book. There the child (and parent) finds a variety of audio and visual activities linked to the book: (1) click on one button and the story will be read in Chinese; click on another button and it will be read in English; (2) the child will be invited to play simple games, with a dialog in both languages; (3) the initial story can be expanded with a series of other experiences, all in multilingual environments with both spoken and written English. The objective at this initial level of the program is to immerse the child in receptive experiences in an English language environment. Many children will require parental assistance for both paperware and webware exercises, and adults will have ready access to give advice in Chinese for both paper-based and Internet-based activities.

Two-year olds, on average, produce 100 to 400 different words in their home language. These words are the most frequent and simplest in the language, and are semantically comparable between languages for the most part—they are about parents, food, other essentials, and everyday activities. The common starting point for the two languages make it possible to employ closely correlated activities in the program; "吃饭" and "eat your rice" have the same meaning when the child sees a picture of a child with a bowl of rice. This commonality is probably one reason why playground bilingualism seems so natural. "Agara la pelota" and "catch the ball" mean the same, though words and grammar may be different. For the child, the goal is communication—exchanging messages.

By three years of age, receptive vocabulary (the words that stand for things and events a child can recognize) is measured in thousands of words, but still centers around everyday words and actions. Sentences are longer and more complex, and children understand increasingly complex ideas, including cause-effect (my friend made me do it) and abstract relations (An apple is a kind of fruit; broccoli is a kind of vegetable). By the age of four, most children are ready to handle ideas of substantial complexity; most of them are actually "ready to read", but it will be another year or two before they are given the opportunity to learn about literacy. They can read "MacDonalds" or their favorite storybooks – if they can go to MacDonalds and have a favorite storybook. The idea behind the current proposal is to open a wide range of rich language opportunities within the home environment for all children.

The learning path sketched in Figure LP displays a variety of activities, including vocabulary development, examples of spoken language patterns, models of sentences and discourse templates (how to exchange ideas with a friend). At the beginning, the path emphasizes informal social language (stories, songs, and games). By four years of age, it covers academic topics (non-fiction reports) for various school subjects. For the oldest children in the program, the activities are explicitly connected to the disciplines for both reading and writing. Games are part of the mix, but so are projects much like those found in school settings. Phonics is introduced in the 5—6 old segment of the progression. *Pinyin* is taught to Chinese children at this age, a parallel to the alphabetic principle used in English for phonics. Chinese characters will have been part of the learning environment, paper and digital, from the beginning of the learning path, but as part of the environment rather than as a subject for study.

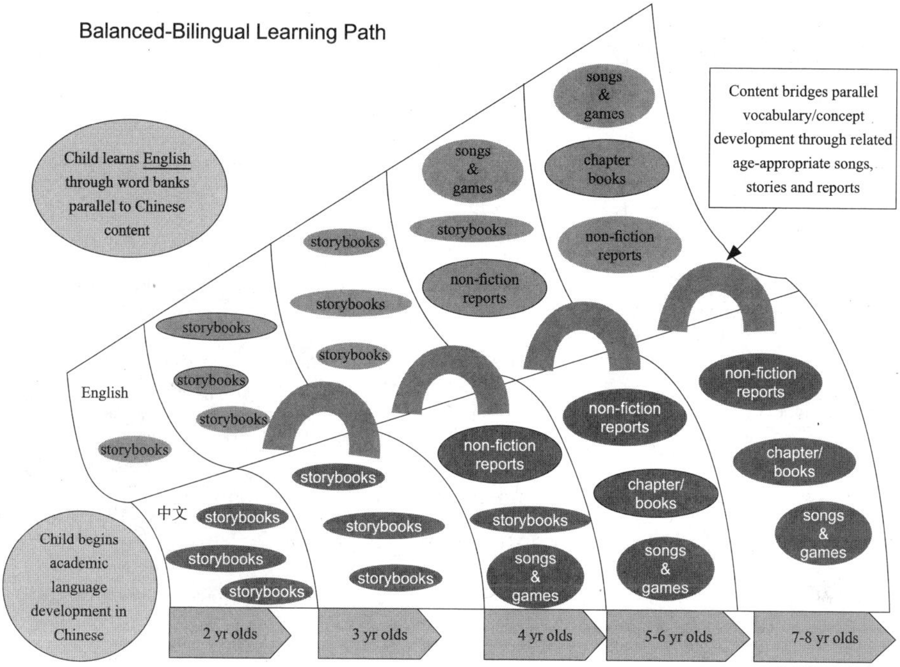

Figure LP (Learning Path). Diagram of the parallel flow of Chinese and English from ages two to eight for a balanced-bilingual program for supporting the acquisition of English, beginning with Chinese toddlers and moving through the primary grades of school.

A different perspective on the learning path appears in Figure S-S, which displays the curriculum scope-sequence design. The figure shows several program features: (1) the progression from receptive language (exposure to Chinese and English) to productive language (saying things in both Chinese and English); (2) coverage of basic reading in both languages, including English phonics and spelling; and (3) the movement from familiar experiences around the home and neighborhood toward larger and less familiar settings, eventually to situations throughout the entire world. The progressions take the child from the known and the informal toward the unknown and the formal, including the world of the school—the language of the "academy".

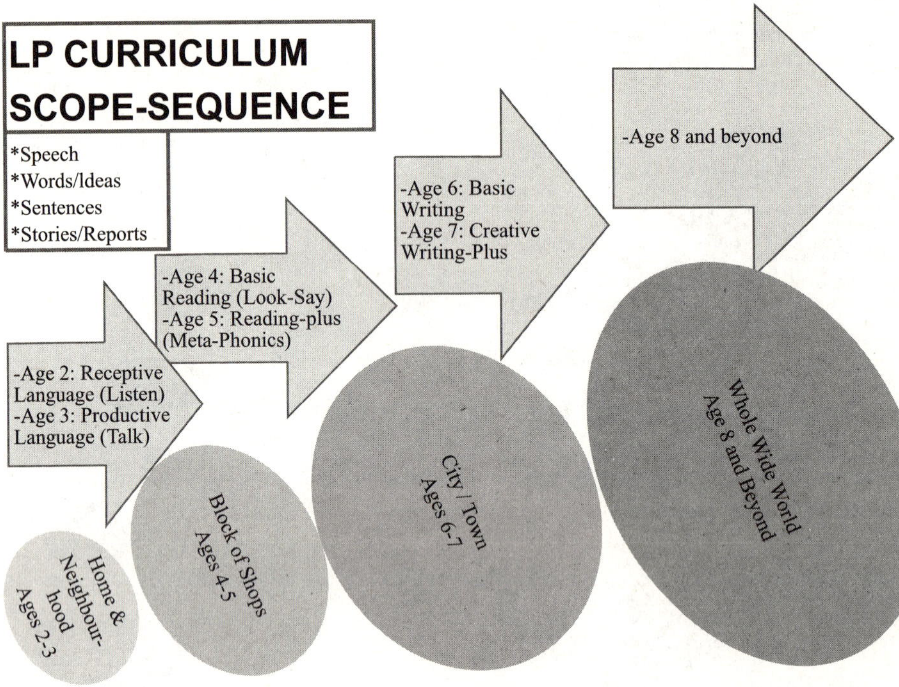

Figure S-S

Figure SS: Scope-and-sequence perspective on the learning path for a balanced-bilingual program that progresses from the informal language of toddlers in familiar settings toward the formal language of elementary school children in school settings.

A key feature of the learning path design is a continuous flow of excellent and engaging texts, chosen from both Chinese and English-language sources (the US along with other English-speaking countries). Figure TXT offers a display of the "table of books" illustrating the concept. Some sources will be chosen from trade book collections, with adaptations as necessary to highlight the contrasts and the complements. *Goodnight Moon,* for example, is available in both English and Chinese, and so the two-page spread strategy described earlier can be applied directly to this text for the youngest children. In contrast, the two "whale" books are quite different, offering older learners the opportunity to synthesize the two works. In addition to books, the paperware packets include *activity sheets* designed to accompany the books, open-ended and game-like, and for the youngest children inviting parents to play along.

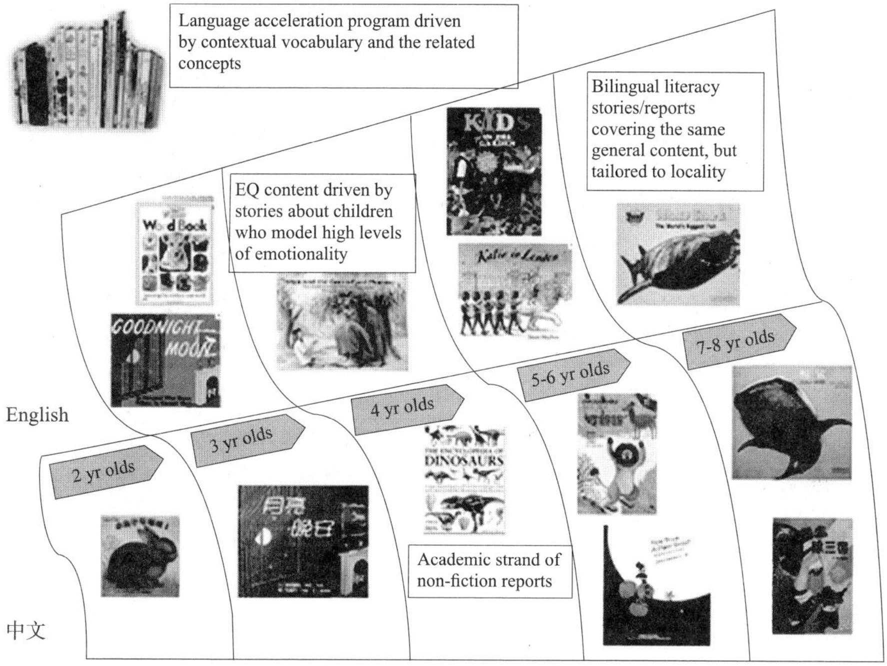

Figure TXT. Examples of "Tables of Books" that provide text support along the Learning Progression. Each book is accompanied by activity sheets for "home & parent work, and an "app link" to the website.

Each book and activity sheet can be directly linked to a website for the Learning Path by an "app" square like those available on today's cell phones. Figure FTSTP shows a screenshot from the *Footsteps to Brilliance* website illustrating the concept. *Footsteps* © is a commercial program designed to help young children learn language and literacy. The website includes engaging books like *The Full Moon Parade* ©. Once a child has logged on to the site, he or she can choose to have the book read with animations and music, to play a variety of games related to the book, or to write a book of his or her own using the original text as the foundation. The "Book Buddies" segment invites learners to collaborate in an activity with an avatar, which can also serve for assessment of skills and knowledge. The child can switch the program from English (ENG) to Spanish (ESP) by clicking the button in the upper right corner.

Figure FTSTP. Screenshot of *The Full Moon Parade* © from *Footsteps to Brilliance* © (www.footsteps2brilliance.com), an early learning platform developed in the United States.

The combination of paperware and webware, along with an explicit "weblink" component, offers many advantages for a toddler-based program like that described in this paper. Paperware has the advantages of familarity to both children and parents, and is available at any time and any place. Storybooks can be read on a parent's lap, on a car seat, just before bedtime. The child's work can be posted on the refrigerator or shared with neighbors. Paperware does not have to be plugged into an electric socket. Webware, on the other hand, is highly interactive and engaging. Webware can read a story and "talk about it" to the child, whereas paper is silent. Webware can provide the young learner with spoken language models from native speakers, when these are not readily available. Web games are exciting, and can promote high levels of motivation. Assessment can be embedded in a game play, allowing the child's progress to be monitored and communicated to the parents as well as the learner. As the child progresses from toddler through the primary grades, the website can support the child in composing stories and reports of his or her own, which goes to the heart of academic language. Computers are increasingly capable of understanding spoken language and responding to complex requests. The day will soon arrive when a toddler can converse with a computer-based avatar—with a "buddy" —in both L1 and L2.

The path ahead. Not that long ago, bilinguality was the mark of an educated person. Today, acquiring a second language is viewed as either "remedial" (e.g., for Hispanics in the United States) or an adjunct to home language necessary for career purposes (e.g., in China and India). The current proposal returns to earlier times, when acquiring a second language meant learning a new culture, new ways of understanding and communicating—an essential part of education.

The proposed balanced-bilingual strategy, which invites toddlers to join a parallel pathway as they spurt ahead in their home language, builds upon natural language growth to promote acquisition of a second language. Research on vocabulary acquisition suggests that the early years are an ideal time for engaging learners in these experiences. The proposed program has several innovative features. First, it lays out a well-defined learning path to guide young learners and inform their parents. Second, it employs a hybrid approach in the application of technologies to support learning. Since its invention in China around 105 AD, paper has served as a significant technology for communication; the arrival of the personal computer in the 1980s opens a wide array of additional opportunities, and linking the two for language acquisition combines the best of both worlds. Third, placing these tools in the hands of parents in a practical and engaging format will allow the family to contribute to their child's learning in novel and effective ways—all of this at a time when expectations for the next generation have increased significantly throughout the entire world, a world that is growing flatter and more connected with every passing year.

Reference:

[1] Calfee, R. C. (1982). Literacy and Illiteracy: Teaching the Nonreader to Survive in the Modern World. *Annals of Dyslexia*, 32, 71-91.

[2] Child Development Institute. (n.d.). *Language Development in Children.* Child www.childdevelopment info.com.

[3] Cummins, J. and Man, E. Y-F. (2007). Academic Language: What Is It and How Do We Acquire It. In J. Cummins and C. Davison (eds.), *International Handbook of English Language Teaching*. New York: Springer. pp. 797-810.

[4] Darling-Hammond, L. (2010). *The Flat World and Education*. New York: Teachers College Press.

[5] Fenson, L., Pethick, S., Renda, C., Cox, J. L., Dale, P. S., and Reznick, J. S. (2000). Short-Form Version of the MacArthur Communicative Development Inventories. *Applied Psycholinguistics*, 21, 95-116.

[6] Friedman, T. L. (2007). *The World Is Flat: A Brief History of the Twenty-First Century*. New York: Picador.

[7] Gil, J., & Adamson, B. (2011). The English Language in Mainland China: A Sociolinguistic Profile. In A. Feng (ed.), *English Language Education across Greater China,* Buffalo, NY: Multilingual Matters. pp. 23-45.

[8] Goody, J., and Watt, I. (1968). The Consequences of Literacy. In J. Goody (ed.), *Literacy in Traditional Societies*. London: Cambridge University Press.

[9] Hart, B. and Risley, T.R. (1995). *Meaningful Differences in the Everyday Experiences of Young American Children*. Baltimore, MD: Brookes.

[10] Howard, E. R., Sugarman, J. and Christian, D. (2003). *Trends in Two-Way Immersion Education*. Baltimore MD: CRESPAR/Johns Hopkins University.

[11] Olson, D. (1977). From Utterance to Text: The Bias of Language in Speech and Writing. *Harvard Educational Review*, 47, 157-181.

[12] Schleppegrell, M. J. (2012). Academic Language in Teaching and Learning: Introduction to the Special Issue. *The Elementary School Journal*, 112, 409- 418.

[13] Soderman, A. K. & Oshio, T. (2008). The Social and Cultural Contexts of Second Language Acquisition of Young Children. *European Early Childhood Education Research Journal*, 16, 297-311.

[14] Tardif, T., Fletcher, P., Liang, W., Kaciroti, N. (2009). Early Vocabulary Development in Mandarin (Putonghua) and Cantonese. *Journal of Child Language*, 36, 1115-1144.

[15] Tardif, T., Gelman, S. A. & Xu, F. (1999). Putting the "Noun Bias" in Context: A Comparison of English and Mandarin. *Child Development*, 70, 620-635.

[16] Tardif, T., Shatz, M., and Naigles, L. (1997). Caregiver Speech and Children's Use of Nouns Versus Verbs: A Comparison of English, Italian, and Mandarin. *Journal of Child Language*, 24, 535-565.

面向幼儿的汉英双语均衡教学策略

[美国] Robert Calfee

摘要： 两岁以前是儿童“像海绵一样”吸收语言的时期。如果把他们放在自然、愉快的语言环境中，他们无需正规教学就可以毫不费力地迅速掌握一门第二语言。本文介绍一种支持一岁半到三岁的中国幼儿习得英语的教学法。该教学法以均衡双语教学策略为基础，在培养幼儿学习第一语言汉语的同时为其提供英语作为第二语言的学习体验。本文重点讨论该双语教学策略的实际效果。在某种程度上，使用这种策略要看这个年龄段的幼儿掌握的双语词汇在多大程度上具有可比性，包括习得的速度、学习的词汇和习得的概念。研究人员使用“沟通能力发展量表”检测中国幼儿双语学习的效果，该研究结果支持如下假设：第一，在输入和输出型词汇方面，两种语言的词汇增长率相当；第二，习得两种语言主谓结构的比例差异是人为造成的；两种语言在概念结构的习得方面十分相似。基于以上发现，研究人员认为，均衡双语教学策略可以为中国幼儿英语习得的项目提供依据。本文最后描述了这种教学策略通过使用一个混合的 Paperware-Webware 平台在实际教学中的应用情况。

关键词： 英语习得；词汇发展；中国儿童；双语均衡教学策略

US-China E-Language Learning Project: Born at 2001 APEC Conference in Beijing

[The United States] Susan Sclafani

Abstract: During the APEC High-Level Meeting on Human Capacity Building in Beijing in May 2001, an informal discussion of economy representatives identified the possibility of using technology to improve the quality of foreign language learning. This discussion blossomed into the later named CHENGO. The project took a technology-driven approach to foreign language learning that integrated gaming, immersion, voice recognition, and problem-based learning tasks. From 2001 to 2005, the two economies worked together, each forming technical work groups composed of experts in language learning content and pedagogy, system design and development, and sustainability and dissemination. The work was collaborative with regular meetings of the two work groups to share content and technology developments. Focus groups of US students in 2004 found the CHENGO Chinese fun and a good way to practice, but requested the addition of *pinyin*. A recent evaluation of the follow-on development of the English program at Coastline Community College showed significantly positive growth in reading and listening for Grade 8 students in western China who had scored in the bottom half of pre-tests of English reading and listening. In addition, 95 percent of their teachers reported they changed the way they thought about teaching languages.

Keywords: APEC High-Level Meeting; human capacity building; Beijing; US-China E-Language Learning Project; CHENGO Chinese

During the Asia-Pacific Economic Cooperation (APEC) High-Level Meeting on Human Capacity Building in Beijing in May 2001, an informal discussion of economy representatives identified the possibility of using technology to improve the quality of foreign language learning. Because of the great interest from the Chinese Ministry of Education, this discussion blossomed into the US-China E-Language Learning Initiative. President George W. Bush announced the initiative at the APEC Leaders Meeting in Shanghai in October 2001. During a visit of the Chinese Minister of Education to Washington, D.C. in 2002, the minister and the US Secretary of Education signed a memorandum of understanding, the first joint government education initiative between the two economies since 1979.

The project took a technology-driven approach to foreign language learning that integrated gaming, immersion, voice recognition, and problem-based learning tasks. The purpose of the project was to determine if such an interactive, online language learning program would be viable and effective. From 2002 to 2005, the two economies worked together, each forming technical work groups composed of experts in language learning content and pedagogy, system design and development, and sustainability and dissemination.

Each economy funded its work, with the Chinese funding the development of a simplified Mandarin course for English speakers at the middle school level and the US creating an English course for Mandarin speakers in middle school grades. It was also the intent of the US Department of Education to develop a program that could be used by US students who were English Language Learners (ELL). The decision to focus on middle schools grades was based on the research that indicated that students at that level have more difficulties learning a foreign language with correct pronunciation than younger students. The question of whether the use of speech recognition and interactive gaming strategies could overcome this challenge became one of the research questions for the project.

The language development work was based on the Chinese National English Curriculum Standard (Education, 2001) and the American Council on the Teaching of Foreign Language (ACTFL) Standards (American Council on the Teaching of Foreign Languages, 1996). The technology started with the animation work done by Little Planet, a sub-contractor of the US Department of Education. It was enhanced through the participation of the Carnegie Mellon's speech recognition research efforts. The design called for learning the language in a virtual learning environment that takes students through a series of adventures or challenges that require the comprehension and use of the target language to respond. Students would also engage in games and interactive exercises to test and build their fluency and proficiency in the target language. In addition, both technical work groups agreed to include opportunities for students to explore and learn about the culture of the speakers of the language they were learning. Starting from those decisions, the work was collaborative with regular meetings of the two technical work groups to share content and technology developments.

After the Chinese technical work group completed its initial set of episodes in 2004, it worked with the US Department of Education staff to hold focus groups with students and teachers from three public schools and one private school who were studying Mandarin. Grades 8—9 students evaluated one of three possible episodes, including the story, practice activities, cultural notes and one game. The students found the CHENGO Chinese fun and a good way to practice, but requested the addition of *pinyin*.

The development of the English program for Chinese students shifted from the Department of Education. All of the source code and scripts were made available to the public on the Internet. In 2007, the Hewlett Foundation funded further development of the program at Coastline Community College. The system was developed as an open education resource available to others to customize to other language groups wishing to learn English. The evaluation in ten schools in Gansu Province in western China showed significantly positive growth in reading and listening for Grade 8 students who had scored in the bottom half of pre-tests of English reading and listening beyond that experience by the students in the control schools. Over half of the students in the treatment schools also reported higher motivation to study English as opposed to 40 percent of the control school students. In addition, 95 percent of their teachers reported they changed the way they thought about teaching languages.

In both evaluations, we saw a positive response to the question of whether online language learning could motivate students to learn a foreign language. However, if that was resulted from the initial discussion, I would not be very excited about sharing the results with you. The real value of the project was the development of a strong relationship between educators in the United States and those in China. Among the members of the US technical work group was Vivien Stewart, the education director of the Asia Society. Stewart had just undertaken this assignment as the work group was formed. She had written the report on a study of what students in the US knew about Asia—very little. The results were clear that a major effort was required to educate US students about Asia and the Asia Society of New York City accepted the challenge.

Through the contacts made during the e-language learning program with the Ministry of Education and Hanban, Stewart initiated a series of study tours to China. She first took leaders of state departments of education to Beijing and Shanghai to meet educators and provincial leaders. It was followed by a speech to the Council of Chief State School Officers annual conference and to the Education Commission of the States by Vice Minister Zhang Xinsheng. Vice Minister Zhang led the Ministry's work on the e-language learning program. The discussion of the Chinese strategic plan for K-12 education opened a lively discussion of comparisons between the education plans of the two economies.

Over the last decade, many states have signed memoranda of understanding with provinces in China, leading to exchanges of students and teachers and better understanding of each other's cultures. Policy leaders and leaders of non-profit organizations and foundations have visited China and participated in Asia. In addition, study tours have taken educators to visit schools in different parts of China.

The result of these experiences has been the development of bilateral relationships of the governmental, public and non-profit sectors in the two economies. Educators in both China and the US have discussed their approaches to improving education and learned strategies that could be adapted to local conditions in each economy. To me, that is an important contribution that participation in APEC has brought to the US and we are grateful for the opportunity and the results.

发端于 2001 年北京 APEC 会议的中美数字化语言学习项目

[美国] Susan Sclafani

摘要： 本文首先介绍中美数字化语言项目的产生背景。2001 年 5 月亚太经合组织在北京召开了以“个人能力建设”为主题的高层会议，与会的经济界代表在一次非正式讨论中达成了技术可能提高外语学习质量的共识。此次讨论促成了后来被命名为“CHENGO”（乘风汉语）的数字化语言学习项目。本文重点讨论该语言学习项目的特点和合作方式。该项目融合游戏、沉浸式教学、语音识别和任务型教学法等多种学习方式运用技术驱动的方法处理外语学习问题。从 2001 到 2005 年，中美两国分别成立由语言学习内容和教学法、系统设计与开发、可持续性发展和传播等领域的专家组成的技术工作组，两个工作组通过定期会晤，以分享内容和技术开发的方式进行合作。本文最后总结中美师生对该项目的评估。2004 年对美国学生的小组访谈结果表明，《乘风汉语》趣味性较强，练习汉语的方法较好，但是学生提出汉字加注拼音的要求。美国海岸线社区学院负责英语项目的后期开发工作，其对该项目的评估显示，中国西部学校初二年级的一些学生在英语听力和阅读方面进步很大，而在此前的预测中这些学生的英语阅读和听力成绩在全年级中位于较差的那一半；另外，95% 的教师指出该项目改变了他们对英语教学的看法。

关键词： 亚太经合组织高层会议；个人能力建设；北京；中美数字化语言学习项目；乘风汉语

Some Experience in Applying Information Technology to English Teaching at Colleges and Universities

[Vietnam] Tran Thi Mai Phuong

Abstract: Information technology has a great influence on education, especially on teaching and learning foreign languages at colleges and universities. Modern equipments in classrooms helps improve teaching and learning quality. Information technology also brings a lot of advantages to English teaching. Students can look for different materials from the Internet; they can practice different language skills with their network-connected computer. Especially, language lessons would be more interesting with illustrations of pictures, videos, or movies downloaded from the Internet or made by teachers with the support of different software. In this article, some issues will be discussed: some experience in applying information technology to English teaching at colleges and universities; some advantages as well as disadvantages in applying it in Vietnam and some suggestions to overcome the difficulties.

Keywords: Vietnam; information technology (IT); colleges; English teaching

Some Experience in Applying Information Technology to English Teaching

Information technology (IT) plays an important role in providing trainees with information quickly, accurately and fascinatingly. Teachers can download various teaching materials from the Internet. Instead of looking for many books, borrowing many dictionaries in the library, teachers can find everything needed only with a network-connected computer. However, important applications of IT are e-lecture design and using slideshow software to design English lectures.

E-Lecture Design

A significant application of IT to teaching is e-lecture design. E-lectures are designed and developed in the computer-based on some specialized software. E-lectures are conducted via the multimedia teaching system or the Internet. PowerPoint is the common software to design e-lectures, besides some other specialized software. Some advantages of e-lectures are as follows:

- Saving time for teachers during the lectures (blackboard writing is unnecessary) ;
- High quality audio-visual equipment helps students absorb lectures easily;
- Rich and vivid source of information (images, sound, speed);
- Helping teachers highlight the topic and focus of the lecture;
- Helping teachers strengthen the lectures, repeat important points when necessary;
- E-lectures are saved on a server or intranet as references;
- E-lectures assist students in their self-study.

Applications of Slideshow Software to Design English Lectures

While teaching English, apart from chalks and blackboards, we can use images, sound, short videos to illustrate English lectures at different levels and for different skills. On each slide, there may be texts, images, pictures, voiced videos and sounds. Slideshow software aims at attracting listeners' attention so that teachers can save and control the time. Lectures are also scripted to improve their quality.

Steps to Design English Lectures with the Applications of Slideshow Software

To have an English slideshow lecture that makes learners attracted and interested, it's necessary to build a script for the whole lecture as well as a logical structure among lectures. Steps include:

- Defining preliminary ideas for the lecture;
- Building a slideshow script;
- Designing slides;
- Testing the slideshow.

Step 1: Defining preliminary ideas for the lecture

Defining the main content: it is necessary to define the main content, the focus of the lecture, thence choose suitable emphasis effects. The contents are ordered according to their importance; more important content needs more emphasis effects.

Defining the way of using multimedia: based on the content of the lecture, the teacher decides the way of using multimedia, the way and the time to display the content via each type of media.

Step 2: Building a slideshow script

Principles:

- Script is the outline of a lecture shown on the computer, so it only includes main ideas;
- Using the same design including the color effects, distance and layout for the same level titles;
- The order of contents is based on the order of the lecture outline;
- Complying with the time according to the lecture content.

Building a slideshow script

This is the step to write voice-overs/explanations and scenes, to distribute the time, and to plan the use of sound and image techniques and emphasis techniques to make the lecture coherent, constant and logical. Scripts are built as follows:

- Based on the lecture size/capacity, define the number of slides;
- Based on the time allowance, define the display time for each slide;
- In each slide, define the number of components (text, video clip, sound clip) and the display time for each of them;

- Define the explanations and actions of teachers while showing each component.

Step 3: Designing slides

After building the lecture script, the teacher starts to design slides. A slide is a page displayed on the screen. Each slide includes text frames, image and sound frames with emphasis effect.

Principles of building slides:

- Complying with the display script;
- The core content needs emphasis effects;
- Avoiding content duplication;
- Co-ordinating harmonically the colors among the slides and the overall lecture.

Step 4: Testing the slideshow on the computer

This step is just a test performance on the computer without the projector. Some contents to be tested include:

- The match between the teacher's explanation and the lecture script;
- The lack of content;
- Reasonableness of time distribution and emphasis effects;
- Reasonableness of color and sound co-ordination.

General slideshow test

Conduct the lecture with the projector. Contents to be tested include:

- Testing the mastery in using;
- Testing the suitability of image and sound effects with the environment;
- Testing the equipment's synchronism;
- Testing the contents of the script.

Giving the lecture in practice with the comments of students is the final test, showing the quality of the lecture in terms of both contents and the form.

Advantages and Disadvantages in Applying IT to English Teaching at Colleges and Universities in Vietnam

Advantages

E-lectures help to save time and improve the quality of the lecture. E-lectures also attract students and makes them participate more actively in activities during the lesson.

Moreover, using computer helps students practice and develop their methods and tactics in study at different levels and with different demands. Students have opportunities to practice skills, such as listening, speaking, reading, and writing; they can choose suitable materials and courses. Online courses are very popular nowadays.

The application of IT brings a lot of benefits to teachers. They can update their knowledge fast with endless sources of materials, modern teaching aids, especially the interaction between teachers and students.

Disadvantages

Apart from the advantages mentioned above, there still remain many disadvantages in applying IT to English teaching in colleges and universities.

Firstly, with regard to classroom equipment: Most foreign language classrooms lack equipment for the application of IT to teaching and learning. In detail, there is a lack of projectors, sound systems, soundproofing materials and screens in the classrooms.

Secondly, the classroom is small with a large number of students (over 50). In such a small space, the "student-centered" teaching method cannot be applied; especially, in foreign language classes, students can neither have opportunities to interact nor communicate.

Thirdly, in terms of syllabus: in order to utilize efficiently the support of IT in teaching and learning foreign languages, it is necessary to set up an outline, and a detailed syllabus, to build a database and exploit them with proper methods and techniques that comply with learners. Today, only a few institutions can deal with such issues.

Fourthly, in terms of learners: students' informatics knowledge is not good at all. Most of them do not have computers and many of them cannot use the computer proficiently. Students are passive and accustomed to one-way acquisition from high schools.

Finally, regarding to English teachers: most English teachers of colleges and universities graduate from language-majored institutions. They receive little training in informatics, so their abilities to apply IT are limited. Moreover, many teachers are not young, which causes difficulties for them to absorb IT knowledge.

Some Suggestions to Improve the Quality of Lectures by Applying IT to English Teaching at Colleges and Universities in Vietnam

Applying IT to teaching is an inevitable trend. However, the IT application at colleges and universities in Vietnam is conducted only in a small and pilot scale. Expecting to improve the quality of applying IT to the teaching of foreign languages, the author would like to propose some suggestions as follows:

- Foreign language classrooms need to be equipped with a projector, and a proper light and sound system. Classrooms are soundproofed and the Internet is connected;
- Teachers are trained to apply IT to their teaching. Training courses for foreign language teachers in terms of IT application (equipment use, material collection, lecture preparation) are organized;
- Colleges and universities should have detailed policies and regulations in order to encourage teachers to innovate their teaching methods, especially the IT application to teaching;
- Colleges and universities should upgrade and invest more in equipment, purchase more teaching materials and software (updated and advanced foreign language teaching programs).

So, I have mentioned some experience in applying IT to English teaching, as well as the advantages and disadvantages in applying it at colleges and universities today. In order to achieve effective application of IT to foreign language teaching, we should pay more attention to some components, including teachers' qualifications, equipment, and especially the policies of colleges and universities.

大专院校英语教学中应用信息技术的经验

[越南] Tran Thi Mai Phuong

摘要： 本文重点讨论了信息技术对教育，尤其是大专院校的外语教学产生的重大影响。首先简述了信息技术为英语教学带来的诸多便利，比如学生可以在互联网上查阅资料，还可以通过计算机互联网练习多种语言技能等。特别值得一提的是，教师可以从互联网上下载或者借助软件工具制作图片示例、视频和影片，使得语言教学更加有趣。本文详细描述了设计数字化课程对英语教学的益处，包括节省教师上课板书的时间，可以提供种类丰富、具体生动的学习资源，方便教师强调教学重点，有助于学生课外自学等。本文还讨论了越南将信息技术应用到大专院校英语教学中的经验、现存的问题和解决的对策等。

关键词： 越南；信息技术；大专院校；英语教学

附录　Appendix

作者职务表　List of Authors' Positions

Paper Title No.	Author	Position
Foreword	李宇明	Secretary of the Party Committee, Beijing Language and Culture University
Speech at the Opening Ceremony	杨军	Deputy Director General, Department of International Cooperation and Exchanges, Ministry of Education, P. R. C.
1	Adriana de Kanter	Education Network (EDNET) Coordinator of APEC HRD Working Group
	Bridget Belknap	Project Director, Leed Management Consulting
2	Hisham Hj. Rahmat	Assistant Director, Educational Planning and Research Division, Ministry of Education, Malaysia
3	李宇明	Secretary of the Party Committee, Beijing Language and Culture University
4	Anna Marie Baligod-San Diego	Education Program Specialist of the Department of Education, Philippines
5	Tunku Ireneza Marina bt. Tunku Mazlan	Assistant Director, Curriculum Development Division, Ministry of Education, Malaysia
6	林文通	Director General, Bureau of International Cultural & Educational Relations, Chinese Taipei

Paper Title No.	Author	Position
7	Usanee Watanapan	Deputy Director of the Bureau of Academic Affairs and Educational Standards, Thailand
8	Cathryn Hlavka	Minister-Counsellor (Education and Research), Department of Education, Employment and Workplace Relations, Australian Consulate in China
9	Timothy Greene	Provost and Vice President, Western Michigan University
	Donald McCloud	Director of the Confucius Institute and Western Michigan University Associate Professor of Political Science and Global Studies
10	Javier Vivaldo Lima	Professor, Autonomous Metropolitan University, Mexico
	Magaret Lee Zoreda	Professor, Autonomous Metropolitan University, Mexico
11	Li-Jiuan Tsay	Professor, Department of Applied English, Ming Chuan University, Chinese Taipei
	Pey-Chewn Duo	Assistant Professor, Department of Applied English, Ming Chuan University, Chinese Taipei
	Min-Hsun Su	Assistant Professor, Department of Applied English, Ming Chuan University, Chinese Taipei
	Hsiang-I Chen	Assistant Professor, Department of Applied English, Ming Chuan University, Chinese Taipei
12	Neungreudee Lohapon	Head of Department of Western Languages, Chulalongkorn University, Thailand

Paper Title No.	Author	Position
13	Michael Byram	Emeritus Professor, School of Education, Durham University, UK
14	Maria Elisa Lidia de la Vega Polanco	English Specialist for Secondary Education, Ministry of Education, Peru
15	Hajah Lena binti Mohammad Hassan	Senior Education Officer of the Ministry of Education, Brunei Darussalam
16	Dang Thuy Chi	Official of the International Cooperation Department, Ministry of Education and Training, Vietnam
17	Shuhan C. Wang	Director, Foreign Language Studies Center, Maryland University, US
18	Alice Murray	Regional English Language Officer, US Embassy in China
19	Cheng Long	Professor, Beijing Language and Culture University
20	Robert Calfee	Emeritus Professor, Stanford University, US
21	Susan Sclafani	Former Special Advisor of the US Education Secretary
22	Tran Thi Mai Phuong	Director, Foreign Language Center of Hanoi Architectural University, Vietnam